# A
# HARSH
# AND
# DREADFUL
# LOVE

*Peter Maurin 1877–1949*
*Founder of The Catholic Worker movement*

[This caption was used for another photo of Peter Maurin in the original frontispiece;
this is how Dorothy Day wished her mentor to be remembered.
Day and Maurin are commonly identified as co-founders.—Phillip M. Runkel]

*#61362118*

## Library of Congress
## Cataloguing in Publication Data

Miller, William D., 1916-
  A harsh and dreadful love : Dorothy Day and the Catholic Worker Movement / with new photos and with a foreword by Phillip M. Runkel.
     p. cm.
  Originally published: New York : Liveright, 1973. With new foreword, errata sheet, and new photos.
  Includes bibliographical references and index.
  ISBN-13: 978-0-87462-012-2 (pbk. : alk. paper)
  ISBN-10: 0-87462-012-0 (pbk. : alk. paper)
  1. Catholic Worker Movement. 2. Day, Dorothy, 1897-1980. 3. Catholic worker.
  I. Title.
  BX810.C393.M55 2005
  267'.182--dc22

                              2005024480

© 2005
Marquette University Press
This new edition includes an errata list to correct errors found in the first edition, a new Foreword by Phillip Runkel, and many new photos taken from the Marquette University Archives.

*Original copyright page information*
First published in the United States by Liveright
and in Great Britain by
Darton, Longman & Todd Limited
85 Gloucester Road, London SW7 4SU;

Association of American
University Presses

MARQUETTE UNIVERSITY PRESS
MILWAUKEE

The Association of Jesuit University Presses

# WILLIAM D. MILLER

# A
# HARSH
# AND
# DREADFUL
# LOVE

## DOROTHY DAY AND THE CATHOLIC WORKER MOVEMENT

Second edition, with new photos and with a Foreword by
Phillip M. Runkel

**MARQUETTE**
UNIVERSITY

PRESS

*To the memory of*
*William Henry and Bertha Heeth Bond*

By the author

*Memphis during the Progressive Era* (1957)

*Mr. Crump of Memphis* (1964)

*Dorothy Day: A Biography* (1982)

*All Is Grace: The Spirituality of Dorothy Day* (1987)

*Pretty Bubbles in the Air: America in 1919* (1991)

*Note from Andrew Tallon, Director, Marquette University Press*
Marquette University Press is very grateful to Phil Runkel for his Foreword, the list of corrections, and the selection of new photos chosen by him and made available to us from the Marquette University Archives. He more than anyone deserves our gratitude for seeing this reprint of Bill Miller's classic history through to publication. Credit and thanks to Phil.

# FOREWORD

We are pleased to reissue William Miller's pioneering history of the Catholic Worker movement. Originally published thirty years ago, it was the first book to draw upon the movement's archives at Marquette, to which Dorothy Day had granted Miller access soon after the records' arrival in March of 1962.

Subsequently, works by Miller and other scholars (including his students) have augmented our knowledge of the Catholic Worker's history, major figures, philosophical and spiritual underpinnings, and present ministries. (There are now over 150 CW communities spread across the United States and in Australia, Canada, Europe, Mexico, and New Zealand.) But *A Harsh and Dreadful Love* remains, to quote Daniel Berrigan, a "masterful and warm-hearted" account of the Worker movement from its origins in 1933 through the tumult of the Sixties. For James Murray, writing in *The Universe* (Manchester, England), the book revealed "another America set over against the America of the inflationary dollar and the inflationary lie. That America is the America of The Catholic Worker and the best hope of the world." Readers may find that these words still apply.

Phillip M. Runkel
Archivist
Raynor Memorial Libraries
Marquette University

# Errata corrigenda

ix, line 4: William D. Miller wrote Dorothy Day [DD] about writing the book on 1 March 1962, not in 1965. According to this letter, he had just learned from librarian Robert Miller [no relation] that the Catholic Worker [CW] papers were on their way to MU.

36, lines 22-23: DD was born in Brooklyn Heights; the family moved to Bath Beach several years later.

55, lines 20 and 33: Last name is "Batterham."

57, line 3: This was in 1925, not '26.

57, line 11. March 4, 1926.

58, line 19: eighteen months [DD was baptized in December 1927].

58, line 26: August 1927.

60, line 24: Batterham.

67, lines 6-7: Eileen Corridan [related to Fr. John Corridan, the model for Karl Malden's character in *On the Waterfront*].

69, line 17: Paul Hanly Furfey.

77, lines 34-35: The name wasn't a "misunderstanding," according to the artist herself [1983 interview by Nancy Roberts]. She explained that early on she'd sometimes signed "A. de Bethune," but "finally settled on the 'Ade Bethune,' which was shorter and easier to spell out for a telephone operator or something."

111, line 28: Gerry Griffin.

121, lines 28-29: Gerry Griffin, Joe Zarrella.

121, line 33: Gerry Griffin.

143, line 31: Zarrella.

# Errata corrigenda

152, line 26: Ratner.

155, lines 3-7. *From Union Square to Rome* was published first, in November 1938. *House of Hospitality* was published in August 1939.

156, line 1: Margaret Bigham.

159, line 33: Zarrella.

163, line 18: Zarrella.

168, line 12: The letter is dated 10 August 1940.

170, line 4: Zarrella, Gerry.

180, .line 20: Zarrella.

182, line 13: Hughan.

192, lines 2-3: Zarrella, Gerry Griffin.

193, line 35: eighteenth, March 4.

208, line 23: Gerry Griffin.

221, line 22: Elizabeth Burrow.

229, line 35: McKeon.

248, line 30: McCormack.

260, line 17: Watkin.

264, lines 5 and 12: Burrow.

271, line 1: Melms [not Nelms].

280, line 10: Melms.

320, line 11: Norman Morrison.

335, line 6: Vogler.

# Errata corrigenda

344, line 3: Zarrellas.

359: Batterham.

359: Bigham, Margaret [not Bingham].

360: Burrow.

·361: Corridan.

364: Furfey, Rev. Paul Hanly.

364: Griffin, Gerry.

364: Harada, Kichi.

365: Hensler.

365: Hughan.

366: LaPorte [not La Porte].

366: McCormack, Charles.

366: McKeon, John.

367: Add Melms, Selma pages 271, 274, 276, 279-280.

367: Morrison, Norman [not Roger].

368: Omit "Nelms."

369: Ratner.

370: Vogler [not Vegler].

370: Watkin.

370: Zarrella.

# PREFACE

The Catholic Worker movement was founded in 1933 by the French peasant thinker Peter Maurin, and Dorothy Day, a former leftist journalist and novelist and a Catholic convert. On May Day that year, Dorothy Day and a few youthful supporters went into New York City's Union Square and sold for a penny a copy the first edition of *The Catholic Worker*. It is now almost forty years since that event, and the *Worker* is still published, still sells for a penny, has a circulation of some eighty thousand copies a month, and calls now, as it did then, for a human and social revolution that would come from the timeless qualities of the human spirit and not from the discordancies of a world in process.

In the decades that followed that May Day, the Catholic Worker movement inflamed the spirits of many who worked in the expectation of reforming society through the Worker revolutionary program. They were beginning, they believed, a new crusade of the Catholic Church that would end the old world. This conviction, so strong in the thirties, remained through the years of the Second Vatican Council, and to many Workers that event seemed a final confirmation of the rightness of their position.

Since those stirring times of Pope John, however, a dryness has fallen on the life of the Church. Time has leaped to a new level of acceleration and a vision once steady has become blurred and lost in the trail of a fast receding past. The Worker movement, which until a few years ago was looked upon by the young as gloriously radical, is regarded by some as an outdated idea. Dorothy Day's belief that the Church yet remains at the heart of the hoped-for new life of man represents an affront to those who declare that the old vision is gone—to those who would keep abreast the sweeping tide of time by an ever-increasing activism and who would ride the wave of sense with its thrilling acceleration.

I disagree with them. Having researched the Catholic Worker phenomenon, I might well have concluded, on the basis of the evidence, that the movement was a well-intentioned but ineffectual pietistic activism. On the basis of the same evidence I might also have concluded that it was a flight from reality and was thus a madness. But I have come to view the Worker movement as expressing an idea that comes truly out of the midst of life and gives to the human spirit its highest due. I hold this position by virtue of no special illumination but because, thinking as an historian, it seems logical, demonstrable. The conclusions of the historian are, of course, affected by his temperament and what he would like to believe about life. This is very true for me, but even so, there was an evolution in my thinking about the Catholic Worker, after I began the research for this book.

My first contact with the movement came in 1951 when I was introduced to a Catholic Worker group in Memphis, Tennessee. For six months or so I went to discussion meetings at the Blessed Martin de Porres house, which had been organized by a Black girl, Helen Caldwell. It was for me an illuminating experience to meet with Helen and with other Blacks who, likely as not, had been in the fields of Arkansas that day chopping cotton, who sat quietly with hands folded in their laps; with those earnest young White couples who sometimes brought to the discussions their growing brood of children; and with two young men who were Marxists. Helen's house eventually folded from nonsupport, and in

1958 I left Memphis for Milwaukee. For the next few years my only contact with the movement came from reading *The Catholic Worker*.

It was not until 1965, when I was teaching history at Marquette University, that I began to think of writing this book. My first action was to write to Dorothy Day to ask for her cooperation in the way of providing sources. She assented and gave me access to the Catholic Worker papers. I had not known, but it was almost precisely at this moment that the university librarian, William Ready, had begun to collect these papers. Father Raphael N. Hamilton, the university archivist, has now sorted and catalogued this voluminous material with great care and devotion.

Since the character of these papers relate to my final judgment about the Worker movement I would like parenthetically to say something about them. The papers include a number of boxes on special topics but the bulk consists of letters to Dorothy Day and to *The Catholic Worker*. There are very few copies of letters sent out, since Dorothy's letters were almost always hand written.

At the pace at which I worked it took me two years to go through all of the Worker papers, but all of the hours I spent in reading those letters gave me some positions from which to focus on the subject. I was brought face-to-face with the people to whom the Worker movement spoke. A great many of them were not intellectuals, or even great activists, but people past whom time swept without their voices registering in any "important" way to direct the course of events. Yet these people felt that there was something in the spirit of the Worker movement that was central to their lives.

The Worker papers showed me something else. After going through them I was convinced that there was no window dressing in the movement. It never tried to create for itself any "images", and the evidence of this is in the record that was kept. It is not a manipulated record. It was one that contained everything that critics of the Worker movement might use to document their points—that the Worker movement sustained the incompetents and the drones; that it gave little thought to simple organizational principles; or that it was shot through with inconsistencies. The record showed that Workers were not very "clever" people.

Essentially, I came to this mass of data as an outsider looking in, and that, some would argue, is the way history should be written. Relate the facts—be objective. Perhaps for certain subjects this kind of objectivity is desirable. They are subjects witnessed to by facts which may indeed be dramatic, but subjects, finally, worthwhile only as symptoms and even then as insignificant symptoms. There are many such on which historians have concentrated their "objectivity," but the final result has been to increase the burden of facticity in the world without adding anything to its meaning. In my judgment to have labored for a pyrotechnical display of "objectivity" in writing the history of the Catholic Worker movement would have been confusing and perhaps even stupid or dishonest. There is nothing so pointless as a fact that is mute or whose significance is contrived. The crucial question I faced when I was in the process of developing my ground of reference was, what is it that the facts are saying? When I thought that I had the answer to this question, I could relate those facts that had such significance as to enable me to tell the Worker story coherently and honestly.

In the course of the six years of gathering material about the movement and, at the same time, trying to see that this material got its due, how it related to the history I knew, how it related to life as I now understood it, I got what Peter Maurin might have called a "clarification." Seven years ago I was a "liberal" Catholic and I regarded the Worker phenomenon agreeably because the Worker movement, I thought, was very liberal. But in studying the Worker movement—not dwelling always on the surface of its life, but trying to grasp its central idea, especially Peter Maurin's idea—it was not only clear that there was no blood bond between the Worker idea and liberalism, but that the two positions were antithetical. The Worker idea is total; it subsumes all, and liberal Catholicism (or liberal anything) is something that flows in and out of the currents of time.

The remaining question concerns the reason for my abandoning the liberal interpretative position and coming finally to accept the Worker idea as logical and credible. First like some others, I can see no solution to the problem of the acceleration of the historical process. Twenty years ago one could still brush off Henry Adams' woeful reflections on this subject as the product of a pessimistic and obscurantist character, but today they seem very plausible. I share, too, Adams' dismal thoughts on the possibility of rescue at the hands of our academic establishment. The scholarly world, it seems to me, is increasingly geared to technique, and more and more the human sense is abandoned in favor of this technique. Those neo-utopian projections of a programmed and presumably blissful future that one hears so much about these days may be ahead—if for many they are not already here—but the bliss may turn out to be hell. In the increasingly valueless life of flow and sense there lurks the growing specter of madness, a vision that when apprehended may cause men to turn away from it.

Perhaps this is where the prophet comes in. As mangled and perverted as are the uses to which the idea of freedom has been put throughout history—the wars, the killing, the hypocrisy—it remains with all of its burden of suffering and tragedy the central theme of history, and it has been the work of the prophet to clarify men's vision on the subject. When that vision is lost it is the prophet who sees it most strikingly and is willing to give up all to attest its reality. Peter Maurin was a prophet. There are prophetic voices today—certainly in Russia—but in many other places, too, They have been heard and are still heard in the Catholic Worker movement, and the spirit of that movement will continue to fire the zeal of those who can take prophetic inspiration.

In writing this history I have emphasized the thinking

and action of Dorothy Day. There are two reasons for this: first, she has been, since the beginning of the movement, the final exemplar/arbiter of what is contained in the substance of the Worker idea and how it is expressed in life. The second reason is that Dorothy Day's voluminous writings on the Worker movement—in *The Catholic Worker*, in her books, and in a number of periodicals—has made her, along with the Worker papers, a prime source of information. One could not write about the movement and avoid a major emphasis on her. This is not, however, a biography. The focus is on the Worker idea and not on Dorothy Day.

From some others who have been associated with the movement from its first days I have received hospitality and help. I spent several days with Bill and Dorothy Gauchat at Avon, Ohio, talking about the Worker movement. On five or six occasions over the past seven years I and my family have visited the Catholic Worker farm at Tivoli, New York. The people at Tivoli: Marty and Rita Corbin, Deane Mowrer, Hans Tunnesen, John Filliger, Alice Lawrence, and Peggy Baird, before she died, soon ceased to be objects of investigation for me and became friends, and I have gone back to Tivoli because I like their company. Stanley Vishnewski is frequently at the farm, and he has been very generous with his help, providing me with good insights from his own reflections on the movement and even serving as a kind of editorial assistant. Without the customarily requisite foundation grant, Stanley has made himself the archivist of the Catholic Worker movement, and I am sure that there will be other historians who will recognize their debt to him. Deane Mowrer, likewise unfunded, has compiled an oral history of the movement and she, too, has worked at this simply to provide a record of something in which she believes. Arthur Lacey has done favors for me and once told me an engrossing story about his days at the Easton Worker farm. I am grateful to these people.

Generally, affairs have gone very well for me in writing this book. On several occasions I found, almost accidentally, books that provided me with key ideas about the Worker movement. For over a year I have spent most of my evenings writing. This has been a happy time for me and I am a little sorry that the work is ending. My greatest fortune, for which I am thankful, is in having Ned Arnold as my editor. It is more than his technical skill that I appreciate. It is his qualities as a person which, sooner or later, show through in a work of this kind. I can not burden him with its faults, but whatever in it is positive he has helped to form. Through him I had the great good fortune of getting Mary Solak as text editor.

David O'Brien of Holy Cross College read most of the first draft manuscript and gave me much encouragement at a time when I wondered if what I was trying to say made sense to anybody else. John Zeugner, my associate at Florida State University before he moved to Massachusetts, read the first draft and gave it a careful and helpful appraisal.

I acknowledge and appreciate the research grants given me by The American Philosophical Society and by Marquette University. Florida State University provided me with a quarter off from teaching, enabling me to avoid the strains of a pressing schedule.

More than anything else, though, I appreciate something I can only describe as the atmosphere out of which I wrote this book and which basically shaped my attitude toward its central idea. Whomever else I might name that went into making this atmosphere, I can place my wife and children at the center. And with them I can now also include two Marquette University girls, Susan Stemper and Cathy Ghiardi, who married my two oldest sons.

WILLIAM D. MILLER

*Lloyd, Florida*
*August, 1972*

# CONTENTS

# A
# HARSH
# AND
# DREADFUL
# LOVE

# Introduction

## THE RADICAL IDEA OF THE
## CATHOLIC WORKER MOVEMENT

The era of history through which the Western world has just passed is one in which the idea of time was virtually equated with that of "progress." There has been, and still is, almost a religious connection between the two. Progress was the increase of things—of the observable, the useful, and, especially, of those things that brought men ease and power. Time was the heartbeat of progress. It was for those who were faithful to its spirit the infallible bringer of the good, the Holy Spirit of the age of science.

In this era the acceptable humanism of progress was located in the dogmas of liberalism. Fervor was in the faith that by keeping abreast of the sweep of time, especially in the institutional forms that order its sweep, the essential goodness of men would bloom and life would be made rich. The method of liberalism was that of knowing the phenomenal world and then in a continued rearrangement of its forms keeping time's flow harmonious. In the midst of this change and flow men, as always, required a basis for community, something to be together in. The national state became the primary source of community; never was its cohesive power stronger than when war invested it with all of those marks of power in the form of military might that bore testimony to its progress.

For the age of technological enlightenment the liberal

outlook was a harmonious vision. Time moved with a regular cadence, governed by a moral order. Now all of this has gone. Time has accelerated, and progress has become flight. It is not change that is anticipated but shock, and the formulas of radical adjustment devised to meet this change never fit, but before they can operate are discarded in the wake of hurtling time.

It may be, as Herbert Marcuse says in his *Essay on Liberation*, that man is proceeding toward a new universe "where the sensuous, the playful, the calm, and the beautiful become forms of existence and thereby the *Form* of society itself." This is the vision of the new age of sense, hailed as the answer to those ideological constructs of the last half century that have produced racism, gas chambers, and everlasting wars. In the time of the new *Form* all of the guilt feelings that have accumulated, from the lynch mob to Auschwitz to Vietnam, will be washed out in an action of playful sense indulgence. A curtain will be dropped on the past and man, smiling to himself in a subdued way, will live forever in the new *Form*.

The radical idea of the Catholic Worker also anticipates form, not one rooted in the kingdom of sense but in the life of spirit. The form of the Catholic Worker will come when time is ended, and it will be ended when Christ, in an active and selfless love, is taken into every aspect of creation. This idea is a return to the theme of eschatological expectation, which was so powerful in the early days of the Christian community. In the minds of the founders of the Worker movement, Peter Maurin and Dorothy Day, it is the only radicalism worthy of the depths of man and sufficient to the crises at hand. It is the only one that can take man from that centrifugal force, now so strongly felt at the periphery of the process of time, and return him to the center of creation. It is radical because it would have history submit to it and would not itself submit to history.

The Worker movement is preeminently radical in its disposition to reject the myths by which modern men have lived and to affirm again the ones it believes is at the heart of creation. Myth is the realm through which ultimate reality is mediated to man in life-arranging values and actions. Its character is recognized and supported in extensive symbolization. The central myths of the Catholic Worker are those of the Garden of Eden and the Fall, the light of beatitude and the darkness of oblivion, sacred community and sinful alienation. From the Worker point of view, the tragedies of our time are found in the rejection of these central myths in favor of a succession of others that have become increasingly manipulated and brutalized.

There are two sources of ideas that have given much of the inspiration for the Worker idea. One, generally transmitted through Peter Maurin, was that body of thought produced in the years immediately after the First World War by a Paris group whose intellectual interactions touched on a common conviction which they called Christian personalism. The principal synthesizer of this approach was the French philosopher Emmanuel Mounier, who began in 1932 to publish articles of the personalist group in his review, *L'Esprit*. Peter Maurin's "idea," which he set before Dorothy Day in the first months of 1933, was his own in certain details of emphasis, but in its large lines it was the idea of the French personalist group. After the appearance of *L'Esprit*, he used it as an aid to his teaching.

Jacques Maritain was another French philosopher who had associations with the personalist group and who influenced Worker ideas by his views on the nature of the state, especially his advocacy of decentralized political institutions. Maritain maintained a personal contact with the Worker movement over many years. In November, 1934, he visited the Worker house at 436 East Fifteenth Street in New York and afterward wrote to Dorothy Day that he had found there a sign of new hope—"a preparation for the future for which we long."

The theme of the personalist idea held commonly by Mounier, Maritain, and the Catholic Worker was that the primacy of Christian love should be brought from its position of limbo where human affairs are concerned and infused into the process of history. The central fact of existence should not be process, with man holding on in whatever spot he found most tolerable; love should redeem process itself.

This redemption began with man, for in the human person was the final, indivisible entity that stood above process. This was the level to which Christ had brought man. Thus a change in the world began with man. He must "put on Christ," an action which began his own salvation and that of the universe, too. Otherwise, to follow only the line that avoided pain and led to sense pleasure was to increase the weight of time in history. On the other hand, to accept the worth and destiny of man in the light of Christ produced an effect that tended to bring history into harmony with itself and to direct it more speedily toward its fulfillment in a final redemption. Since all creation was finally one, there could be no such thing as a personal salvation unrelated to that of history.

And what in the personalist-Worker view did "putting on Christ" mean? It certainly did not mean a further refinement and extension of the analytic temper of the modern mind, so dear to the hearts of those whose first thought was to "study" the problem. This, as the Worker saw it, was a technique of altering process and not of changing it. Putting on Christ was an act of freedom which would be a leave-taking in spirit, mind, and even body of the institutional forms, manners, and values of a world of process—of, more particularly, the bourgeois world—for all that remained of a dynamic that had brought the modern period of history into existence was a shell. Those ideas that had borne the Western world along what it thought was the certain route of "progress" were lifeless.

It would be a leave-taking without revolution, slogans, banners, and mass demonstrations. These things were the symbols of change in external forms, more frequently attended by violence than not. In a phrase that Peter Maurin introduced to the Workers, and one that he appropriated from that radical labor union founded in 1905, the Industrial Workers of the World (Wobblies), the task was one of "building the new within the shell of the old." The "shell" was that fossilized myth that had structured a time of bourgeois ascendancy and that had passed. Personalism did not primarily require the destruction of old forms. "We are to be announcers of a new social order and not denouncers of the old," Peter Maurin had said. The repeated counsel of Dorothy Day has been to begin where one is—begin simply, build from the bottom up.

This is Catholic Worker personalism—the personalism of Mounier and Maritain. There is one thinker, however, who stands in relation to the life of the Catholic Worker movement as a particular prophet, a man who was profoundly a personalist, but whose philosophic penetration is such that it goes beyond the label of personalism; one who with the gift of his genius has explored the meaning of the life of the spirit in the twentieth century. That man is Nikolai Berdyaev, the Russian émigré who lived in Paris during the thirties and forties and who participated in the study sessions of the personalist thinkers there. A Socialist during the Russian Revolution, he was expelled from his country in the early twenties because the impulses of his philosophical speculation brought him to ideas about the nature of freedom and the reality of spirit that were considered inimical to the intellectual formation of a Communist state.

Berdyaev, above all others, is the contemporary world's philosopher of freedom and spirit, and it is remarkable to what degree his ideas have been mirrored in the thought and experience of the Catholic Worker movement. In the following sentence of his can be found the philosophical statement of the Catholic Worker personalist idea: "The end of history is the victory of existential time over historical time, of creative subjectivity over objectivization, of personality over the universal-common, of existential society over objectivized society." It is the war against historical time and "objectivization" that contains the substance of the Worker idea. Berdyaev died in 1949, knowing nothing, probably, of the Worker movement. From the Worker side,

it seems that Workers were not extensively acquainted with
him. True, there was a time when they studied his books,
but young Workers of a later period have seemed unaware
of the extent to which the Worker idea is contained in the
religious and social philosophy of Berdyaev.

The second source for the Catholic Worker idea comes
from the Russian novelist Dostoevsky, and it was mainly
from his writings that Dorothy Day derived key elements of
her personalist sense. Since Berdyaev, too, found in Dostoevsky the illumination and power that Dorothy Day had
found, one can find in Dostoevsky themes common to Berdyaev and the Catholic Worker movement. In his book,
*Dostoevsky*, Berdyaev says that the Russian author was
"among the most brilliant and keen-minded men of all
time," and to read his *The Brothers Karamazov* could be a
baptism of fire. This was certainly true for Dorothy Day
who, even in her adolescent years, read him and reflected
on those questions he raised that seemingly went to the final
depths. It was from Dostoevsky that she saw so strikingly
the dialectic of radical love as against the procedural and
pragmatic character of history.

From *The Brothers Karamazov*, she has quoted many
times a phrase from the statement on love made by the
monk, Zossima. The scene, familiar to all Dostoevsky readers,
is at a monastery where a number of travelers have gathered, seeking counsel from the monk whose wisdom and holiness are well known. One of the persons hoping to be
helped is an attractive society woman who tells him that she
is suffering from a lack of faith. "Lack of faith in God?" he
asks. No, not that, she says. She is worried about immortality. It is such a problem; no one can prove it, "and I say to
myself, 'What if I've been believing all my life, and when I
come to die there's nothing but the burdocks growing on
my grave?' as I read in some author. It's awful! . . . How
can I prove it? How can I convince myself?" Father Zossima
responds with the Worker's radical answer, the one that
Dorothy Day has repeatedly given as the substance of the
Worker philosophy. To the woman's final demand of how,

the monk replies: "By the experience of active love. . . . In as far as you advance in love you will grow surer of the reality of God and of the immortality of your soul."

And what was meant by "active love," the woman asked. She loved humanity. Often she dreamed of a life of service to the unfortunate that filled her with warmth. She could nurse the afflicted; she would be ready to kiss their wounds. But sometimes she wondered how she would react if she were not repaid in gratitude for her service. What if the patient "began abusing you and rudely commanding you, and complaining to the superior authorities of you (which often happens when people are in great suffering)—what then?" She could not bear ingratitude. "I expect my payment at once—that is praise, and the repayment of love with love. Otherwise I am incapable of loving anyone."

The radicalism that seeks to change the time-formed arrangements of values and institutions has time as its ally, but the radicalism of love ignores time, and its course for the bearer of love is the most difficult to follow. When the woman stated that she had to have gratitude as a repayment of the love she gave, Father Zossima answered in words that Dorothy Day has many times repeated: "Love in action is a harsh and dreadful thing compared to love in dreams. Love in dreams is greedy for immediate action, rapidly performed and in the sight of all. Men will even give their lives if only the ordeal does not last long but is soon over, with all looking and applauding as though on the stage. But active love is labour and fortitude, and for some people, too, perhaps a complete science. But I predict that just when you see with horror that in spite of all your efforts you are getting further from your goal instead of nearer to it—at that very moment you will reach and behold clearly the miraculous power of the Lord who has been all the time loving and mysteriously guiding you."

For Peter Maurin, Dorothy Day, and many others who have lived in the spirit of the Catholic Worker, the first mark of their desire to redeem the universe has been to live at the "harsh and dreadful" front of active love. In the early period of the movement, Dorothy Day wrote in *The Catho-lic Worker* an editorial on love, and much of it was based on the reflections of Dostoevsky's monk. "Hell Is Not to Love Any More" was the editorial's title. It was a statement of the Worker's faith in love as the ultimate reality: "When one loves, there is at that time a correlation between the spiritual and the material. Even the flesh itself is energized, the human spirit is made strong. All sacrifice, all suffering is easy for the sake of love. . . . This is the foundation stone of The Catholic Worker movement. It is on this that we build." And she made the point again that with Workers there could be no spirit of that sentimental unreality that came from an expectation of "miracles" of love occurring to grace their days and comfort their nights with the pleasant sense that comes from living in the glow of gratitude of those whom one has helped. Love in practice was harsh and dreadful.

The "hardness" of the Catholic Worker way has another aspect of Dostoevskian emphasis. It is found in the Worker's view of freedom. To those contemporary cultists of the "new sensibility," freedom means the removal of all barriers to sense probing, but to the Worker freedom means to turn away from the tyranny of sense toward spirit over a course that involves suffering and even tragedy. This freedom is the highest value, the way to God, in the Worker view. Indeed, says Berdyaev, "the justification both of God and of man must be looked for in freedom, of which the tragic process of the world is only a function, its issue subordinates to the progress of the main theme."

As Berdyaev observes, historically, Christian thinkers have swung between two positions: the tragic pitfalls that come with the good of freedom, as against the evil of the enforced good. Christianity, Berdyaev declares, must choose the whole of freedom, "otherwise it would have to renounce the possession of that truth of freedom which is the very truth of Jesus Christ." He concludes that "Doubtless this long passage through the experience of good and evil could be made much shorter and easier by limiting, or even entirely suppressing human liberty. But what is the value of men coming to God otherwise than by the road of freedom and after having experienced the harmfulness of evil?" It is to this view of freedom that the Catholic Worker has subscribed—which it has practiced and which has surely brought it hurt and tragedy.

This freedom has been personalized in the founders of the movement. Dorothy Day thought that Peter Maurin's greatest quality was that he was free in those ways that represent the very opposite of the contemporary sense-object definitions of the word. He had no concern with Berdyaev's "object world." Robert Ludlow, one of the most thoughtful of those who over the years have written for *The Catholic Worker,* observed that "Peter was a free man. . . . He achieved to a remarkable degree the liberty of the Christian."

For her part, Dorothy Day in her life with the movement has accepted the divisions and catastrophes that are the part of freedom. There have been divisions within the movement. From the first, there were those who would have it follow a more moderate course, who would trade the precariousness that went with freedom for an organization of their lives. There were divisions accompanied by that particularly bitter type of recrimination that occurs when zealots with tormented minds find that the course they have charted as absolute is not followed.

There were outside pressures, some powerful, for the movement to cease its groping and stumbling after the vision of a redeemed creation, and to turn back to some of the main marked routes on which modern man travels. The state has exerted its pressures for conformity. Where the state would be violent, Dorothy Day and those who shared her pacifist convictions chose nonviolence. There were pressures from churchmen who used finely spun traditionalist arguments, sincerely offered, about "just" wars, and who advised the exercise of the virtue of prudence when she and other Workers spoke against injustice. It would be better to leave the world to the Caesars, she was told.

There was the inner pressure from a protesting flesh to turn from the harshness of life at a Worker house to the security of an organized life, conforming to certain state "guidelines" that would assure a generous financial assistance. Worker life might then be glamorous with its soup lines and colorful characters, but there was no glamour in the smell of the old and diseased, in the fathomless pettiness of some, in the quarrelsome and sometimes drunken rages that occasionally erupted, and in the cabals and intrigues carried on by those who felt that they had not received their due. It was these things, borne day after day and year after year, that revealed the hardness of the personalist idea.

Obviously, the Catholic Worker idea is at odds with the contemporary myth forms that dominate the world and with none more so than that which has manifested itself in bourgeois culture—its institutional forms, values, and manners. It has seen these as principal impediment to redemption, and in this view it has been faithful to the thought of the personalist philosophers. The following, one of Peter Maurin's "easy essays," a paraphrase of Berdyaev, illustrates the personalist attitude:

This middle-class mentality
ripened and enslaved
human society and culture
at the summit of their civilization
Its concupiscence
is no longer restricted
by man's supernatural beliefs
as it was in past epochs
It is no longer kept in bounds
by the sacred symbolism
But even when the triumph of mediocrity
was complete
a few deep thinkers
denounced it
with uncompromising power
Carlyle, Nietzsche, Ibsen,

Leon Bloy, Dostoevsky, Leontiev
all foresaw
the victory of the bourgeois spirit
over a truly great culture
on the ruins of which
it would establish
its own hideous kingdom
History has failed
there is no such thing as historical progress
the present is in no wise
an improvement on the past . . .
The will to power, to well being, to wealth
triumphs over the will
to holiness, to genius
The highest spiritual achievements
belong to the poor
spirituality is on the wane
and a time of spiritual decline
is a time of bourgeois ascendancy

Most specifically, the Worker has protested the dehumanizing aspects of those two phenomena of the bourgeois period of history: nationalism and capitalism. The nation,
which derived much of its initial dynamism from what
seemed to be its tangible dimension for community, had put
too much of its use to the ends of competitive power. In the
context of nationhood, the spirit of community seemingly
could reach its fullest height when the nation was engaged
in war, yet who could say, finally, that any of these wars
had been just? Dorothy Day, especially, has viewed warfare
among nations as an aberration, a colossally organized extreme opposition to the principle of active love. It was clear
to her that the Gospel message was peace, and it is she who
has contributed nonviolence to the personalist idea. It is this
principle, brought to bear in a world still seething with conflict, that tests to agonizing depths the personalist idea for
many who are attracted to it.

The Worker has also objected to the increase in the Or-

wellian 1984 characteristics of the state. As life becomes
rapidly more complex and interactions among men increase,
it is, in the Worker view, a critical necessity that the final
authority for the extension and regulation of these interactions should not be given to the state. The advancing sweep
of the modern explosion of process could quickly turn any
state into the most tyrannical Caesardom. Dorothy Day has
frequently expressed her suspicion of the state by the use of
the phrase, "Holy Mother State."

Capitalism, like nationalism, is opposed because its
mythic lineaments have been saturated with the glorifica-
tion of struggle. Capital, always in pursuit of its own ag-
grandizement, had used the mythology of the state for its
own imperialist ends. In its more immediate and obtrusive
form, it had thrust itself upon man by advertising its wares
to the point where the possibility of a reflective mood or humanizing grace had been isolated out of existence. Man
does not live by suburbia alone, the Worker has repeatedly
said, and it sees the institutions of modern capital actively
trying to convince man that suburbia and the enlarging
areas of sense delight are its handiwork.

These criticisms are not, of course, original with the Catholic Worker. Nor can the Worker's program for getting at
the problem be considered original. Worker history in action is to build the new within the old, and its "new," both
for nationalism and capitalism, has been aimed at institutional redirection toward voluntary communities, then regional associations. But the Worker has been vague as to
the specific form the new social organization would take,
and when Peter Maurin was pressed for a blueprint he
would answer that he only enunciated the principles. The
application of these principles to specific situations would
be the continuing work of the committed.

Dorothy Day, always the apostle of social decentralization and simplification, has tried to bring the Worker idea
into life by a succession of community ventures. Their
course, like Worker history, has been precarious, but Workers cast their failures into hope. Their goal is not success in

the world, as the world accounts success, but to establish
the reality of spirit in the world. Thus in the Worker view,
to "fail" is to succeed.

Over the years Dorothy Day and her friends have been
accused of harboring a profound naïveté on Communism,
the other major contemporary myth form. To the more choleric, the movement has not only been "soft" on Communism
but was its knowing agent. Fundamentally, the two philosophies are profoundly at odds. They are at odds on the question of freedom. For Communism, freedom comes when
time's flow is brought into a humane material alignment.
The Worker, too, believes in this alignment but not through
the instrumentality of force and state organization. The material is the means to transcendence, the means by which
man practices his charity, shows his love, and through
which in the beauty of nature he can find God. In the Communist sense, freedom harmonizes time; in the Worker and
Christian sense, it is time that gives to freedom its "tragic
principle," and it is divine grace only that can at last bring
man through the snare of time.

Communism and the Worker differ in their sense of community. Communism has said, with the evidence of history
to back it, that historical Christianity has been only a pawn
in centuries of international rivalry and warfare. It, to the
contrary, offers men the idea of the universal state and universal peace. But from the Worker's Christian point of view,
this universality is an illusion, since it can never be anything
more than a point running in the track of time. Communism's promised community represents a deification of historical time, an attitude against which the Christian must
rebel, since real love has no fulfillment except in the completion of time. This final community, "The Mystical Body
of Christ," is, as Dorothy Day has said many times, "the
doctrine which is behind all our effort."

Finally, the radicalism of the Catholic Worker is opposite
from that of Communism in the way each chooses to reach
its end. If the completion of community is a state of work
and play running in time, of which the past with its inequi-

ties is a preparation, then drastic and forcible realterations in the forms of the object world are legitimate. These changes, effected by war, revolution, or the firing squad, fill the tenderhearted with abhorrence, but the very sternness of the Communist's method is, within the logic of his mythic form, a testimony of his devotion to man.

The Worker viewpoint, seeking an end to time, requires with a logical insistence equal to the Communist's that force not be used. Violence is of time and process. A Christian radicalism is above all time. "All the way to Heaven is Heaven," St. Catherine of Siena had said, and Dorothy Day has frequently cited this. To give in charity, to turn from violence, to die for love, is time-ending.

The Catholic Worker, however, most emphatically has not regarded Communism as the ultimate force of evil in relation to the good of a bourgeois culture. Rather, the Worker (Peter Maurin, especially) has said that Communism was more the immediate evidence of a failure of historical Christianity, most strikingly revealed in the bourgeois period of history. And insofar as Communism has helped to raise the human level of the world's forgotten masses by giving them bread and stirring within them a vision of community, it is an advance over the past. But finally in its mythic form it settles on the ideal of science, and in the Worker view, man has depths, and a vision, too, that science can never reach.

# 1

## PETER MAURIN

Once, in answer to the question of who founded the Catholic Worker movement, Dorothy Day responded, "Peter Maurin is most truly the founder. I would never have had an idea in my head about such work if it had not been for him. . . . Yes, he was a leader, a teacher, a founder. I was a journalist, a doer, but without the theory, I would have gotten nowhere." Again, she commented that he was her master, and she was his disciple; that he gave her a way of life and instruction, and to explain what has come to be known as The Catholic Worker Movement in the Church throughout the world, she must begin with him. He was in her view "a genius, a saint."

Maurin was born on May 8, 1877, on the family farm in the Gevaudan area of Languedoc, southern France. His parents, John Baptist and Marie, named him, their first child, Aristide Peter. His mother died when he was seven, having by that time borne five children, only three of whom survived. Two years later the father married again, and over the course of the years his second wife bore him nineteen more children. It was, apparently, a simple, well-ordered, and happy family community, directed and secured by a tradition that came from fifteen hundred years of Maurin ownership of the family land. Years later Maurin would exclaim, "I am neither a bourgeois nor a proletariat. I am a peasant. I have roots!"

Dorothy Day met Maurin when he was fifty-four years old, and her impression of him then was of a "short, broad-shouldered workingman with a high, broad head covered with greying hair." His face was weatherbeaten, but he had warm gray eyes and a wide, pleasant mouth. She recalled that he had on a dirty shirt, but he had tried to dress up for the occasion by wearing a tie and a suit that looked as though he had slept in it—which, as she found out later, had actually been the case.

What sort of man was this Maurin whom Dorothy Day, after fifteen years of firsthand acquaintance with him, would label a genius? There were others who on meeting him concluded that his ideas, such as they could glean through his heavy French accent, were fanciful constructs of a distracted mind that had little to do with the world of experience they knew. Academicians were seldom impressed. It was not only that intellectually he stood outside of prevailing notions of what was current and vital in the realm of ideas, but also that he wore none of the standard marks of intellectual involvement. He was associated with no university; he spoke without the mantle of authority that comes from a higher degree; and he did not "publish." His teaching techniques seemed simplistic. To those who wanted ideas explicated in a scholarly jargon, his ideas stated in short, phrased sentences seemed juvenile. Reducing to several alliterative phrases an analysis and solution to a major problem of civilization could only appall those accustomed to a careful and extensive refinement of even the most insignificant backwash of history.

Yet others besides Dorothy Day attested to the power of his mind and spirit, albeit they were Workers who had lived for some years in the atmosphere of his teaching. John Curran, a member of the Worker household during and after the Second World War, said that usually those who met Maurin briefly ended up by calling him a "pest and a nuisance," but those who lingered long enough truly to confront his mind and person recognized his brilliance. Julia Porcelli, the young Italian high-school graduate who in the

Peter Maurin in his room in St. Joseph's House of Hospitality,
115 Mott St., New York City, 1930s.

thirties gave devoted service to the Worker, registered her own passionate conviction: "Peter was a poet, he was an agitator, and the gentle, strong voice of truth. This was the voice of the Holy Ghost and it wasn't listened to." There was an occasional bishop, an occasional priest who had caught a part of Maurin's vision, but even they failed due to "their lack of understanding of all that he meant."

Certainly, at first glance there was nothing about Maurin that conveyed to the world of affairs the power he possessed. He was, in fact, a poor man, "a bum," as indifferent to the accepted amenities of dress and toilet as he was of intellectual style. He was "a real St. Benedict Joseph Labre in our day," Dorothy Day recounted, thinking back to that saint who went unwashed and accoutered in rags alive with vermin.

Because of his apparent and absolute indifference to the accepted standards of dress, Peter was sometimes rejected by those in the mainstream. Once, when Dorothy Day had recommended Maurin to a pious acquaintance who had asked for someone from the Worker house to speak on the Worker idea, the response was negative. "With all due respect to your Apostle on the Bum, I do not think that he is the man for up here."

Workers could tell stories in which Maurin's unconventional attire involved him in cases of mistaken identity. Dorothy Day recalled a time when he went to a Westchester town to give a talk to a woman's club—"He always went where he was asked." Several hours after he had gone, she received a frantic telephone call: Where was Maurin? "Since I had put him on the train myself, I told them he must be in the station. 'There is only an old tramp sitting on the bench asleep,' was the reply. We knew it was Peter."

Once, it was in 1939, Maurin was invited to dinner at the home of the eminent Columbia University professor Carlton J. H. Hayes. When he arrived, Mrs. Hayes thought he had come to read the gas meter and directed him to the basement, and there he sat until it dawned on the professor that it was Maurin who was sitting submissively below.

He liked to travel, and during his Catholic Worker years he spent much time wandering about the country, stopping at the homes of *Catholic Worker* readers or sleeping in bus stations, never changing his clothes and never bathing. At night, if he found a bed, he would roll his coat around his feet and fold his pants into a pillow under his head. He had a small suitcase but he never carried clothes, only books. Dorothy Day recalled that once she and Maurin were at Notre Dame University, where Maurin was the guest of Emmanuel Chapman, the latter a Thomist philosopher and Jewish convert–friend of Jacques Maritain. When the visit was over, all went to the bus station together, Dorothy Day to go in one direction and Maurin in another. Although Maurin's ticket read Cincinnati, he boarded the bus for Cleveland, an error that a friend and Chapman hurried to point out to him. "That's all right," he said. "I know people in Cleveland."

One might suspect that Maurin's vagaries where time and space were concerned were calculated artifices, designed to build an aura of romantic imagery about himself. But they were utterly true to his nature. He was a teacher, consumed with an invincible sense of his missionary purpose to awaken others to think. He wanted to be an instrument of what he called the "clarification of thought," and he scarcely heard at all the call of the world to concede to its terms.

He was a persistent talker. Dorothy Day said that "he was one of those people who talked you deaf, dumb, and blind; who each time he saw you began his conversation just where he had left off at the pervious meeting. He never stopped unless you begged for a rest, and that was not long." He made her think of St. Paul, "how he talked all through the night and how one of his listeners, sitting on a window sill in a close room, hot with the lamp light, fell out of the window and had to be restored to life by the speaker, who then went on indoctrinating regardless!"

"Clarification" apparently went on whatever the circumstances. The Jesuit John La Farge recalled a summer night in 1934 when he went up to Harlem to visit Maurin, who had opened a storefront hospitality center. There had been no money to turn on the electricity, or for candles either, so Maurin received his evening caller in the dark, with only a faint illumination from the streetlight outside. Father La Farge remembered that night because "all he could see in the . . . gloom was Peter's forefinger, motioning in the air as he was making his points."

He talked even while riding a bus. Talking, presumably, to a Worker traveling companion, he would raise his voice so that others might be brought to listen and thus enter into the thinking process. There is a story that once when he was staying in a flophouse in Chicago, a prostitute knocked on the door and asked him if he wanted to "have a good time." He invited her in, only to indoctrinate her in what having a good time meant from his point of view, offering her a "clarification" that turned out to be something different from what the lady had had in mind.

He suffered disabilities as a talker. Some, it was said, did not like to listen to him because of his heavy French accent. Others complained that he talked too much, maintaining that "it was never a dialogue with Peter, but a monologue." But Dorothy Day said this was not so. "Actually," she said, "Peter explained to us very carefully the technique he used to follow. . . . First, he (or the other fellow) would talk at length and say all he had to say. Then the listener had his turn to hold forth. To interrupt was a failure in technique. It was also to be understood that one really listened and did not spend the time while the other was talking in preparing one's own speech." Maurin was full of little aphorisms, and one of them, on talk, was, "I will give you a piece of my mind and you will give me a piece of your mind and then we will both have more in our minds."

He did not consider himself a writer, but in certain circumstances he saw the worth of writing his ideas. All of his writing was, as Dorothy Day described it, in phrased sentences, broken up to look like free verse. It was a device that he thought would compel attention and make for reflection. But what really prompted him to express his ideas in this manner was some ancient cultural sense that led him to attempt a form of folk communication in the transmission of those thoughts and feelings that lay close to the heart of myth formation. All of his writings had a swing, a rhythm like verse, and, as Dorothy Day observed, "he liked to consider himself a troubadour of Christ, singing solutions to the world's ills."

He was also fond of pamphleteering. As he traveled and walked the streets of New York, his pockets bulged with pamphlets, some of his own composition, which he passed out indiscriminately. He would do without food and walk rather than pay bus fare, to have money for pamphlets. As Dorothy Day remembered, every day he would present himself at the desk of one of the men who had taken over that most ubiquitous of all jobs in the Worker household, that of "business manager," and put out his hand for a dollar. "Nothing more or less." Then he would go to a noonday Mass at St. Francis of Assisi Church, on West Thirty-first Street, or at St. Andrew's on Duane Street near City Hall, after which he would breakfast on Bowery stew, costing fifteen or twenty cents, and then, "walking slowly with his hands behind his back," he would go to Union Square to begin his pamphleteering and talking.

If some found him a bore and a nuisance, those around the Worker house came to feel a great force that rose through his vagaries, his accent, his unkempt appearance, and his curious teaching techniques. "Liking" Maurin was not the issue, Dorothy Day said. She recalled a point made by a French priest who later died in a concentration camp. He had said that man's freedom was so precious that no one should ever exert a personal influence to win another to an idea. It was the truth alone that should attract. Maurin, she thought, exemplified that approach. It was not the attractiveness of his personality that won people to him; it was simply what he was. She has given a description of his impact on her:

❁ ❁ ❁

Peter made you feel a sense of his mission as soon as you met him. He did not begin by tearing down, or by painting so intense a picture of misery and injustice that you burned to change the world. Instead, he aroused in you a sense of your own capacities for work, for accomplishment. He made you feel that you and all men had great and generous hearts with which to love God. If you once recognized this fact in yourself you would expect and find it in others. "The art of human contacts," Peter called it. . . . But it was seeing Christ in others, loving the Christ you saw in others.

Maurin was, more than anything else, a free man, for he wanted nothing. Over the years that he lived in the Worker house of hospitality in New York, he seldom had a room of his own. Some of the young, especially those who helped edit the paper, had their own desks and were jealous of their privacy. But Maurin, said Dorothy Day, "had no chair, no place at the table, no corner that was particularly his. He was a pilgrim and a stranger on earth, using the things of this world as though he used them not, availing himself of only what he needed and discarding all excess baggage."

He was not a pious recluse who shunned the world. To be free meant to free others. This was a problem that a better social order could help solve, but the social order was not of itself the provider of freedom. It could be an instrument of freedom only insofar as it enabled men to rise above misery and drudgery and gave them the opportunity of making more significant choices with reference to freedom. The ultimate significance of the social order was in terms of its personalist reference. One became free in the *action* of freeing others. This action began with the person and extended through institutions to all of the universe. The action of freedom was the action of love, and it had no racial, religious, or institutional bounds.

Maurin's conviction that it was the action of love that came before any other consideration has given the Catholic Worker movement a constant motif in its approach to the problems of the world—one from which Dorothy Day, as her critics have charged, has intransigeantly refused to depart.

The world must be changed, but, again, the change must begin with the person. There could be no quick or revolutionary leap to the good society that could ever put aside, even for a moment, personalist action. Mass political and social pressures that ignored the poor at one's doorstep were false. The action of love came before the action of the world. With both Peter Maurin and Dorothy Day, there was a settled antipathy against all action that took on the spirit of a crusade, for crusades traditionally indulged those flights from the hard level of personalist action.

In those early years of Worker history, Maurin set the example for personalist action. Oblivious of the exigencies to which the larder at the Worker house might be subject, he brought home whomever he found that was hungry, and his concern for those sleeping on the benches in Union Square led the Worker to rent apartments where people could be sheltered. When anyone who had shared in Worker hospitality made attempts to thank Maurin and the Workers, Maurin would respond by saying that it was the guest who should be thanked, for in his view the man who came to share their food and shelter had been the means by which they progressed in freedom. He literally accepted the Gospel injunction that he should give his own coat to whoever asked him for it. He gave away coats—or whatever else he had. Dorothy Day remembered how Maurin had returned to the Worker house one summer evening with a swollen eye, and he explained that he had been robbed in Morningside Park. "And when we indignantly asked him how anyone had dared to strike him, he replied that he only had been trying to tell the thief that he had the money in the other pocket!"

He never saw his life in any other way than in relationship to the Catholic Church, nor did he seem to have any disposition to examine critically any aspect of that relationship. Dorothy Day sometimes met him at St. Andrew's Church so that after Mass she could discuss the affairs of the Worker house without interruption. She described him

as quiet and very attentive at Mass, after which he would sit
for long periods lost in thought.

He hoped and believed that the Church would be the
agent of the new synthesis, if only she would "use some of
the dynamite inherent in her message." The following is one
of his "essays" on this theme:

> If the Catholic Church
> is not today the dominant social, dynamic force,
> it is because Catholic scholars have failed
> to blow the dynamite of the Church.
> Catholic scholars have taken the dynamite of the Church,
> have wrapped it in nice phraseology,
> placed it in an hermetic container
> and sat on the lid.
> It is about time
> to blow the lid off
> so that the Catholic Church
> may again become the dominant social dynamic force.

It is perhaps because he was free and so full of his program that Maurin seemed never to have found it necessary
to expend any of his energy as a critic of the Church. Personalist radicalism found the idea of the Church no obstacle
to its philosophy or methods; to the contrary, it was only
through personalist radicalism that the dynamite of the
Church could be ignited. Maurin thus united orthodoxy
with radicalism, and this principle was understood and has
been faithfully followed by Dorothy Day.

Though the Church had failings, Maurin was not the kind
to be turned from his vision by institutional or human faltering. Unweighted by cynicism or pessimism, he was certain
of deep reservoirs of human goodness that could be brought
forth to take man along the path to the Kingdom of God. To
people who viewed him from a distance he seemed unreal,
but to Dorothy Day his reality was a powerful and permanent force in her life.

Maurin also impressed many young people who came to

the Worker house in the first years, and one young Worker especially, Arthur Sheehan. It was his opinion that Maurin was "the greatest Catholic of our times," a conviction that led him to write a biography of Maurin. In *Peter Maurin: Gay Believer,* he has written of Maurin as he knew him in the Worker movement, and to this personal familiarity he has added a considerable amount of research pertaining to Maurin's early years. Sheehan provides practically all that is known of Maurin's life before the Catholic Worker years— a significant contribution, since Maurin almost never discussed the circumstances of his past life except in the most general terms and then only to make a point.

When he was fourteen he went to a boarding school near Paris, run by the Christian Brothers, a teaching order which in that time was dedicated to providing an education for those ordinarily without the necessary resources. In 1893 he entered the Brothers as a novice, but formal teaching did not seem to suit him. When he was twenty-three he discovered an idea that seemed more meaningful than any in which his life had been involved. He found it in *The Furrow* (*Le Sillon*), the publication of a religiously inspired youth movement organized by the young enthusiast Marc Sangnier. On January 1, 1903, at the expiration of his annual religious vow, he left the Brothers to make his own way in the world and to work with the Sillon movement.

The Sillon was something new in Catholic action, certainly of a different stamp from the well-established *L'Action française,* with its longing backward look at the days before the French Revolution when there was royalty and special privileges for the clergy. The Sillon, to the contrary, was one of the first of the modern Catholic movements to say that the Catholic Church had a central role to play in the social processes of the age of evolution and the machine, and it saw the rise of democratic forces as a development in keeping with the essential spirit of the Church. In the turbulent days of 1905 in Russia, Sangnier upset Catholic traditionalists by praising the revolutionaries as "these anarchists with a mystical and profound soul" who were disturbing the "sweet dream holy Russia held in its vast heart" by spreading germs of a "strange redemption."

The Sillon, too, was in sympathy with a Tolstoyan kind of pacifist opposition to the rising spirit of nationalism and militarism. As a movement it was decentralist—there were "no dues, no rules" and no elections. One entered and left freely, and there were no salaried positions. In all of these things there are parallels with the Worker movement. But beyond the close similarity in their programs and organizational characteristics, the two movements held in common one pervading idea. They were hostile to the bourgeois spirit and especially to its presence in the Catholic Church.

Maurin began his association with the movement as a member of a study club. "It was the time of Charles Péguy, but I didn't know him nor was I influenced by him," Maurin observed to Arthur Sheehan when the latter asked him about the well-known Catholic poet. Rather, Maurin was interested in a group that published a weekly paper, *The Democratic Awakening (L'Eveil democratique)*. He took a room in a poor section of Paris and went out each day to sell the paper. Maurin's brother, Brother Norbert of the Christian Brothers, has told of Maurin's enthusiasm for the movement. "He busied himself profoundly in the . . . movement. . . . The ideas set forth and propagated by this movement struck deeply and were close to his most intimate desires," especially as it aimed at a "program for peace —religious peace, social peace, international peace."

But Maurin's ardor as a Sillonist cooled. Sheehan gives seemingly logical reasons for this. Maurin wanted a deeper analysis of the social problem than Sillonists were willing to make. Sangnier had placed little value on scholarship, saying, "Are many books necessary for one to have the Sillon spirit?" Maurin would think that "many books" were indeed necessary—if not for the Sillon spirit, then, certainly, for a right spirit. Nor is it difficult to see another aspect of the Sillon that was not to Maurin's taste: its disposition to view itself as a crusade—parades, oratory, and its *Jeune Garde*, the "knights" of the movement who sometimes fought street battles with rightists—affronted his inherent personalist disposition. In his view, emotional flights were always susceptible to taking one away from the substance.

Maurin presumably ceased his Sillonist activities shortly after the turn of the century. Sheehan has little on Maurin's life during the next few years, except that he worked as a chocolate salesman and read widely. Sheehan states Maurin was influenced considerably by *Mutual Aid,* a collection of a series of articles by Peter Kropotkin, the first of which appeared in 1890. The main theme of this book is worth noting, since it set forth an idea that has been strongly emphasized by Maurin and the Worker movement.

Kropotkin was a late nineteenth-century anarchist and biologist. As a biologist, his observations led him to a conclusion as scientifically radical as were his social views. In the last half of the nineteenth century, the Malthusian doctrine, combined with the thinking of Herbert Spencer and some facile generalizations about the Darwinian hypothesis, had raised a new value standard for men and nations. "Woe to the weak" was the new doctrine, one which, in the words of Ashley Montagu, was quickly "raised to the height of a commandment of nature revealed by science." By the beginning of the twentieth century the idea of the endless goodness of "competition" had ramifications in all aspects of human association.

It was this new dogma of science that Kropotkin attacked. T. H. Huxley's famous "Struggle for Existence Manifesto," an article published in 1888, took an extreme position on the ultimate beneficence of ruthless competition. As a response, Kropotkin published his *Mutual Aid.* Opposed to struggle and survival as the evolutionary vehicle, he found another principle—cooperation—more profound and pervasive than the Malthusian principle. It was the operation of the cooperative principle in social relations he had witnessed at work among Russian peasants that led him to his anarchism.

This idea appealed to Maurin, and it is easy to see why. It provided a wide expanse in which man's creative freedom could operate, and it presumed that there were untapped sources of goodness in man that would lead him to exercise this freedom. The influence of Kropotkin through Maurin on the Catholic Worker can be seen in the Worker's continuing concern to restore the communal aspects of Christianity.

Kropotkin's *Fields, Factories and Workshops* introduced Maurin to another idea that appeared in the Worker movement. Kropotkin believed that the intellectual could find in manual labor, especially in intensive gardening and fine craft work, an enriching dimension to intellectual work. This idea appears in the Catholic Worker movement in Maurin's emphasis on the unity of the scholar and the worker, a concept that apparently has much currency in contemporary Red China.

In 1909, when he was thirty-two years old, Maurin joined the 140,000 immigrants who entered Canada that year. There was much advertising in France at that time about the advantages of Canada, and Maurin, the peasant, was probably interested in the prospect of free land. Never having married, and still without a certain vocational commitment, he was free to go.

Little is known about his Canadian years except that somewhere on the frontier he and an unnamed partner homesteaded a parcel of land. When his partner was accidentally killed while hunting, Maurin gave up homesteading and took to wandering, picking up jobs here and there as a laborer. He entered the United States in 1911, moving from one place to another, as the job market shifted. He was arrested twice for vagrancy, once for riding the rails and once for an attempt to get a drink of water. In later years he described the latter episode: "I wanted a drink of water, so I knocked on a door. The woman tried to open it, but it was stuck with the frost. I started pushing to help her. The neighbors thought I was trying to break in. So, to please the neighbors, the chief of police put me in jail. Two days later, to please the neighbors, they let me go."

In the winter of 1912 he worked in the coal regions near Brownsville, Pennsylvania, for the H. C. Frick Coal and Coke Company. He made $1.50 a day, and he lived in an unused coke oven which he shared with a Black fellow workman. Stark though his habitat sounds, in Maurin's view it possessed the fundamental attributes of genteel living: it was warm and dry. An adjacent oven was in operation, and the heat from it kept the two of them warm. "All you had to do was to crawl in and lie down, and you were at home." There were additional pluses in the situation. His roommate was a "gentleman," and, besides, he did all of the cooking.

He worked for a time on railroad gangs and then settled down in Chicago as a janitor. The latter occupation kept him employed until 1925, a year that was apparently one of a major redirection in his life. He left Chicago for New York City and the area around it. At this time, too, says Sheehan, he "underwent some great religious experience. He never explained it to anyone, but from this time on his actions were different." What was this religious experience? One can only guess. His reading and thinking had brought him to a new insight. He saw things in a new Church-centered focus.

There were signs of his change, and leaving Chicago may have been one of them. It seems reasonable to think that the idea of voluntary poverty took on new meaning for him. There is a picture of Maurin taken during his Chicago days that suggests he paid attention to his grooming and dress. How different from the Maurin the Workers knew—the man who wore whatever covered him: even his glasses, ill-fitting and damaged, hung precariously on his nose. Possibly his penchant for "indoctrinating" had been exercised in his Chicago years, but it becomes clearly apparent after his move to New York, taking on the techniques that were peculiar to him in trying to awaken others to think and achieve a "clarification" of their own.

It is interesting to speculate on what he might have read during the 1920s that helped him toward his insight. It is in this period Sheehan mentions the impact that Leon Bloy had had on him, and it may have been Bloy who helped to bring Maurin's religious-intellectual quest into focus, for

there is a great deal of Bloy's spirit in Maurin. According to
Sheehan, Maurin was one of the first to bring Bloy's writings to the attention of Americans.

It was probably from Bloy that Maurin got his sense of
the anti-Christian character of bourgeois culture. Bloy, who
died in 1917, was a herald of the French Catholic thought
of the twenties and thirties, and he, before Maritain and
Mounier, was disposed to treat the modern period of history
with the shocking acid of his pen. Bloy regarded bourgeois
culture as a grotesque abomination, so corrupt that "even
sows would recoil from . . . [its] body."

Maurin and the Worker have shared Bloy's sense of the
mystery of poverty: that voluntarily embraced, it can be a
freeing and purifying force; that suffered, it is a hellish
thing. As Bloy described it: "The Saints who espoused her
from love and begat many children of her assert that she is
infinitely lovable," but others "die from terror or from despair at her kiss, and the many of men pass 'from the womb
to the grave' without knowing what to think of this monster." But voluntary poverty was the straight path to
freedom—to God—and Bloy might have written of Maurin
as he wrote of St. Francis of Assisi: he was "a lover and not
a poor man. He was in need of nothing, since he possessed
his God and lived . . . outside the world of senses. He
bathed in the gold of his shining rags." But for those vast
hordes who knew poverty and who had not willed it, they
had "been excommunicated from life and turned into a people damned." And so it was with the Catholic Worker which
advocated voluntary poverty as an act of freedom, only to
condemn it more for its diabolical consequences to the spirit
of men who were forced, against their will, to bear it.

Maurin and Bloy were otherwise dissimilar types. Maurin
was a teacher and he had the optimism of one who saw a
path even though the times were dark. Bloy, on the other
hand, was sickened and angered by what he saw as the intellectual pretension, the spiritual vapidness, and cruelty
of bourgeois culture. He used words that slashed and
shocked, and his outlook was bleak.

When the Depression hit America, Maurin was working without pay at a summer camp for boys in Mount Tremper, New York. On weekends, with a dollar given him by Father Joseph Scully, the camp manager, he went to New York City to read in the public library and to talk with the radicals who congregated at Union Square. At night he got a bed for forty cents at Uncle Sam's Hotel on the Bowery. As the Depression deepened, the radicals at Union Square increased in number, and to a casual onlooker Maurin probably appeared no different from the rest. But he seemed to have been looking for some special person—someone to whom he might communicate his clarification. It was George Shuster, then editor of *Commonweal* magazine, who advised Maurin to seek out Dorothy Day.

# 2

# DOROTHY DAY

In 1932, the universe still had some semblance of traditional order. The nation-state was as yet unchallenged as the ultimate factor in shaping human destiny, and when on June 10 the cadets at West Point assembled to hear their commencement address, they were assured that they had an honorable and godly calling, not to be affected by "disarmament conferences and pacifist conventions." As the speaker accurately predicted, the cadets would soon have an outlet for their professional expectations, since it seemed "all too likely that some day in your lifetime our streets again may be filled with marching men."

It was a time of "old-fashioned patriotism," and a time that caught some of the lingering iridescence of the twenties. Late in November, Noel Coward arrived from England to appear in *Design for Living* with Alfred Lunt and Lynn Fontanne. At the Barrymore Theater, Cole Porter's *Gay Divorce* opened, and soon Americans were singing "Night and Day."

In Washington, Herbert Hoover strove, in his humorless, high-starched-collar fashion, to preserve the fixed points in the firmament that he knew about—the gold standard and the sanctity of international war debt commitments. After November his problems took on substance. It was not only the threat of Keynesian economics to ancient economics verities that disturbed him: it was the prospect of the newly elected Franklin D. Roosevelt taking over the Presidency, a man who apparently had no sound grounding in any category of formal truth, to say nothing of the gold standard, and who was breezily unconcerned about the awful threats to traditional order that lurked in the shadows. Moreover, the chorus of groans from those nations having to make their annual war debt payment indicated that the federal financial structure would receive no propping from that source.

The reality most immediately disturbing to Hoover was, despite some palliative federal measures in 1932, the persistence of the Depression in a seriously aggravated form. In May and June, some twelve to fourteen thousand World War I veterans descended on Washington to demand that they be paid "adjusted compensation certificates" in paper money for their wartime service. On June 15, the House of Representatives passed a bill to issue the paper money to pay the veterans, but under strong pressure from Hoover the Senate refused passage. Some of the veterans went home, but about six thousand remained, and on July 28 a riot occurred in which two were killed. Thereupon, President Hoover summoned the Army Chief of Staff, General Douglas MacArthur, who sent a small army with machine guns and tanks into the veterans' shantytown on Anacostia Flats, dispersed the occupants, and either accidentally or deliberately burned the town. It had to be done, said Hoover in a public statement on July 28, because Communists and persons with criminal records were stirring up violence.

By fall the economic situation had worsened again. Bank resources continued to decline, and the strain of runs and withdrawals started to erode the foundations of the nation's economic system. Communist agitation found increasingly fertile areas to cultivate. In November the Communist-organized Unemployed Councils began to organize a "hunger" march on the capital. The New York contingent assembled at Union Square on November 30 to be fed and loaded into trucks bound for Washington. While Cole Porter's songs were being heard uptown, the marchers in Union Square

had their own composition whose melody had been traditionally much appropriated for any number of other themes:

Hoover's having a helluva time
Stopping the hunger line
Hinkey Dinkey—Parlez Vous!

And *The New York Times,* reporting the event by use of a
stereotype faithful to the era, made the central theme of its
story "A high-stepping Georgia Negro in a rainbow-colored
beret."

While the trucks carrying the marchers made their rick-
ety way to Washington, Congress and the city's population
indulged in dark speculation as to what might occur after
the capital had been invaded. Fearing the worst, the police
held them up on the outskirts of the city for three days, confined to their conveyances. After protests from spokesmen
for liberal groups and the threat of legal action against the
District government, the police permitted the marchers to
have their parade and to present their petitions to Vice
President Charles Curtis and House Speaker John Garner
on December 6.

As the marchers passed through the streets in the bright
morning sunshine, the scene moved and evoked a very personal response from a woman who observed it: "I . . .
watched them, joy and pride in the courage of this band of
men and women mounting in my heart, and with it a bitterness too." Her bitterness was due to a sense of loss: for
five years before she had become a Catholic and now, witnessing this "ragged horde triumphant with banners flying,"
she sensed an isolation from them which she knew must be
deeply alien to the spirit of the faith she professed. Two
days later, on December 8, she went to the crypt of the un-
finished Shrine of the Immaculate Conception at Catholic
University. "There I offered up a special prayer, a prayer
which came with tears and with anguish, that some way
would open up for me to use what talents I possessed for
my fellow workers, for the poor."

The crisis in the life of Dorothy Day and the prayer that

followed were the result of a convergence of two conditions. One was the absence of a specific purposefulness in her life in the Church, made more acute by watching the marchers, because, as she saw it, Church leaders had provided no modern example of identification with that socially abandoned class, the one she had instinctively known all of her life as first in that community of man for which she longed. The other condition was the feeling she had always had about herself, that she existed for a special purpose.

That she existed at all registered upon her as an awesome thing. It was a miracle for which in time she would have to render due account. It was the miracle that took her out of the abyss of nothingness, an abyss that stood as a terror lurking at the edge of her consciousness. One of her first memories was of this terror. One time when she was a child she left her yard alone, "spending what I felt to be long hours one sunny afternoon, blissful enchanted hours until the sudden realization came over me that I was alone, that the world was vast and that there were evil forces . . ." She was overwhelmed with "black fear" and ran all the way home.

Dorothy Day was born on November 8, 1897, at Bath Beach, Brooklyn. Her father was from Cleveland, Tennessee. The circumstances of his family background were something she knew little about, she relates in her autobiography, *The Long Loneliness*. The Days were Scotch-Irish, from the same stock that for more than a century had lived in the Southern plateau regions and had produced men like Daniel Boone and Andrew Jackson. They were Calvinists who lived by the work ethic, and insofar as they philosophized about life, they saw it in the light of a universe that was complete and where all the big questions had been answered. Her mother was a Satterlee from Marlboro, New York, a family that, like the Day family, went deep into the region's history. They were merchants and craftsmen, and belonged to the Episcopal Church. While there are no available pictures of Dorothy Day's parents, one would guess that her height and the angularity of her face came from the

Scotch-Irish forebears of her father, and, possibly, too, the tempered quality of her will was something that came to her from him.

When she was six her father, a sportswriter, took the family (two older brothers and a baby sister) to California, first to Berkeley and later to Oakland. In Oakland, when she was eight years old, she attended a Methodist Sunday school and church with a friend, and from that visit she began to experience "the sweetness of faith." Her parents, not accustomed to an outward show of piety, could not answer when she asked her mother "why we did not pray and sing hymns." At the same time, she began to "be afraid of God, of death, of eternity." As soon as she closed her eyes at night "the blackness of death" surrounded her. "I believed and yet was afraid of nothingness. What would it be like to sink into that immensity?" Then when she fell asleep, "God became in my ears a great noise that became louder and louder, and approached nearer and nearer to me until I woke up . . . shrieking for my mother. I fell asleep with her hand in mine, her warm presence by my bed."

When the great San Francisco earthquake occurred, the plant of the newspaper for which her father wrote was burned. Unwilling to accept the charity that had been organized to help the victims, the father sold all of the furniture that had laboriously been shipped from New York around Cape Horn to California. With this money the family moved to Chicago where her father tried to earn money by writing short stories and a novel. Unsuccessful, he took a job as sports editor for a Chicago paper, *The Inter Ocean*. The first year in Chicago was a time of straitened circumstances for the family, and Dorothy Day, then eight years old, later recalled how ashamed she was of the apartment house on Thirty-seventh Street in which the family lived. Walking home with her school friends, she would turn away before she reached home, pretending that she lived somewhere else. But after three moves the Days found a more genteel place on Webster Avenue near Lincoln Park, and it was there she spent her girlhood years.

Until she went to college, she led a protected life. Her father permitted no "trash" in his children's reading, and because he worked at night, they were not permitted to interfere with his daytime rest by having friends in the house. For herself and her sister, books became the chief release. Looking back on her childhood, she thought of those years as a "happy" time and expressed gratitude to her parents for the quietness and security of her life. "To draw the curtains at night on a street where people bent against the wind, and where a steady whirl of snowflakes blurred the outlines of trees . . . and to turn to a room where a fire glowed . . . this was comfort, security, peace, community."

But all was not uninterrupted tranquillity. She suffered from periods of moodiness and sadness, induced by a sense of the transient character of joy and beauty. It was a perception that came from the clarity of childhood, before the necessity of choices and struggle took over. "I walked the streets at sunset gazing at the clouds over Lincoln Park, recognizing the world as supremely beautiful, yet oppressed somehow with a heavy and abiding sense of loneliness and sadness." This was a mood that came over her again and again.

When she was fourteen she fell in love, with all of the romantic intensity of young innocence. He led the band in Lincoln Park on Sunday afternoons and Wednesday nights, and she arranged confrontations with him as he walked to the park. She involved him in a dreamworld of her fancy. The fact that he was married and the father of children made no difference, she relates in her novel, *The Eleventh Virgin*. His wife was remote and ineffectual; it was only she who fulfilled the most basic artistic and spiritual needs of his sensitive nature. She even saw herself saving one of his children when it became ill. Yet actually they never exchanged a word.

Her fourteenth year brought another love into her life—the birth of a baby brother, John. She took him over, mothered him, and rolled him along the streets, hoping to meet her other love. The two loves seemed to go together, for the love of the baby was "as profound and never-to-be-forgotten" as her love of the man who led the band in Lincoln Park.

It was 1912, and the world clung precariously to its order. That fall, after the summer of band concerts and searing love, a new fervor entered her life. Her brother Donald began his newspaper career on a journalistic experiment called *The Day Book.* The dime-novel-size book, whose name had nothing to do with her family, told of the struggles of the labor movement, especially those in Chicago. She learned of the greatness and nobility of Eugene Debs, of the Industrial Workers of the World, and of the Haymarket anarchists. She read Jack London's books and from him was led to attempt a reading (brave soul) of the ponderous and then godlike Herbert Spencer. After reading Upton Sinclair's *The Jungle,* the strolls with her baby brother were no longer directed toward the park and the lake, but toward the West Side. With her sister Della holding on to the carriage, she walked for miles through slums, imagining in the drab scenes a re-creation of some of the things she had read about in Sinclair's book. During her last year in high school she, too, read the Russian anarchist Peter Kropotkin and wrote a paper in her English class about the martyrdom of one of the Russian revolutionists. Kropotkin especially had brought her to an awareness of the plight of the workers. Walking Chicago's streets, she felt from then on her life was to be linked to theirs. "I had received a call . . . a direction to my life."

Dorothy Day, sixteen years old when World War I began, was unaffected by it. "I was going away to school. I was grown up." She had ranked fifteenth in a test to select the twenty best high-school students in Cook County to receive a scholarship of three hundred dollars to go to college.

Her college career consisted of two years at the University of Illinois at Urbana. Formal academic disciplines produced little reaction in her. Missing her baby brother terribly, she developed insomnia and spent the night hours reading. She read everything by Dostoevsky, who impressed her profoundly, and the stories of Gorky and Tolstoy. She became preoccupied with poverty, misery, and the class war; she joined the campus Socialist club. She was frequently without money, and to provide for herself she washed for a poverty-stricken instructor who had five children. She baby-sat for a family whose father was involved in several local sublegal activities, and when he sought to enlarge the dimension of the conditions of her employment, she left. Occasionally she made a little money by writing for the local newspaper, but it was not much. She sometimes went hungry.

She was one of the campus nonconformists. She missed classes, disdained the customary patterns of college social mixing, and, with the long strides of a singularly self-sufficient determination, went forward to grapple with the universe. Full of the invincible spirit of life in full dawn, when there is no death, she gave up religion when a professor whom she admired suggested that religion was a prop for the weak. She felt that she must ruthlessly cut it out of her life. She even began to swear!

Describing herself during these years as tall and gawky, and recklessly pursuing the inner directions of her spirit, she must have been considered odd by other students who were content to drift in the stream. Yet, perhaps more than most, she was responsive to friendship; she needed someone with whom to share the intensity of her nature—a generous and loving person who could comprehend what she wanted to say and be. She found such a friend in Rayna Simon, the daughter of a Chicago merchant.

She first saw Rayna on a train filled with Chicago students going to Urbana. She stood out like a flame with her red hair, brown eyes, and vivid face, and it was this flame-like quality, surrounded by an aureole of joyous purity, that Dorothy touched on again and again in describing her.

They became acquainted in a college writers' club. Rayna and the student to whom she was engaged, Samson Raphaelson, called "Raph" by his friends, had been impressed with a personal account of hunger that Dorothy had written for the college magazine. Meeting, the three discussed their writing interests long into the night. Rayna and Dorothy found themselves drawn to one another immediately, and the generous Rayna, touched by her new friend's poverty, immediately provided for her. She paid her room rent and then insisted that Dorothy share with her the daily pint of cream that her parents had insisted she drink, for Rayna "was a fragile creature and all of her flowing vitality was of the spirit." In a short time they became close friends, and when Dorothy's room rent again came due, Rayna asked her to move in with her.

With the coming of May, Rayna, Dorothy, and Raph went into the prairie countryside for Sunday afternoon picnics. Taking their books and a portable phonograph, they breathed an air filled with the sweet smell of clover and listened to a Beethoven symphony amidst the songs of the meadowlarks. Nearly forty years later Dorothy Day remembered: "I can see Rayna lying on her side in a dull green dress, her cheek cupped in her hand, her eyes on the book she was reading, her mouth half open in her intent interest."

It was, in Dorothy Day's words, an idyllic year. Her friendship with Rayna was as if a "new love" had come into her life, "as clear as a bell . . . with no stain of self-seeking." They shared their clothes, thoughts, feelings, and even at times the disconsolate Raph, who would like to have had a more exclusive dominion over Rayna.

In June, Dorothy left the university, not to return, and while she saw Rayna after that, the days of their close friendship had ended. In the light of the later course of Rayna's life, it is interesting to speculate on some of the basic elements of that friendship. Both were generous, open, and intelligent. But most fundamentally, Rayna must have recognized in her a passion of seeking that produced a strong response in her own nature. In college, Dorothy had committed herself to the poor and had ignored academic discipline and her own physical well-being to study and read in areas that brought her to a spiritual communion with the poor. Rayna, with her Jewish reverence for scholarship, thought answers lay in the minds of her professors and the facts she absorbed. Rayna used to laugh at her friend's absorption in Socialism, Dorothy Day once observed. "She felt that I was unbalanced on the subject and was looking at life from only one angle." But shortly Rayna would move beyond the level of academic formalism to give her life to a cause.

In 1934, Vincent Sheean published his *Personal History,* and in a chapter entitled "Revolution," he gives the sequel to Rayna's life. She became a Communist, and in 1927 Sheean met her in Hankow, China, where she was working in the revolutionary cause. Weeks later, he met her again in Moscow where she was preparing to enter the Lenin Institute to be trained as a revolutionary. He saw much of her that summer and tried to dissuade her from the course she had set upon. His arguments had no effect; she was serenely determined to give her life to the cause in which she had found meaning. But Rayna died the day before she was to enter the institute. Deprivation and the intense pace at which she drove her frail body had induced an encephalitis that raged quickly to its fatal end.

She died on Monday, November 21, and was cremated the following Thursday. Sheean described the funeral—the mourners following the bier behind a band playing funeral marches—trudging through a falling snow in the early darkness of a Moscow evening—the great bells of a nearby convent ringing for evening services. After what to Sheean seemed an interminable journey, the procession arrived at a new crematorium outside the city. "It was brightly lighted, square and spare." The bier, draped in the Red flag and covered with asters and chrysanthemums, was placed on a platform. After speeches, a signal was given "and the golden mass of Rayna, her hair and her bright flowers and the Red flag, sank slowly before us into the furnace."

Dorothy Day was much affected by Sheean's account of the last days and death of Rayna. She read it shortly after its publication and wrote that she would be at least one person who would pray for Rayna, "for I am the only one she knew who has a faith in the resurrection of the body and the life everlasting." It was at the same time that Rayna was making her decision to enter the Lenin Institute that Dorothy was making hers to become a Catholic, for it was not long after Rayna's death that she was baptized.

# 3

## THE YOUNG JOURNALIST

Dorothy Day left the university to follow her family to New York where her father had gotten a job as racing editor for the *Morning Telegraph*. She left college because the formalisms of academic life seemed to suggest not paths but byroads toward that as-yet-unnamed objective to which she felt her life should be directed. She spent some time looking for a job. She became depressed, suffering from loneliness and the impact of the squalor she found, and as she walked about the city the rancid smells that welled up from the basements of tenements made her ill. Finally, she cajoled the editor of the Socialist *New York Call* to hire her as a reporter for five dollars a week.

Thus freed from a dependence on her family, she took a room in the largely Jewish Lower East Side, drawn, as she explained, to share the life of those whose state had so depressed her. It was also an exciting adventure for an eighteen-year-old girl to move into the teeming center of a people who were poor, yet immensely rich in heritage. She lived on Cherry Street near Manhattan Bridge, within walking distance of the *Call* office on Pearl Street just off Park Row, amidst saloons and warehouses.

Cherry Street, as she found it, was cheerful and lively. In the afternoon children swarmed in the street, and on the fire escapes that faced the buildings, mothers hung over the railings to shout admonitions to their errant young. Every half hour or so, a horsecar carrying passengers came through.

Above these sounds, a street organ could be heard playing the latest popular tune, and every once in a while a merry-go-round set on a wagon was drawn through by an ancient horse, which from time to time was directed to the curb where waiting children surrendered their pennies for a ride. Then the operator, energetically turning a crank, sent the carousel spinning and piping a music that drew customers from blocks around.

She bathed with the other women in a public bathhouse and lived up three flights of stairs that were dirty and dark. But her room was clean and cheerful, and she described it in an article she wrote for the *Call* on December 3, 1916. She would have to keep it spotless, she said, because her landlady was an Orthodox Jew and could not have dirty premises.

Her first assignment (her own idea) was to act as the *Call's* "diet squad" of one, in an emulation of other "diet" squads then in vogue. Their purpose, it was said, was to show how frugally a person could live and still maintain a semblance of health. Her plan was "to live on five dollars a weak [sic] all by myself one month" and then tell *Call* readers what her experiences had been. She was sure that she could fare better than another diet squad, then operating in Chicago.

The experiment did not last the month. Reader interest was not high and the young reporter acknowledged that "it is a frightful bore to have to state specifically what you ate, what you are eating and what you are going to eat." Anyway, there was a new interest in her life. She had bought a phonograph for fifteen dollars on an installment plan of a dollar a week, and "you don't know how cheery it is to have a tribe of young ones of all ages, nationality, and state of cleanliness sit all over your bed when you are trying the wakening effect of a piece of ragtime." Thereafter she reported strikes, picket lines, and peace meetings, and interviewed Leon Trotsky, who was bitterly critical of the parliamentarianism of the New York Socialists and as critical generally of the movement's failure to end the war.

These were the days of fateful signs, and to one she reacted with ardor. On March 21, 1917, at Madison Square Garden, "I joined with those thousands in reliving the first days of the revolt in Russia. I felt the exultation, the joyous sense of victory of the masses as they sang . . . the workers' hymn of Russia," described by the *Call* the next day as a "mystic, gripping melody of struggle, a cry for world peace and human brotherhood."

In April, 1917, she left the *Call* because of a dispute with the city editor over her behavior in affronting a down-at-the-heels radical at the Anarchist Ball. "With all my radicalism, I was extremely conventional," she explained, and when the man, with "his long hair, his ragged clothes, his emotional speech," made an attempt to embrace her, she slapped him. He, in turn, slapped her, whereupon several reporters from *The Times* and the *World* moved with traditional male gallantry to the rescue and forcibly ejected the offender from the hall. The *Call*'s editor could have charged his young reporter with bourgeois morality and with insensitivity to radical communitarian demonstrativeness. Possibly, too, he was thinking of the five dollars a week he would save.

That was the month the United States went to war. Woodrow Wilson had concluded that only by entering the conflict could the large problems of human destiny be set aright. Toward that end he appealed to the whole panoply of the sacred symbols of nationalism to launch America on its "great crusade," and it was a piping to which most Americans joyously submitted. But there were some who did not, and among them were Dorothy Day and the young Socialists whom she knew. With some of these, and a group of Columbia University students, Dorothy Day joined a haphazard expedition to Washington to protest the draft. On her return to New York, she found a job on the staff of *The Masses*.

Founded in 1911, *The Masses* was the voice of revolution and the new freedom of the young. In 1912 it came under the capable editorship of Max Eastman and aimed its attack

at the whole range of values and practices associated with
middle-class America. In addition to Eastman, among its
writers were Floyd Dell, Merrill Rogers, and John Reed,
and its principal artists were Hugo Gellert, Maurice Becker,
and Boardman Robinson. All were talented and joyously set
against prevailing conventions.

For several months Dorothy Day worked as an assistant
to Floyd Dell, who, in his book *Homecoming* recalled her
as a "charming young enthusiast, with beautiful slanting
eyes." Dell wanted to write that summer and satisfied that
his assistant could handle the job of editing the magazine,
he left for a cabin in New Jersey. His departure left vacant a
place in the Greenwich Village apartment used by the staff
of *The Masses,* and Dorothy Day moved in.

In *The Long Loneliness* Dorothy tells of the summer. It
was one that burned itself into her memory, for the world
was erupting, and with the passion of youth she and her
companions set out toward that vision of a new kingdom
that they saw with such clarity. Rayna came, and with Mike
Gold and Maurice Becker they walked the streets of New
York, "sat on the ends of piers singing revolutionary songs
into the starlit night, dallied on park benches, never wanting to go home to sleep but only to continue to savor our
youth." In love with all mankind, they embraced the world.
Coming home late at night, they took back to their apartment the men they found sleeping on park benches, and
gave them whatever bed was empty. And even then life was
upon them with such force that they sat up talking through
the night.

That summer was the last time she saw Rayna. When Raphaelson, back in Chicago, heard of the joys of the bohemian life that Rayna was living, he took the next train and
descended on the apartment to insist that she return home.
He and Rayna were married the next year, but quickly divorced, and Rayna went to follow her own adventure.

Dorothy Day saw much of Mike Gold that summer and
the year following, and, indeed, they were on such terms of
friendship that she was taken to visit the strict Jewish Or-

thodox household of Gold's parents. For a while they found something in common—their revolutionary excitement and the literary ambition that fired both. But Gold's social concern crystallized into a rigid Marxism, and he came to regard Dorothy as too impressionable. "He used to make fun of my religious spirit," she observed in *The Long Loneliness*.

Gold, born Irwin Granich, did go on to fulfill a writing vocation. He wrote a semibiographical novel, *Jews Without Money*, but it was not a major literary accomplishment. His main reputation was based on his hard-boiled Marxian attacks on everything that was not in line with his revolutionary expectation, ranging from the style and subject matter of his literary contemporaries to the political and social institutions that sustained bourgeois life. Beginning in 1926, he was for some years the editor of the *New Masses*, and he also wrote regularly for the Communist *Daily Worker*.

It was on a Monday night, June 4, that the group in the apartment stayed up until the morning hours of the next day, discussing what their attitude should be toward the draft registration scheduled for Tuesday. One, at least, refused to join the crusade, the younger brother of the artist Hugo Gellert. He refused to put on a uniform because it was a "capitalist war." He was put in a guardhouse on Long Island where Dorothy Day, Gold, and his brother Hugo visited him. He seemed cheerful then, Dorothy Day recalled, but some weeks later he was reported dead. It was said that he had taken his own life, but she could not believe it because he had been so cheerful when she had visited him. Had he been killed? she wondered. It was a mystery which left her shuddering.

In November the government suppressed *The Masses*, and the summer of close comradeship and millennial expectation ended for the young radicals. It had been like the early days of the Christians—giving, taking, and sharing all. But after 1918 the lines that marked the radical course became more rigid. Mike Gold might assent to doctrinal requirements, but Dorothy Day could not, and after a while she fell away to follow the paths the inspiration of the moment presented.

One night, shortly after *The Masses* had been shut down, she sat talking with a friend, Peggy Baird, and impulsively decided to go with Peggy to Washington to picket the White House with a group of militant suffragists. There they succeeded in doing what they obviously had set out to do: they were arrested and, when they refused bail, were sentenced to thirty days in the Occoquan prison, some distance out of the city. In *The Eleventh Virgin* she gives an account of the train ride to the prison:

> June [Dorothy Day] pressed her face against the window and watched the blue twilight pierced with the bare black shapes of many scrawny trees. Here and there lamps glowed in the farmhouse windows. In the west the sky still held radiance which gradually faded. It was drearily beautiful at that time of night, and all feeling of excitement dropped from the girl. . . . Billy [Peggy Baird] sitting across from her also gazed silently out of the window.
>
> "Somehow," June told her when they reached the little country station which was their destination, "life and struggle seem very tawdry in the twilight. This bleak countryside makes me feel that I should struggle for my soul instead of my political rights."

Confinement, a physical struggle with a guard, and the hunger strike to which the suffragists had committed themselves brought her close to despair. For six days she was alone in the cold darkness of her cell, refusing food. She lost all consciousness of the cause that had brought her there, having, instead, a black conviction of the unending pointlessness and futility of life. She would never be free again. She was united with those around her and with all those the world over who were constrained, tortured, and isolated for crimes for which, in some basic way, all men were guilty. "I felt that we were a people fallen from grace and abandoned by God."

On the fourth day an attendant brought her a Bible, and she read it "with the sense of coming back to something of

my childhood that I had lost." The Psalms comforted her.
She prayed without realizing that she was praying. Yet she
decided that the comfort she received from religion was a
sign of weakness. She should develop the strength to wage
the struggle alone.

After six days the hunger strikers were put in the prison
hospital, a considerable improvement over the cold, dark
cells. There, she broke her fast when Peggy, in the next
stall, passed her a crust of toast that had been soaked in
warm milk. On the tenth day concessions were made to the
strikers' demands, and they were all shortly taken to the
Washington city jail. It was almost a triumphal return. They
were transported in limousines through the sparkling air of
a day following a snowfall, and at the jail she and Peggy
were permitted to pick their own cell. During the remain-
der of the time they had to serve, they were treated almost
graciously.

Back in New York she began to work for *The Liberator*,
the successor to *The Masses*, edited by Crystal Eastman.
But things had changed; unhappy, she left to do free-lance
writing. It was cold, that winter of 1918, and the rooms in
which she lived, first one and then another, were inade-
quately heated. Seeking the warmth of friends and places—
"no one ever wanted to go to bed, and no one ever wished
to be alone"—she began to hang around the Provincetown
Playhouse, where Eugene O'Neill was beginning to fashion
his career as a playwright. "I walked the streets with Gene
. . . and sat out the nights in taverns, in waterfront back
rooms," she said, writing about O'Neill forty years later.

What she wrote was in a six-page manuscript called "Told
in Context," which she put in the Catholic Worker Papers,
and one of the points that she wanted put in context, as she
understood it, was the matter of O'Neill's religion. He had
been described as having no interest in religion, but she
thought that religion was at the center of his life struggle. It
was on one of those cold, bitter nights, sitting around a
table in the back room of Jimmy Wallace's saloon at Fourth
Street and Sixth Avenue, just around the corner from the

Provincetown Playhouse, that she heard O'Neill recite from memory Francis Thompson's "The Hound of Heaven." In the smoke-heavy air he had sat there, head sunk, giving the lines "in his grating, monotonous voice, his mouth grim, his eyes sad."

Yes, she thought, if ever a man had a tragic sense of life, it was he—"if ever a man was haunted by death it was Gene." She remembered that he had told her "how he used to swim far out to sea when he lived at Provincetown and how he played with the idea of death in those deep waters in the ocean from which all life springs." He was tortured by the "big questions" to which only religion could provide an answer. And so crucial were they to him that he did not dare believe that there could be an answer; he would not be beguiled in affirming a redemption when it was possible that there was only the void. "Like Ivan [in *The Brothers Karamazov*] he wanted to reject, he wanted to turn back to God his ticket. His whole life seemed to be like that terrible dialogue of Ivan with Alyosha, and the problem of evil, and God's permissive will."

As for herself during this time, she mentions in *The Long Loneliness* that "the life of the flesh called to me as a good and wholesome life, regardless of man's laws, which I felt rebelliously, were made for the repression of others." She was self-sufficient—beyond good or evil, for "the satisfied flesh has its own law."

Even then, there was "many a morning after sitting all night in taverns or coming from balls at Webster Hall" that she went to an early-morning Mass at St. Joseph's Church on Sixth Avenue. She knelt in the back, not knowing what the Mass was about, but feeling comforted. She did not consciously pray—only to go into the church was a need she felt "again and again. . . . I put myself there in the atmosphere of prayer—it was an act of the will."

Then, suddenly, she relates, there were some things that happened with which she could not cope. She did not explain, saying only that she could no longer endure the life she was leading. And so she broke with her bohemian existence, and on January 1, 1918, she began nurse's training at Kings County Hospital in Brooklyn. It was an exhausting, disciplined work which she liked. But feeling an urge to write, she left after completing one year, troubled in conscience, wondering if she somehow had been at fault for failing in this effort to determine what her life was about.

The year 1919 is one about which, she writes in *The Long Loneliness*, she prefers to say little. She went to Europe—to London, Paris, and to Capri for six months. In Italy she spent her time writing *The Eleventh Virgin*, a time of joy she says, but also of heartbreak.

Perhaps it was the latter that brought her back to the United States. Whatever the case, she returned to live in Chicago. She had a room in a slum, and to live she wrote and held odd jobs, among which were modeling for artists and working as a clerk at Montgomery Ward's. Again, her companions were radicals, and she mentions one in particular, a black-bearded young man who had been among the group in 1917 when she had gone to Washington to protest the draft. He had gone to Russia to attend the Third International and was now in Chicago "engaged in underground party business." She was not too interested in that business, but seeing him made her happy, and for a while she went with him to workers' meetings and Sunday-afternoon picnics.

In Chicago she had another experience with jail. The Washington episode had been for a cause, in the company of educated women, but this was different—ugly and sordid. In *The Long Loneliness* she related the story in detail. It must have been in the year 1920 (she mentions being twenty-two at the time) that she came to know a woman who had a history of thievery, drug addiction, and prostitution, but who had managed to overcome many of her problems. She was in love with a newspaperman—with whom Dorothy Day was also infatuated—so a certain bond was established between them. Perhaps it was because of some despairing reaction in connection with her love that the woman tried to commit suicide by taking poison. She was hospitalized, survived the crisis, and in a few days she had mustered enough strength to sign herself out. Not wanting to return to her room, she went to the headquarters of the Industrial Workers of the World, popularly known as the "Wobblies." There, in Chicago's Skid Row, the union maintained a cheap rooming house for their men. Seeing that the woman was obviously ill, they took her in, and it was then that she called Dorothy Day to ask her to bring her food and clothing.

Dorothy Day went at once, and when she saw the woman's circumstances, she decided to remain and assist her. It was that night the authorities, reflecting the inflamed popular concern over the presumed red menace, decided to raid the Wobbly residence. Dorothy Day and her friend were summarily arrested on charges of prostitution. She was jailed for only a few days, and when the case came to court it was dismissed. It was, nonetheless, a shocking and humiliating experience. Yet she could say when it was over that during her several days of imprisonment with drug addicts and prostitutes, she found a generosity and community not commonly found outside.

Early in 1923 Robert Minor took over the editorship of *The Liberator,* and with her previous experience on *The Masses,* Dorothy Day now assisted Minor, who edited the journal from Chicago. Because the subject of Communist subversion produced near hysteria in the years following World War I, Minor did his work covertly. Dorothy Day, however, was not caught up in the cloak-and-dagger aspects of the situation, although Minor seemed to relish its dramatic potential. "I only knew," she relates, "that when I took dictation from Bob, he kept telling his friends that he was being followed. Pacing up and down the room, glancing out of the window he would say, 'At this moment of writing there is a man standing in the doorway across the street. . . .' This was repeated in each letter."

She was not especially attached to any group. She found Marx incomprehensible and dull. She liked the Wobblies because they had good songs and a rich symbolism, like the everlasting pot of stew to which everyone who came in was supposed to contribute whatever food they had and to take from it what they needed. It was not to ideology but to people that she felt drawn. She spent her time in the company of radicals because their free and open life, for the moment, suited her taste.

But it was a freedom that sustained her only briefly. She was in love again, this time deeply—and unhappily. She does not mention who the man was except to say that he shared his reading experiences with her. At the same time he took a proprietary attitude toward her literary taste, and once while they were riding a North Avenue elevated he wrested from her hands a copy of James Joyce's *Portrait of the Artist as a Young Man* and hurled it through the window as unfit for her.

She spent a winter—it must have been 1923—in a furnished room that belonged to a Catholic family. Sometimes she saw them kneel to pray, and again she was stirred as she had been back in 1917 when she had gone to those early-morning Masses in New York. She read the New Testament, inspired to do so by the account of Sonya's reading the Gospel to Raskolnikov in Dostoevsky's *Crime and Punishment*. Her life came to seem not free, but encumbered and disordered. With her sister, Della, she decided to go to New Orleans.

She had no trouble getting a job there. She wrote a few articles for the *New Orleans Item* and was soon given a full-time assignment. It was not one, however, that offered her the means of directing her life into more serene channels. She was to get a job as a taxi dancer in a Canal Street dance hall and write stories about the girls there. In the afternoons, though, before beginning her night work, she would stop in at the cathedral that faced Jackson Square for Benediction and tentatively say the Rosary with beads that her sister Della had given her.

In the spring of 1924 *The Eleventh Virgin* was published, and soon after she got a long-distance telephone call informing her that the publishers had sold moving-picture rights for five thousand dollars. What to do with this stupendous fortune? Her friend Peggy Baird suggested that she get her own house where she could study and write. Many of her radical friends had succumbed to the temptation to acquire property. Max Eastman and Floyd Dell both had little homes up in Croton-on-Hudson, New York. Jack Reed had a place of his own. Most of the others on the staff of *The Masses* had bought old farms. So she bought a small bungalow on Raritan Bay on Staten Island.

The move into her beach bungalow brought a time of tranquillity and reflection in her life. It was, as she said, a time that was joyous and lovely, a prelude to that moment that brought direction to her existence. Every afternoon she walked for miles along the beach, collecting shells and mussels, returning to the little house which she had furnished simply and roughly.

Several months after moving into her cottage, she entered into a common-law relationship with a man who spent much of his time boating on the bay and investigating marine life. Forster Battingham had been in the service during World War I, had gotten flu in the great epidemic of 1918, and as a result had spent practically the duration of his military service in a hospital. He was an anarchist, a position that was obviously associated with a temperamental predilection, and he was not a part of the literary or radical groups with whom Dorothy Day had associated in the past. His sister, Lily, however, had married Kenneth Burke, philosopher, literary critic and language authority, and it was Dorothy Day's friendship with Lily that represented the connection. Their first meeting had been at Malcolm Cowley's Village apartment, Cowley having only recently married Peggy Baird.

So when she and Battingham went into the city for weekends, much of their socializing was done in the company of the Cowleys and Burkes. In the winter, when it was too cold to live in the cottage, they moved in to share with sister Della her New York apartment. Allen Tate and his wife, Caroline Gordon, lived across the street, and Hart Crane used to drop in at all their places for coffee and talk.

But Dorothy Day never pretended to dwell in the inner circle of the intellectual and literary set that habituated Paris and the Village in the twenties and that gave such grace to that era. She was impulsive and direct, turning away impatiently from ideas abstracted from the flesh-and-blood situation or which never seemed to relate to that central and ever-recurring question that intruded itself upon her—where is that point of truth by which I bring my existence into focus and depart from vanity? "I can remember," she wrote, "one conversation among Malcolm, Kenneth, and John Dos Passos which stood out especially in my memory because I could not understand a word of it."

Back at the cottage she read, did some writing, and socialized among the beachcombers and radicals who lived in the area. Mike Gold and his brother, George Granich, were frequent visitors. Malcolm Cowley and Peggy moved to the island and achieved some fame in the community for having a house with steam heat and hot water. Sometimes Dorothy went there to take a hot bath.

"I was happy," she wrote of this time in her life, "but my very happiness made me know that there was a greater happiness to be obtained from life than any I had ever known." To her surprise she found that she was beginning to pray daily, and when she walked to the village for the mail, she took her rosary and tried to recite its prayers. Peggy Cowley, recognizing her friend's interest in religion, had given her a wax statuette of Mary and she found herself addressing the Virgin. Prayer became a central part of her life, and she began to go to Mass regularly on Sunday mornings.

Then she asked herself what it was she was slipping into. Was not religion a crutch for those incompletely formed; was it not an opiate, a delusion for those in grief and despair? But then, she thought, she was not unhappy; she prayed because she was happy. She gave up her weekends in the city, the cocktail parties and the dancing in smoke-filled rooms, so that she could walk along the beach and think. When she and Forster rowed about the bay or took walks in the woods, she tried to talk to him about belief and faith. But he was not interested.

It was 1926, a beautiful day in June, that Dorothy, Forster, and Malcolm and Peggy Cowley set out for a neighboring town for a picnic and to see a circus there. To her the day was eventful because she experienced unmistakable signs of pregnancy. She was supremely happy, but Forster was not, wondering what point there was in bringing another person into the world to suffer hopelessness and injustice.

Tamar was born on March 3, 1927. It was an occasion of such happiness for her mother that she wrote an article about the experience which Mike Gold published in the *New Masses*. The note of joy in her account, she was later told, had caused the article to be reprinted in Communist publications in other countries.

The baby was six weeks old when Dorothy Day took her back to the cottage, and as she wheeled Tamar about on sunny days, spring began to burst about them. In the evening, when she had put the baby to bed, she sat in contented exhaustion, watching the evening fall. At times of happiness in her life she seemed to become rapturously sensitive to the world about her. This was such a time, and in her book, *From Union Square to Rome,* the story of her conversion, she expressed it in her description of nightfall as she watched it from her cottage window:

Outside dozens of fleecy pink clouds were caught in the top of the hickory trees at the head of the bank and below them were whole fleets of lavender gondolas, then the deeper purple shadows of the Jersey shore. The three lighthouses stood out black against the silver water and there was not a wave, only a rippling, a scalloping along the yellow beach.

Soon the pink and rose clouds faded to a dingy smoke color, and those nearer the horizon changed to a purplish gray. The water remained silver with a peculiar surface glow which the sky did not have though they were the same color. Away off, miles away, through the bare trees on the point, the lights of a roadway flickered like candles.

As she watched the deepening night, she was conscious of the life in the room with her, "throbbing silently." Already she had made up her mind that she was going to have Tamar baptized in the Catholic Church, and she knew, too, that this would be a point of separation in her life with Forster.

Several afternoons later, as she wheeled Tamar down a neighborhood road, she met a nun from a nearby home that was run by the Sisters of Charity, and impulsively she approached her on the matter of baptism for the baby. For the nun it was no doubt a surprising encounter—to be broached on such a subject by one known to have about her the aura of Communism and bohemia. But Sister Aloysia was matter of fact about it all, and under her tutelage matters were eventually arranged for the baptism, which occurred in June.

During the next six months much of Dorothy's joy vanished. With Tamar baptized, she knew that she, too, wanted to become a Catholic, even though it meant breaking with Forster at a time when his presence in her life seemed most logical and necessary. Aside from her need for him, there were his own feelings at stake, his feeling for the baby in whom he had come to take delight.

But there was no accommodation. In August the impending execution of Sacco and Vanzetti added to their own private misery. Dorothy Day was sickened by the prospect, so much so that every breath she drew pained her because of the knowledge that the joy of life would soon be taken from the two men. Forster was numb with misery; he ceased to eat and escaped to the solitude of the bay, where he spent days sitting in his boat.

A terrible tension developed between them. Forster left and returned, then left again. In December, in New York City, he sought her out, but she would not see him. She was determined to end finally the torture that both were undergoing. The next day she took the ferry to Tottenville, Staten Island, to be baptized. The action was almost wholly mechanical, with no sense of peace or even the conviction that she was doing the right thing. As the ferry made its way through the foggy bay, she wondered if she was being too precipitate. When it was over and she had gone to Confession, there was still no consolation. It had been done and that was that.

Her action came from a long-developing passion of her heart that ignored positions arrived at solely by a rational reflection on science and history. That was her failing, thought her friend Rayna—Rayna, so recently dead, yet consumed at the end by her own passion. She had indeed made her leap without philosophy or history, yet it was one that she had been nurturing for at least ten years, witnessed in those episodes in her life when, seemingly having surrendered beyond recall to those beguiling allurements of sense and time, she would turn away, looking for eternity. Now she had registered her new course with that finality and decisiveness that marks the rite of baptism in the Catholic Church. "The trouble with Dorothy Day is that she is a romantic," her critics are apt to say. But there was no romantic soaring to enrapture her spirit that day she took the ferry to Tottenville. She had taken the hard course, and it would never be anything else. There would be no more of Forster in her life—or any other man.

What now? Move into the comfortable positions of mainstream—join in parish activities and perhaps even write a book to condemn in a superior moral tone her life just past and her associates in it? Not that. From the first she knew that what she sought in the Church was an involvement with man that went beyond anything she understood from her association with Communist friends. But how? The answer would have to wait. For the moment there were the immediate problems of adjusting to the daily life of the Church.

She was confronted by priests whose social vision scarcely went beyond the bounds of their parish and who were more concerned with the "sound" financial management of an easeful parish life than they were with the great masses of the poor in the world about. Later, she realized that there were many who "gave their lives daily for their fellows" and would themselves have given much to have escaped the stifling effects of parish existence. When she asked about the poor, the answer given to her question was that there was, indeed, a vast Catholic charitable undertaking—hospitals, homes for the aged, orphanages, and poor relief.

But who wants that kind of charity? she wondered. "Charity" was a word to choke on, and Catholic charity was like all the rest, taking help from the state and rendering to the state. What man needed was less of this "charity" and more of basic social justice. But pursuing that subject would quickly lead her into deep waters. It meant questioning the traditional values by which most Americans lived—those values that preserved the interests of the dominant class and that churchmen seemed not at all inclined to affront. "No wonder," she wrote in *The Long Loneliness*, "there was such a strong conflict going on in my mind and heart." Even so, she subjected herself to the direction of priests, humble men who for the most part gave her sound spiritual guidance.

With Battingham gone, the next five years were ones of exploring her faith and increasingly adapting it to her life. Rearing Tamar limited her movement, and she had no settled work. She wrote and sometimes did menial labor. On August 15, 1929, after a summer of housekeeping for some Marist fathers, she got a telephone call from a Hollywood moving-picture company offering her a contract to write dialogue for pictures. Someone in the company had read a play she had written. She was compared to Chekhov; there were great things ahead.

The experience in Hollywood was depressing. She sat all day in her small office with nothing to do. Occasionally she was summoned to join a group in a comfortable lounge where they viewed a picture and were invited to comment on it. The pictures were silly, juvenile, but the business was carried out in such an atmosphere of pretension that she was unable to summon much enthusiasm for her work. When her three-month contract expired, she was dismissed. She used her last paycheck to buy a bus ticket for herself and Tamar to Mexico City.

She remained there six months, living very cheaply with a poor family, washing her clothes and dishes in a canal and carrying the water she used from the town pump. She lived off the income she got for writing articles for *Commonweal*. These were the days of a politically directed anticlericalism in Mexico, but she wrote sparingly of politics, saying that the subject was beyond her competence. Instead she wrote graphically of the life of the poor among whom she lived.

When Tamar began to suffer from a chronic digestive disorder, Dorothy Day returned to New York, arriving in May, 1930. The next two years, despite the worsening Depression, were a happy time in her life. She found a library research job where she could manage her time as she wished and was thus able to read and write. In the summer of 1931, she moved back to her cottage on the bay to find her garden overgrown with weeds, but she was "glad to be home again, to be cultivating my own bit of soil, to be living in my own house and to feel, for the time at least, that I am never going to leave it again."

But her declaration about not leaving home again was not very realistic, as she well knew. To travel was for her a near compulsion, and in the following spring she was off to Florida, where her mother was visiting. There was a new sight: "The Florida pines rear their plumed masts to the sky, and under them, dotting the open fields, are seedling pines, bright and green," she wrote in *Commonweal*. There was a new experience, too. She saw at firsthand the life of the Southern Blacks and recognized something of their great spiritual fortitude when she wrote of the death of the eighteen-year-old daughter of the woman who worked for her mother.

Back in New York—"very refreshing after the torpid heat of Florida"—she took an apartment on East Twelfth Street, but shortly moved to a tenement on Fifteenth Street because the rent was eight dollars cheaper and there was a backyard in which Tamar could play. With two bedrooms she could also have her brother John and his Spanish wife live with her. John's wife could take care of Tamar when she went off on writing assignments.

Since becoming a Catholic, she had gradually lost track of her radical friends, but that summer Mike Gold dropped in often and with him frequently was his brother, George Granich. It was George, working with the Communist-dominated Unemployed Councils, who set in motion the circumstances that led to her presence at the Washington hunger march. He told her of his plans and urged her to go. She decided that she would go and report the event for the Jesuit periodical, *America,* and for *Commonweal.* Getting an advance, she bought a bus ticket to Washington.

Dorothy Day, her critics and friends would sometimes say, was too disposed to take great leaps and thereby ignore the due process of history. But for her, history had a way of crystallizing its message in a striking sign. Witnessing the hunger marchers, she knew, without extensive documentation on the subject, that somewhere the faith she had so recently embraced had been turned aside from its true historic mission. It would be her own task to try to discover how the mission of the Church might become vital to the welfare of the world which was already entering the swirl that would soon sweep it far from the time that it had known. "And when I returned to New York," she wrote, "I found Peter Maurin—Peter, the French peasant, whose spirit and ideas will dominate . . . the rest of my life."

Dorothy Day, ca. 1930s.

# 4

## UNION SQUARE

Dorothy Day thought of her meeting with Peter Maurin as "heaven's answer" to the prayer she had said at the Shrine of the Immaculate Conception, and she has always insisted that Maurin's place in the history of the Worker movement be remembered and honored. He had given her "an instruction and way of life." It was, according to one of her accounts, the very evening that she returned from Washington that he knocked at the door of her Fifteenth Street apartment. When her sister-in-law admitted him, he began immediately to talk, "casually, informally, almost as though he were taking up a conversation where it had been left off."

For more than four months he came daily to visit her. Arthur Sheehan relates that he followed the form of St. Philip Neri's "Easy Conversations" by talking to Dorothy Day from three in the afternoon until ten or eleven at night. When she moved about the house, he followed her, giving a history of the Church and then interpreting the significance of comtemporary events in the light of that history. He brought her books to read: lives of the saints, Church history, and others that were important to his "clarification." He wrote his own digest of Peter Kropotkin's *Fields, Factories and Workshops* so that she might easily get the important ideas from it.

In time his "Easy Conversations" became not so easy. The

manner of his thinking and the books he would have her read were new to her and difficult to digest, she recounted. The constant talk sometimes became oppressive, and she developed a technique of redirecting it to others so that she could escape and get relief. Sometimes Maurin brought an itinerant sculptor and musician with him, and as the ideas streamed from Maurin, the musician idly played a flute, nodding an occasional assent to the points that Maurin was making. When eleven o'clock came and Dorothy Day could stand no more, she sent Maurin and his companion out into the night. But even then the words went on. On a bench in Union Square, Maurin continued to expound and the flute player continued his serenade.

The focus of Maurin's hours of teaching was the necessity for an immediate institution of radical personalist action. Grasping the idea, Dorothy Day recognized it as the bridge between the faith she had professed and life around her. But where to start? Personalism was first a disposition to grow in "active" love toward all creation. It was "making love" by using such "weapons" as one possessed in a vocation of pursuit to change institutions so that man might find the freedom necessary to live in the fullness of spirit.

Dorothy Day's vocation, clearly, was journalism, and it was Maurin's idea that she should get out a paper for the workingman in which the personalist principles would be set forth. She was interested and immediately began to plan the makeup and the stories she would write to go with Maurin's essays. Then came the obvious question: Where was the money coming from? At first Maurin had talked hopefully of possible assistance from a priest friend, but this assistance never came. Anyway, he thought of himself as the theorist, not to be bothered with practical matters. And what theory had he for this situation? "In the history of the saints," he answered, "capital was raised by prayer. God sends you what you need when you need it. You will be able to pay the printer. Just read the lives of the saints."

During the winter—while reading the lives of the saints—Dorothy Day planned the paper, and by April she took stock of her resources, hoping to have an issue ready by May 1. She had a small check coming in for a research job she had just finished; two checks were due for articles she had written, but these were needed for overdue rent and light bills. Then the Paulist priest Joseph McSorley paid her generously for a small bibliographical job she had done for him; the pastor of a Black church in Newark, a Father Ahearn, gave her ten dollars; and a nun gave Dorothy a dollar that someone had just given to her. Deciding that the rent and light bills could wait just a little longer, she went to the Paulist Press and found that for fifty-seven dollars she could get twenty-five hundred copies of a four-page, tabloid-size paper.

In the meantime Maurin had come to the city from time to time, leaving his caretaking job. In April, with excitement rising over the forthcoming issue, he remained. But when printed copy began to come in and a dummy paper was tentatively put together, Maurin seemed disappointed. Reading Dorothy Day's stories about the plight of sharecroppers, child labor, the wage-hour issue in factories, and racial injustice seemed, in his view, to have missed the point. It was just another paper. "Everybody's newspaper is nobody's paper," he said, and left again for Mount Tremper.

What had troubled him? Dorothy Day explained that he had wanted only his essays printed. She conceded that while his attitude could have "looked like conceit and vanity to the unknowing," he was in reality only concerned with his "clarification." He probably thought that the paper suggested more the radicalism of the class struggle than that of personalism. True, perhaps, she later thought, for had not her whole life in journalism been lived from the position of viewing the world in terms of the class conflict? She was, after all, an ex-Socialist, ex-Wobbly, and ex-Communist. She thought of St. Augustine's observation that a bottle will still smell of the substance it once held. This applied to her. Besides, she concluded, her own temperament was involved.

May 1, 1933, was to be a day for massive demonstrations of the strength of Communist sentiment around the world.

The crisis in capitalism had reached new depths, and National Socialism in Germany was daily revealing new and more fearful aspects of its cult. Both would provide themes for leftist May Day orators. In New York, Socialists and Communists planned parades and rallies that would fill Broadway from Times Square twenty-five blocks southward to Union Square, from early morning until late afternoon. So many were expected to converge on Union Square that the police department assigned one thousand men to preserve order there.

Fifty thousand persons packed the square that bright, warm day. Setting out from her apartment at 436 East Fifteenth Street, Dorothy Day and three young men sent by a priest to assist her walked west on Fifteenth Street the four blocks to Union Square, lugging the first issue of *The Catholic Worker*. In an editorial the paper declared that it was for the unemployed and those who suffered from social injustice. It was a Catholic voice that stood with them; a voice, no less, that bespoke truly the mind of the Church as found in the social encyclicals of the popes.

Tensely, the four moved into the mass of men, crying the paper at a cent a copy. Any focus on the word "Catholic" in Union Square on May Day in 1933 was not something that would produce concerted enthusiasm. Reaction occurred with jibes in such volume that two of the newsmen left. But Dorothy Day remained, and so did Joe Bennett, a tall, gangling young man who occasionally had to sit because of exhaustion that came from a heart damaged by rheumatic fever.

When they returned to the apartment, they had not sold out their supply, but there were stories to relate of their encounters, and Dorothy Day felt satisfied with their effort. In the following week she sent copies of the *Worker* to editors of diocesan papers and to prominent Catholics. The mailing produced an extensive response. Encouraging letters and contributions began to come in. A second issue was assured.

Anticipating a larger operation, the working area for making up and mailing the paper was expanded. A vacant bar-

bershop on the ground floor below the apartment was acquired. Behind it was a bedroom and then a kitchen with a
door that opened onto a small backyard with a paved space
in front of the garden area—a patio where guests could be
served tea, Dorothy Day thought. Two women came to help
with the second edition, Eileen Corrigan and Dorothy Weston. Miss Corrigan had been a newspaperwoman, and Miss
Weston had recently graduated from Manhattanville College where she had majored in journalism. Both remained
with the *Worker* for some time. Then Maurin returned, and
Dorothy Day thought she saw a change in his attitude toward her. He no longer looked at her as "a Catherine of
Siena, already enlightened by the Holy Spirit," but as she
was, a person in whom he might find some concordance,
some basis on which to build. And the building began immediately from where he had left off; he pulled a book from
his pocket to continue his teaching.

The June edition of the *Worker* was primarily Maurin's.
He wrote a statement explaining that he did not want to be
an editor, but simply a contributor. "As an editor it will be
assumed that I sponsor or advocate any reform suggested in
the pages of *The Catholic Worker*. I would rather definitely
sign my own work." Then he outlined his program: round-
table discussions because he wanted a clarification of
thought; then "houses of hospitality" set up as ventures in
community living to take care of the unemployed; and, to
complete his scheme, "agronomic universities," or farm col-
onies. People will have to go back to the land, he said, because the cities have become overcrowded. The whole idea
was "a Utopian, Christian communism. I am not afraid of
the word communism. . . . I am not opposed to private
property with responsibility. But those who own private
property should never forget it is a trust."

Elated by the volume of complimentary mail the first
issue produced, Maurin announced in his statement that he
was pressing ahead with his program and would hold his
first round-table discussion at the Manhattan Lyceum at 66
East Fourth Street on the last Sunday in June. For ten dol-

lars he could rent a hall for eight hours. He had made a deposit of three dollars, he said, then added, "I have no more money now but I will beg the rest. I hope everyone will come to this meeting. I want Communists, radicals, priests, and laity. I want everyone to set forth his views. I want clarification of thought."

The event was heralded in a mimeographed broadside, passed around to friends, and distributed in Union Square, but the results were meager. Fifteen people showed up for the meeting. Nor was there much "clarification." One speaker from the floor claimed that the Church was inextricably bound up with the capitalist system. He was, of course, "refuted." Maurin tried two more times in the Lyceum, but the temperate exchange of ideas he had hoped for turned out to be shouting matches.

The idea, however, caught on—and essentially had a remarkable success. That fall lectures and discussions were held in the ground-floor offices before small groups made up of students and those aging and rootless men and women who sensed a new respect for their person in the atmosphere of the house. Ordinarily, these lecture-discussions came under one of the headings in Maurin's trinitarian approach to the problem of modern life: "cult, culture, and cultivation." "Cult" had to do with man's spirit, expressed in liturgical worship; "culture" concerned institutions and the kind of life and values that had been built around them; and "cultivation" involved nature and the instinct for workmanship. "Cult" and "culture" belonged to the scholar, while "cultivation" was the domain of the worker. Maurin believed that it was only by integrating these three aspects of existence in freedom that man could reach toward his highest human potential.

The exceptional thing about the lectures of the winter of 1933–1934 is the character of those who came to Fifteenth Street to sow ideas and share in discussions that sometimes went on for hours. European history professor Carlton J. H. Hayes of Columbia gave the first lecture. He spoke on "The History of Nationalism," emphasizing the fragmenting effects that this force had had on the human community. His associate in American history, Professor Harry Carman, came later, speaking on "Cultural Interests vs. Business Interests."

Distinguished priests came. Father John La Farge had attended Maurin's first round-table session. As a missionary priest in southern Maryland, later as an associate editor of *America,* he had become interested in the cause of interracial justice. In the small Worker group he found a similar concern, and it was he who focused discussions on the interracial theme in the early days of the movement. Father Wilfrid Parsons, *America's* editor, came to speak, and so did Father James Gillis, the Paulist oratorical and journalistic gadfly.

Two priests who had an early contact with the *Worker* and whose spirit and ideas were closely involved in it were Paul Hanley Furfey and Virgil Michel. Furfey, a young sociologist at Catholic University, would in the 1930s advance the idea of a "personalist" sociology. Accumulating and arranging data could not alone, in his view, provide the vision or the way by which society could become better. It took the radical action of persons who would live as closely as possible to the spirit of the Gospels, taking active love to those "other Christs" whom the world had forgotten.

Furfey was popular in the early days of the *Worker* with a group of young Catholic activists who called themselves "Campions," organized into their particular Campion Propaganda Committee. The committees were begun by Tom Coddington, a student who took up with the *Worker* in its first days and who married Dorothy Day's first editorial associate, Dorothy Weston. Coddington and some of his friends thought that the *Worker* needed to become involved in a more dramatic way in the issues of the moment, principally by demonstrations and picketing. On such matters Dorothy Day stood with Peter Maurin—these activities could lead away from the hard substance of personalist daily living to the excitement of crusades and action. But, as she noted, "I allowed this though [I was] not in favor of it."

It was Father Joseph McSorley who proposed that these activist works be separated from the Worker and organized under another name. On this she was reluctant, too—"sounded too much like Communist tactics to me."

For a while the Campions were strong. The New York committee, following the lead of Dorothy Day and her friends, picketed the Mexican and German consulates (the latter to protest Nazi anti-Semitism). On weekends they went to a shore house on Staten Island to ponder their interest in sociology and liturgy. There were also active groups in Boston and Washington. Furfey had close contacts with all the Campion groups, and he was impressed with their work.

But the world of the Campions was not that of Peter Maurin. Thereafter, the relationship between Furfey and the Worker was not close. Yet he kept abreast of the Worker movement and, over thirty years after his visits to Fifteenth Street, he wrote to Dorothy Day to tell her how much *The Catholic Worker* had meant to him. "I owe you a great debt," he said.

In Virgil Michel, the Benedictine liturgist, Peter Maurin found a source of ideas that bore on the "cult" part of his formula for personalist action. Michel, says his biographer, the Benedictine Paul Marx, saw the liturgy as "the basis of social action, of Christian social reconstruction and the very springboard of Catholic Action." Maurin's principle that culture was an aspect of spirit was underwritten by Michel's insistence that there could be no separation between social action and the liturgical action of worship. "What a changed outlook the Christian would experience," he exclaimed, "if he saw penetratingly—or rather lived intensively—the implications of the membership in the Mystical Body of Christ, the very core idea of the liturgy!"

Over the years the Workers tried to live the integrated life that Michel believed to be the necessary foundation for a new society. For his part, as a steadfast spokesman for the lay apostolate, Michel supported the Worker movement, even in its most controversial moments. He was a clear-

sighted man of rare spirit and intelligence who expected no
happy and quick solutions to society's problems. Like most
of the personalists, he felt strongly that "we are definitely
at the end of an era of human history." He died in 1938 in
his forty-ninth year. Writing at the time in *Orate Fratres*,
the liturgical journal that he had founded and edited, Dorothy Day told of the close association that this "Fellow
Worker in Christ" had had with the Catholic Worker movement.

There were other distinguished guests and speakers who
came in 1933 and 1934. There was Columbia historian
Parker Moon, the English historian and writer, Hilaire Belloc, and even French philosopher Jacques Maritain. The
"Workers' School," as Dorothy Day called it, raised such enthusiasm that meetings were held every evening and usually
went on until eleven o'clock and sometimes later. Jacques
Maritain stated his feelings to Peter Maurin in a letter
shortly after his visit. Maritain asked Maurin to tell Dorothy
Day how happy he had been to visit her, adding, "I wish I
could have said all that was in my heart—never was I more
vexed by inability to speak fluent English. It seemed as if I
had found again in The Catholic Worker a little of the atmosphere of Peguy's office in the Rue de la Sorbonne. And
so much good will, such courage, such generosity!"

What those "workers," recruited off the benches at Union
Square, got out of it was an open question. One, at least, felt
that the group was up to no good. An Irishman who had listened intently to the discussion following a lecture rose at
its conclusion to deliver a judgment: "You are all a bunch of
bloody Communists," he shouted. "I've sat here all evening
and nobody has once mentioned the name of the Blessed
Virgin!" But, for the young students who were beginning to
associate with the movement, the lectures were an experience that not only opened ideas to them, but also, in the
drab and close atmosphere of the old barbershop, added to
the growing excitement that came from the feeling they
were moving toward the heart of creation.

Another sign of the vitality of the new group was the

rapid increase in the circulation of *The Catholic Worker*. The November, 1933, issue reported a circulation of 20,000, which, by March, 1934, had risen to 25,000. One year later it stood at 65,000. It might be said, of course, that most of this growth came as the result of the energy of a relatively small number of enthusiasts who thrust the *Worker* pell-mell into whatever hand would receive it. But if many put the paper aside, dismissing it as another crackpot Depression phenomenon, there were also many for whom the paper touched a profoundly responsive chord. In the thirties there were Catholics, and indeed others, who felt as had Dorothy Day that the Church and the spirit of religion had said nothing of hope or concern to those millions who suffered from the Depression. The Communists were saying so much about misery and injustice. Ought not Christians to say more?

For others who did not think so explicitly about the problem, the *Worker* was simply a Catholic answer to Communism. That Dorothy Day and her friends had taken the first *Worker* to Union Square was a vigorous offensive tactic. A Fordham Jesuit praised the paper as "the best literary antidote I know against its mendacious namesake, *The Daily Worker*." Other letters, largely from priests and nuns, expressed a like sentiment. On September 18, 1933, a notice was sent to the universities, colleges, academies, and high schools of the Archdiocese of Chicago by the regional director of the National Catholic Alumni Federation. He had, he said, asked the editors of *The Catholic Worker* to send copies of the September issue to every Catholic school in the Archdiocese of Chicago. "The purpose of this paper is to fight communism and atheism by fighting for social justice and by popularizing the encyclicals of the Popes on social justice." *Commonweal* took note of the phenomenon. "A Catholic Paper vs. Communism" was the title of an article explaining what the new paper was all about. It was to give the laboring man "a journal that is essentially and peculiarly his; to offset the polemics of Communism with a clear exposition of the principles of social justice enunciated in papal encyclicals; and to oppose Communism and atheism by fighting for social justice for the working-man."

Such publicity quickly made Dorothy Day a prime candidate to lead in the always popular cause of anti-Communism. Invitations came in to lecture: "We are all waiting in anticipation for [your] view-point on the subject of Communism," a nun wrote. The Immaculate Catholic Club of New York was so impressed with the potential sweep of the thing that it "duly moved and unanimously passed" a resolution that the *Worker* could use its clubrooms for "meetings, teas, etc." In 1934, when Dorothy Day lent her support to the protest against the persecution of the Catholic Church in Mexico, there was applause. Two thousand singing and marching Catholic high-school students joined a handful of Workers in picketing the Mexican consulate. It was seen as a striking example of militant faith. The Catholic Action Club of Detroit wrote to the *Worker* that its activity "in combating the . . . fanatical persecution of the Church in Mexico deserves the most unstinted praise. You may rest assured that the forces of Catholic Action in Detroit will not lag in the struggle against the vanguard of militant atheism. . . ."

During the first years Workers found a certain attractiveness in the proposition that they were the Catholic front-line force against the Communist threat. "We must put over Catholic pamphlets and the Catholic press with the same tactics that the Communists use in putting over their literature," Dorothy Day declared, although "Heaven knows" that the Communist literary fare was itself "dull enough often." For a time *The Catholic Worker* ran a feature called "Specimens of Communist Propaganda," where it would print examples of some of the more outlandish statements in the *New Masses* when its subject was the Catholic Church.

Concentrating on the shortcomings of Communism was not a sustaining enthusiasm for *The Catholic Worker*, nor could it be. Its personalism precluded an expenditure of any major portion of its energy in the denunciation of outside forms and processes. "We must never cease to emphasize a personal responsibility," Dorothy Day would say. "The work we must do is strive for peace and concordance rather than hatred and strife." And no less than any other, "A Communist beaten and kicked reminds us of Jesus as He fell beneath the weight of His cross."

In the long run, the continued expansion in the circulation of the *Worker* was due to those who, caught by the attractiveness of its personalist idea, supported it with contributions and through work to get subscriptions. A seminarian wrote to Dorothy Day to tell her of his joy at reading the paper, and he enclosed an order for sixteen subscriptions. A priest sent in $8.50 which he had collected from friends and said he would distribute the *Worker* himself. Another priest, crippled with arthritis, sent in $25 and suggested that Dorothy Day "say a prayer at least that they won't stop manufacturing aspirin. . . ."

Indeed, contributions would in time come from sources so disparate as to indicate the Worker idea's ability to touch depths of feeling ordinarily not reached. An inmate of a prison in Trenton, New Jersey, sent two dollars, asking the *Worker* to keep one-half "for the continuance of the glorious work you are doing . . ." and to forward the other half to "The Harry Bridges Defense Fund." He had heard of Peter Maurin from another inmate who had described him "as the only near Franciscan he had ever met," and he hoped that if Maurin ever got to Trenton he would stop for a visit.

On the other hand, a high executive in a large New York investment house contributed generously in the early years. And through all the history of the Worker movement there would be those persons, too tired and alone to be caught up in the issues discussed in the pages of *The Catholic Worker*, but yet who sensed in it something of a hope and charity for which they reached. "Today is the anniversary of a brother's death," came one note with a donation, "and I feel there is no better way to remember him outside of masses than to help the poor."

The contributions were put to use increasing the volume

of *Workers* sent to whoever seemed a likely candidate to distribute them. Indeed, the enthusiasm of *Worker* staff members for attaining higher levels of circulation sometimes caused bundles of the paper to land in the hands of a reluctant distributor. Donald Davidson, a member of the Agrarian group at Vanderbilt University during the thirties, found himself buried in copies. "For some time," he wrote, "I have been intending to suggest to you that you find another distributor to take care of the copies of *The Catholic Worker* which have been coming to me. . . . I admire what you are doing and am in sympathy with many of your aims; but I am really not the person to pass out the copies of the *Worker*."

The contributions, however, could not catch up with costs. "We live in the daily hope," Dorothy Day wrote in the second issue "that someone will come in and offer to pay the printing bill or the rent." One year later matters had hardly improved: "The printer called this morning wanting to know affably when we were going to finish paying our bill. . . . We told him he had better get busy and pray for it right hard." And it would always be this way—a sign that in the financial management of *The Catholic Worker*, as in all other matters that touched on the movement, Dorothy Day never presumed to deny to Providence a prominent role in the disposition of events. To those who entreated her to put the operation on a businesslike basis, she answered, "But this isn't a business, it's a movement. And we don't know anything about business around here anyway. Well-meaning friends say—'But people get tired of appeals.' We don't believe it. Probably most of our friends live as we do, from day to day and from hand to mouth, and as they get, they are willing to give. So we shall continue to appeal, and we know that the paper will go on."

Beginning with the second issue, Peter Maurin's essays were featured on the front page amidst news that illustrated the paper's concern with social justice. Papal encyclicals were quoted to indicate the Church's attitude on social issues, and when members of the clergy wrote or spoke

against human abuses, the *Worker* featured them prominently. Shortly, good reviews of new books appeared. With
her daughter Tamar six years old, Dorothy Day even included a feature in the early issues called "Our Children's
Corner." Much of the news was related to workingmen's
concerns. Michael Gunn, "a brushmaker of Brooklyn, and
street speaker," wrote a column on labor news, and there
was an attempt made to keep abreast of what in the New
Deal's unfolding program related to the interests of labor.

Yet *The Catholic Worker* was not a news medium, and in
time its half-formed concern to be so gave way to a clearer
concentration on its particular mission. It became a personalist paper, setting forth personalist approaches to those
great human problems of the 1930s and the decades following.

It was the paper of labor's poor in spirit. To the discomfi-
ture of established persons, it declared a communion with
the heroes and martyrs of radical labor. When Tom Mooney, dubiously incarcerated for the 1916 San Francisco Preparedness Day bombing, was freed in 1939, the *Worker* editorially rejoiced. The Wobblies were looked upon as close
brothers, and Workers tried to emulate some of their
customs—like the everlasting pot of soup from which all ate
and into which all put what they could. Annually, Sacco
and Vanzetti were memorialized on the anniversary of their
execution in August, 1927. Vanzetti, the *Worker* said, "fulfilled the characteristics of moral and Christian heroism.
. . . He approaches comradeship with Jesus." In 1967, when
John Nicholas Beffel (who had reported the Sacco-Vanzetti
trial for the Socialist *Call*) organized a memorial service for
the two men, Dorothy Day was asked to speak.

*The Catholic Worker* was Dorothy Day's paper. She
chose the "news," wrote the copy, and composed the editorials. In the first editions she began her own column,
called "Day by Day," but shortly changed to "All in a Day."
In 1946 she began calling her column "On Pilgrimage," a
title that peculiarly caught the mood of her life in the
Worker movement. The column has long since become the

Readers of *The Catholic Worker*, Union Square, 1940.

Stanley Vishnewski (left), distributing *The Catholic Worker*,
at Union Square, ca. 1 May 1940.

heart of *The Catholic Worker*. When in March, 1943, a reader wrote in to say that the paper "breathes a deep spirituality which I do not find in any other Catholic publication," he certainly must have been thinking of her columns. Dorothy Day did not write of religion as a segment of life, but as the substance of life. The penetration of her insights on the subject of man's spirit in the contempory world was rare and clear.

In addition to her special kind of personalist writing, the paper has enjoyed another distinction. The artwork alone made a powerful personalist statement. Its woodcuts, depicting Christ and the saints as workers, have helped to fuse a sense of the divine in the performance of menial labor. Christ was shown working in a carpenter shop; Mary was a housemaid who swept the floor; and St. Joseph worked at his sawbench. It was an artwork that gave the feeling of the humanity of Christ and the community of man, signified in the performance of those menial tasks that represented the foundation on which men could reach for higher things.

The artist who did this work, Ade Bethune, came to Dorothy Day and Peter Maurin in January, 1934. A recent graduate of New York's Cathedral High School for girls, looking for an outlet for her talent, she was sent to the *Worker* by the editor of *Liturgical Arts* magazine. It was Maurin who told her to depict Christ and the saints as workers. In the March, 1934, issue, Dorothy Day editorially expressed her thanks to St. Joseph (who was taken as the patron of the movement) for sending them an artist.

Miss Bethune thus began her long association with *The Catholic Worker*, but not without an initial editorial liberty taken with her name that was to register permanently. The Bethunes were World War I refugees from Belgium whose name properly was "de Bethune." The young artist signed her work "A. de Bethune" which through a "misunderstanding" came out in the *Worker* as "Ade Bethune." And so it remained.

# 5

# FIFTEENTH STREET

Inevitably, the personalist orientation of *The Catholic Worker* led it into controversy. For American Catholics of the 1930s, it was difficult to accept the idea of religion as a force that did not admit of two separate worlds of the heavenly and secular, each operating in its own sphere, without much reference to the other. From the days of Orestes Brownson, back in the 1840s, liberal Catholics had been insisting that Catholicism and Americanism were completely harmonious. David J. O'Brien, who has studied the modern aspect of this subject in his *American Catholics and Social Reform*, aptly quotes Bishop John England to illustrate the point: "Let Catholics in religion stand isolated as a body, and upon as good ground as their brethren," but also "let them as citizens and politicians not be distinguished from their other brethren." Thus, socially aware Catholics of the 1930s, as O'Brien points out in another instance, "had few doubts that common Americanism provided a secure basis for cooperative efforts with others to promote the realization of goals at once Christian and American." Both, it was assumed, "upheld the ideals of liberty and equality, human rights, social justice and the general welfare. . . ."

In the 1840s, when the ideals of Jeffersonian democracy tended to structure certain areas of American life, the assumption was plausible. But in the 1930s, when American ideals were defined more in the competitive terms of William Graham Sumner, the assumption was not so plausible. Yet it was one that persisted uncritically, underwritten all the more strongly by millions of Catholics, just recently immigrants, who were beginning to move into the mainstream of American life. For them, especially, the personalist idea could only seem un-American and anti-Catholic. Nonetheless *The Catholic Worker,* in the excitement of its vision, plunged into those areas where it thought it saw man victimized by bourgeois traditions, frequently supported by the state and meekly acquiesced to by the Church.

One of the most obvious of the inhuman conditions that existed in American life of the 1930s—one that had deep roots in the peculiarities of the American past, yet that was more than adequately nourished in the climate of modern industrial bourgeois culture—was the demeaning status of the Black man. Although the revolution that would begin to alter his condition was still two decades away, even then, as John Cogley has said, "While the Workers did not coin the idea that black was beautiful, they acted as if they knew it was."

The first issues of the *Worker* took up the case of the "Scottsboro boys," in which nine Alabama Blacks were convicted of rape and threatened with execution. Dorothy Day wrote of her prayer that the nine would be spared, saying the episode was the consequence of an "antagonism which . . . is often built upon the struggles of the poor whites and the poor blacks," both of whom were "victims of industrialists who grind the face of the poor."

The *Worker*'s Scottsboro emphasis could have been a response to the energetic way in which the Communists had involved themselves in the case, but it was at the same time a response that was entirely its own. "We believe in the complete equality of all men as brothers under the Fatherhood of God," *The Catholic Worker* declared. To this Dorothy Day added that "We want no revolution, we want the brotherhood of men. We want men to love one another. We want all men to have sufficient for their needs."

When the *Worker* saw Catholics taking positive steps toward equality for Blacks, it noted them with pleasure. In the May, 1934, issue it discussed the work of a Catholic University anthropologist, Father John M. Cooper, who had been denouncing racial discrimination. It frequently noted the work of Father John La Farge, who wrote on the subject in *America*, and it recognized the creation of Catholic interracial councils in some cities. But it also noted and discussed the infamous concurrence of Catholic institutions, schools, and hospitals in policies of segregation that were the same as those of society generally. "We Have Sinned Exceedingly" was the judgment contained in one editorial on the subject.

For their part, there was the house of hospitality Peter Maurin opened in Harlem in May, 1934, an unrented store that had been donated to them. Harlem was tense that summer. Blacks had been the first to be fired from their jobs when the Depression hit, and in their attempts to preserve for themselves some economic security, they had met complete frustration. Maurin's biographer relates some of the problems Workers found there. The three hundred thousand inhabitants of this enclave had petitioned the Fifth Avenue Bus Company to hire Black drivers. The company refused to see the petitioners. The mills would not hire a Black. The chain stores were excluding them. All that remained for them was to go into the White man's world to take porters' jobs and shine shoes, or do other tasks that White men did not care to do.

The Harlem house was a demonstration of Maurin's thought that those who would best represent the personalist leaven must go where lives had been blighted most by injustice. He and his friends did what they could. Ade Bethune held drawing classes for children, and meals were served to the hungry. Unpaid bills were placed beneath the statue of St. Joseph, who was importuned daily to do something about them. The Harlem house did not last long. Dorothy Day gave the reason for its closing: "We were put out of the store in Harlem by the owner, who did not agree with our pacifism. . . . He thought we were subversive. . . ."

The *Worker*'s frequent denunciation of racial injustice and the honest way in which it discussed racist practices in Catholic institutions brought a letter from the chairman of the interracial commission of the Chicago Urban League. Arthur G. Falls was "struck with wonder" when he saw his first issue of *The Catholic Worker*. "Certainly those who have 'labored' with Catholics, both of the clergy and laity, in an endeavor to get them to face practical issues, are more than joyful to see your publication." He thought it would be "interesting to see one of the workmen at the top of your front page shown to be a colored workman. . . ."

Dorothy Day saw his point, so in the same issue with Falls' letter, the change was effected: one of the workmen was made black. Curiously, the Black man was garbed in a tee shirt; the White man was bare to the waist. This contrast evoked a letter from a woman who wrote only to make "some suggestions . . . for Catholic advancement." She urged that "the front page of the *Worker* be changed by the addition of the lines I have drawn [she had drawn lines putting skivvies on the white man too]. Why . . . do we have the heading of a Catholic paper (standing for equality, justice, and propriety), portraying the White Catholic worker as justified and virtuous *without* covering the upper portion of the body . . . ?" This matter of proper dress led to other things. What was "the Catholic Worker's attitude toward the attire in 'Catholic' boxing exhibitions. . . . What is the effect of said exhibitions on peace—between individuals and nations?" The *Worker*, in her view, was not thinking through its art very well!

The Catholic Worker movement and the New Deal began life at about the same point in history, and as the Roosevelt Administration brought specific programs before the country, the *Worker* took its first steps toward charting a personalist course on the fundamental question of how could man best become free in the face of the increasing complexity of his institutionalized life. The central legislative action of the first New Deal was the NIRA or NRA (National Industrial Recovery Act). In the first issues the NRA was supported by

Workers because it was following the lines laid down by Pope Pius XI in his encyclical *Quadragesimo Anno*. Two issues later it opposed the NRA because, it said, the Chamber of Commerce wanted to make it into a "superorganization of industry" where strikes would be eliminated. Even so, it might be justified because it believed with the pope that whenever the general interest of any particular class suffered and was threatened with evils which could in no other way be met, then the public authority, the state, must step in to meet them.

The NRA matter was indicative of the problem the Worker movement faced when it came to defining its position with respect to the economic order. Peter Maurin might say, as he often did, that it was his concern "to make the encyclicals click." Some analysts, however, believed that a social application of *Quadragesimo Anno* would result in a Fascist-type corporate state. Yet Maurin stated his ideal as a "Christian communism," never indicating what institutional form his idea would take. There were also differences between Maurin and Dorothy Day. Surveying the great labor-capital conflicts of the 1930s, Maurin would say, "strikes don't strike me," but Dorothy Day put the movement in the active service of labor formation and strike activity.

What would be the institutional characteristics of the system best suited to achieve the ends of personalism? Socialism, said Berdyaev, for it is the projection of Christian personalism. Socialism is not necessarily collectivism, as in the Marxist definition; it may be personalistic and anticollectivist. This, too, was the Worker view, for, as Dorothy Day wrote, there was still a way for man to be his "own master and not a slave, as he is under both finance capitalism and under a dictatorship whether of the proletariat or of a militarist class."

The socialism of *The Catholic Worker* was thus an economic voluntarism. Maurin called it Christian communism, and Miss Day, too, used this description at times. In a further definition of what she meant, she described it as a "worker ownership of the means of production and distribution as distinguished from nationalization." This was to be accomplished by decentralized cooperatives and the elimination of a distinct employer class. It called for widespread ownership of property by all men as a stepping-stone to a communism that would be in accord with the Christian teaching of detachment from material goods and that, when realized, would express itself in common ownership.

Dorothy Day's voluntarism suggests a close affinity with anarchism, and on occasion both she and Peter Maurin have referred to themselves as anarchists. Of the various "proposed roads to freedom" set forth by nineteenth-century social and economic theorists, the social ends of Christian personalism were most like those of anarchism. But though they were anarchists, Dorothy Day has said, it did not mean that the movement opposed organization. It meant that it wanted radical decentralization and the delegation to smaller bodies and groups what could be done far more humanly and responsibly through mutual aid, as well as charity.

The particular kind of economic and social anarchism that she and her friends did espouse was one that had been set forth in the thirties by a group of English Catholics who styled themselves "Distributists." Hilaire Belloc, G. K. Chesterton, and Father Vincent McNabb urged a rejection of machine technology and urban civilization in favor of a system where the value of creative work would take precedence over mass-production goals. This would be done by a return to a simple, self-contained agrarian, handicraft society, which, in view of the industrialist-capitalist crisis at hand, seemed plausible.

In the thirties this mood came to more than the English Distributists. Throughout the twenties, artists and writers had depicted, sometimes fancifully, the dehumanizing impact of the machine on life—as in Karel Čapek's *R.U.R.* and Elmer Rice's *The Adding Machine.* In 1938 Lewis Mumford's *The Culture of Cities* appeared. It characterized modern urban culture as sterile, dominated by the value of massiveness, whereas, by contrast, in the medieval city all the life was governed by an ideal of spirit, possessing an integrating, humanizing quality. In the South the Agrarian *Fugitive* group at Vanderbilt University took the crisis of the times as a basis for recalling a golden past extracted from the South's agrarian tradition, into which they wove themes of a quasi-medieval synthesis.

The crisis of the thirties provided the mood and even a certain repose whereby thinkers might reassess the past, free of the dogma that whatever was newest was best. But with the advent of World War II, with its emphasis on mass-production goals, the attacks on the machine ended and machine-tending became a noble rite.

Some workers did not go along with the Distributist idea. One was Harvard graduate John Cort. He had read the *Worker*, and then he had heard Dorothy Day give a talk to the Boston Workers. Before she had finished he decided to go to New York and join the group. Interested in economic issues, he found the Worker's decentralist enthusiasm unrealistic, especially when some of them, without much thought, indiscriminately put whatever it was they believed about economic institutions under the heading of anarchism. The Industrial Revolution, he believed, could not be repealed and any serious effort to do so was anachronistic. "I do not think," he wrote in retrospect in *Commonweal* in November, 1952, "that there is aid and comfort for anarchism in the wisdom of the Church. And this despite extended, and often eloquent, efforts on the part of the Catholic Worker movement to find such aid and comfort."

In 1937 Cort helped to found the Association of Catholic Trade Unionists, whose purpose was "to promote democratic trade unionism free from criminal, Fascist, Communist and state control." But Dorothy Day did not go along completely with this idea, which was one of working within the system. As she wrote in *The Catholic Worker* of February, 1949, "All they want, what they will settle for, is a share of the profits, instead of a share in the ownership, and the decentralization of the physical business of factories and production, and not a decentralization of control by widespread ownership."

As *The Catholic Worker* began to define a personalist position on the institutions of social and economic life, it produced a rolling wave of reaction. To those Catholics established in the manners and values of the bourgeois era a personalist world was so strange and radical that its inspiration could appear to be rooted in a demonic heresy. "Your entire production," said one letter writer, "is a hoax and camouflage,—it is the most poorly and thinly disguised sheet of Communistic, rabble-baiting literature it has been my misfortune to see." Dorothy Day wrote to a friend to say that "We've been investigated by the Detective Bureau at Center Street on complaints that we were communists masquerading as Catholics." And it was not long until an official of the New York Chancery Office questioned her about the *Worker's* opposition to capitalism. Their position, she answered, was "no new thing," adding innocently that only recently "The Vatican paper warned us . . . of regarding Americanism or Communism as the only two alternatives. . . ."

The movement's personalist sweep to the heart of the bourgeois structure would in time eat at the roots of American Catholic establishmentarianism, but in those years its position was so novel that some kind of Chancery Office review was urged for the *Worker* by those who stood on established ground. The first specific issue that brought Dorothy Day and the *Worker* into a controversial focus within the Church was one currently being debated within the context of public policy. In 1924 Congress passed the Child Labor Amendment which, by 1934, had been ratified by thirty-six states. The amendment, under discussion in New York, was the subject for the Fifteenth Street "Workers' School" meeting on the Sunday evening of February 18, 1934.

As usual, the speaker was well known. Monsignor John A. Ryan, "the Right Reverend New Dealer," had been the director of the Social Action Department of Catholic University, and he was widely known for his social concerns, one of which was the Child Labor Amendment. To the twenty or so assembled there that evening, Ryan expressed the hope "that those Catholics who believe in the Child Labor Amendment will some day realize to what extent they have permitted themselves to be misled by the dishonest propaganda emanating from the National Association of Manufacturers and other agents of social injustice. . . ." The opponents of ratification, he said, had been claiming that the backward states would take note of the movement for federal control and adequately improve their own statutes. But this had not happened. "Hence there is nothing left now but federal action." Ryan's remarks were immediately used as *The Catholic Worker's* "Case" for the Child Labor Amendment, and the paper henceforth strongly supported it.

However, all eight of the New York State bishops opposed the amendment, as well as most of the others throughout the country. Cardinal Patrick Hayes of New York stated his objection (one which was held by most of the other bishops) that it was the parents and not the state that should exercise authority over the lives of children. If the children did indeed need further protection, it should be given by local governments which, as the legend ran, were in close touch with local conditions. One bishop summed it up by quoting Methodist Episcopal Bishop Warren Akin Candler on the subject—that the amendment tended "to discredit parents and subvert family government, substituting for parenthood a paternalistic government at Washington. . . . This is nothing less than a monstrous proposal."

What the bishops professed further to see in the amendment was a doorway through which the federal government might enter into the area of regulation of other aspects of the lives of children, even to the point of endangering the parochial school system. But by many the bishop's position was taken, at least in part, as an unwillingness to question positions assumed by those who represented high bourgeois respectability.

*The Catholic Worker*'s stand on the Child Labor Amendment raised, in the minds of some, a question of the paper's position in relation to a stand taken by Church officials. The Chancery Office received many letters urging it to take some action against *The Catholic Worker*. Not having before been confronted with such a situation, the office probably wondered what, if anything, it ought to do. Finally, Monsignor Arthur J. Scanlan, Office of Censor of Books, sent a letter to Dorothy Day. He had received some mail, he said, that concerned *The Catholic Worker*. It might be a good idea if Miss Day would give him some names of some priests "who are both interested and sympathetic with the work you are doing." He then thought it would be advisable to have "His Eminence appoint one of them to look over the matter before publication and be responsible for it." This course would "avoid criticism and . . . be of assistance in the future development of the work." Apparently wishing to avoid the appearance of giving an ecclesiastical order, Scanlan followed up his letter with a personal visit. He was concerned about the "great many attacks" on *The Catholic Worker* he had received, Dorothy Day explained in a letter to a friend.

Dorothy Day readily accepted Scanlan's proposal, suggesting that her spiritual adviser, Father McSorley, be chosen as her editorial adviser. Scanlan agreed to this and then relayed information from Cardinal Hayes that McSorley's name was not to appear in print and that he had "received no official appointment to act as censor. . . ."

When, in time, Monsignor Scanlan did intrude the opinion of his office, through Father McSorley, on some of the material in the *Worker*, the subject was the Child Labor Amendment. Dorothy Day's response was temperate. "The stand we take is also the stand taken by Monsignor John A. Ryan . . . and others. It is, after all, a matter of opinion, and it has nothing to do with faith or dogma, so we did not think we were treading on dangerous ground in upholding this piece of legislation." After all, she asked, was there not room for a difference of opinion on the subject?

Possibly Monsignor Scanlan felt a little foolish about the matter, but another Scanlan—Patrick—the editor of the Brooklyn *Tablet,* the diocesan newspaper, had more positive feelings. Writing to Dorothy Day, he informed her that she had taken the wrong position on the subject and he then added an instructive personal observation. He noted that "everyone in my family except one worked before they were eighteen. Two of my brothers who, I believe, glorify the clergy, used to carry orders out for a grocery store at two cents an order when they were small." He had observed that there were boys in his neighborhood who made a good income by delivering newspapers. "It is a pleasure to see them making their few dollars than [sic] to be hanging around the corner shooting crap or playing some of the games which are more destructive to health, character and vitality than the harmless task in which they are at present engaged." He understood that Dorothy Day had quoted from Pope Leo XIII to support her position on the amendment. "The quotation in question has nothing to do with the . . . amendment. I believe Pope Leo would be opposed to the . . . measure."

With the passage of the Fair Labor Standards Act in June, 1938, the bad effects of child labor were so reduced that the subject was no longer one for discussion in *The Catholic Worker.* At the same time, the issue of ecclesiastical review for *The Catholic Worker* seemed to have been dropped. Nor was it ever revived, for some time later Dorothy Day observed that the Chancery Office had "given us absolute freedom and shown us courtesy and kindness." Even so—as she would later say to Dwight Macdonald when he was preparing an article on the Worker movement for *The New Yorker*—"If the Chancery ordered me to stop publishing *The Catholic Worker* tomorrow, I would." This statement, which she has repeated on other occasions, suggests her sense of the importance of the visible Church in the personalist revolution.

There was yet another issue brought up by *The Catholic Worker*'s personalist intrusion into the world of affairs. What right, Dorothy Day was asked on many occasions, had she to use the word "Catholic" as a part of the title of the organization and its paper? The answer that she gave was that its inclusion had no official significance, since the group never concerned itself with doctrinal matters, but as Catholics working in a community effort toward Church-defined ends, they used it as an identification of their spirit and aims. When she was questioned by the Chancery as to the use of "Catholic" in the paper's title, and the suggestion was made that she and her friends should consider changing it, she responded that "None . . . wishes to change the name," adding that she was sure "none thinks the Catholic War Veterans (who also use the name Catholic) represent the point of view of the Archdiocese any more than they think *The Catholic Worker* does. . . ."

Some years later she admitted that she could understand the position of those who questioned the use of "Catholic" in the paper's title. She had been reading Evelyn Waugh's life of Ronald Knox, and in it she had found that Knox, who was the fourth Catholic chaplain at Oxford, had, unlike the others, refused to call himself a Catholic chaplain of Oxford. Wishing to be more precise, he styled himself the chaplain of Catholics at Oxford. Hence she could see how the title, *The Catholic Worker,* sounded official, as though it spoke for all. She added that she had recently been accused in a Congressional committee hearing of usurping the name "Catholic" and that Cardinal Francis Spellman had threatened Workers with court action to make them change the title. But this was untrue. "Cardinal Spellman has never spoken to me on the subject," she wrote.

The problems faced by the movement in these early days did not overly disturb Dorothy Day. In the summer of 1934 she was thirty-six years old, and her life, she believed, was full on the course that had been reserved for her. Julia Porcelli went to live in the Worker house at this time, and she provides a recollection of Dorothy Day as she remembered her then: "I compared her to Greta Garbo who was very popular then—Dorothy's beautiful jaw and her features and her coloring, beautiful bone structure. . . ." But more than her looks was her "presence." "When she enters a room . . . you are very much aware of her. You can't ignore that she's there. There are so few who have this quality."

In the early thirites the world was beginning to shake with the outcries of the Caesars who called for a community of violence. But for Dorothy Day the Worker personalist idea was launched almost in a spirit of joyous tranquillity. Time slowed, and the life around her took on sharpness and color. In the summer of 1933 she wrote in the *Worker* of that life around her: "New benches have been set out in front of houses and boys sit around tables on the sidewalk playing cards. . . . The Italians in the neighborhood are making cherry brandy. All the babies are tanned brown and the benches in the square are crowded. Street cleaners flush the streets and the children run screaming." In the small backyard "petunias are in bloom and the asparagus plant waves its feathery stalks, eight feet tall in the breeze." At night there was "a pier down by the East River where you can sit and watch the moon come up."

Three months later she noted that fall had come. "A haze hangs over the city. Fogs rise from the river and the melancholy note of the river boats is heard at night. There is the smell of chestnuts in the air. . . ." But she underlined the mood of romantic dreaming with reality. The smell of chestnuts might be in the air, but "if you buy the chestnuts, most of them are wormy." Another reality was that "all our Italian neighbors are too poor this year to buy grapes and make wine," one dire consequence of which would be that "Mr. Burino will not be dropping into the office of *The Catholic Worker* when he sees our light late at night, to console us for our long hours by the gift of a milk bottle of wine." It would be a hard winter. "Evictions are increasing, people come in to ask us to collect winter clothes and to help them find apartments where relief checks will be accepted." She noted that the latest game of society was the "scavenger hunt." It was "asinine" while there was another kind of scavenger hunt going on every morning up and down Fifteenth Street, with people going through garbage cans looking for food.

In December she wrote an editorial on the progress of the movement and recalled that it had been on December 8, 1932, that she had spent the morning at the Shrine of the Immaculate Conception in Washington. She recalled the hunger marches and affirmed again that there had been justice in the demands made then by the Communists.

One "bitterly cold" night in February she went to see a Eugene O'Neill play, *Days Without End*. Returning to the office, she "could not forbear to sit down and report on it" with the "kettle singing on the potbellied stove" and "still time before twelve for a cup of tea. . . ." She recalled the O'Neill she had known over a decade ago and saw something of him in the play, "the struggle of a man's soul between belief and disbelief, between hate and love for God. . . ." Belief, she knew, was difficult. "To go on one's knees to pray is a hard thing. . . . It is a struggle to take a physical attitude of humility."

Whatever private life she may have had before meeting Peter Maurin she surrendered when he took up his abode at the Worker house. "Although you may be called bums and panhandlers, you are in fact Ambassadors of God," Maurin wrote of the poor he knew so well on the Bowery and at Union Square. Shortly he was bringing his "Ambassadors" to Fifteenth Street. "They have no place to sleep," he would say.

Among the first in a long and rich succession of Ambassadors was a pair, in that summer of 1933, called Dolan and Egan. Earlier, in the spring, they had been Peter's most solemn and attentive listeners as he discoursed in Union Square. Grateful for their attention, he symbolically designated this "thin, shabby, and rather furtive-looking pair," "The Workers." That summer they visited regularly, announcing their presence to Dorothy Day with an intoned "Dolan and Egan here again." It got so, she related, that her personal friends, knowing how exasperated she got at having her time so taken up, would call out upon arriving, "Dolan and Egan here again."

Dolan and Egan were not only Maurin's "Workers," they were also charter members of the *Worker* sales force. Selling on the streets, they kept the money for "eats and tobacco." But other salesmen, soon recruited, caught the enthusiasm of the new venture and sold the papers with a spirit that more than made up for those first hesitant moments when Dorothy Day and her friends had gone into Union Square. There was "Big Dan" Orr. Dorothy Day remembered how he had come to Fifteenth Street, "groaning and shouting," and when he was asked what might be done for him he bellowed that he could know no higher bliss than to soak his feet. So a tub of hot water was brought to him, and, roaring out his joy, he stripped off his dirt-caked socks and ecstatically lowered his feet into the water. He had been sleeping around the piers on the waterfront and eating out of garbage cans. Shortly he was out selling the *Worker*, and the paper never had a more flamboyant and aggressive salesman. Renting a horse and wagon from a Nazi on East Sixteenth Street, he made deliveries around town. Once he used the horse and wagon to move some Jewish neighbors. "It rejoiced our hearts," Dorothy Day wrote in *The Long Loneliness*.

Steve Hergenham, a German carpenter who had lost in the Depression the home he had built for himself, came to Fifteenth Street from Union Square. Margaret, from the Pennsylvania mining region and far along in pregnancy, arrived to take on the cooking chores. After her baby came, she went into the streets to sell the *Worker*, taking the infant with her. There was a professor who spoke a number of languages and an old Armenian who wore a long black coat and a black hat over his white hair. He wrote poetry and kept a cat named Social Justice.

But it was upon the young that the new movement registered a vital force. One day a seventeen-year-old Lithuanian boy, Stanley Vishnewski, watched Dorothy Day and some

Dorothy Day (r.), Dorothy Weston (l.) and co-workers in the Catholic Worker office, ca. September 1934. Henry Beck photo.

friends selling the *Worker*. Attracted by the style and enthusiasm of the group, he approached her and asked what he might do to help. She was eating something and offered to share it with him. Then she said, "Join us." This is one of the stories that Vishnewski tells today, some four decades later, of how he came to join the Worker movement. He can, of course, tell others. He likes to recall those days, and he has recounted a description of the Fifteenth Street house and aspects of its life:

The office itself was one of those railroad flat stores. There was a big plateglass window and you walked down the stairs and entered this room, sort of a dark room. The room itself was long but narrow and as you walked in onto your left there was a big packing box full of clothing that people were bringing into the Catholic Worker. Anybody in the neighborhood could open the door and help themselves to clothing that was there. And as you walked in to the left there was a small bookcase with many books there that people were donating . . . and next to the bookcase was an antique rolltop desk that Dorothy Day used. This desk was rather shabby . . . in fact it had to be supported by a few books to keep it on an even keel. Next to it was a metal table that Frank O'Donnell used as a circulation table . . . [with] two little filing cabinets under it which comprised the entire circulation of *The Catholic Worker*. In fact it was a very easy job to put the paper out because we used to hand address the envelopes. . . .

In this office also there was a pot bellied stove. . . . Peter Maurin used to love to take care of . . . the stove.

As you left the office you walked into a little room in which there were no windows whatsoever. This was a dark room and here they kept back issues of *The Catholic Worker,* and also back issues of magazines, the *Sign* magazine, *Commonweal, America* . . . there was a big rack in which they kept suitcases and bundles for people who had no place to live and they just stored their suitcases there while they went out looking for work.

I used to set the table every night and we always had a ritual setting one extra plate for whoever came to the Catholic Worker was always invited to stay.

In the back we had a lovely little garden. Dorothy used to love to sit out there and write the editorials or articles for the paper, and when visitors would come, if it was warm they would sit out there and drink coffee.

For Vishnewski and the others there was also action. As Dorothy Day observed in the *Worker,* they could not write of poverty and injustice without being drawn out into the streets to picket and demonstrate. They picketed businesses that they believed were dealing unfairly with labor, and they picketed the German consulate at the Battery, protesting Nazi anti-Semitism. Sometimes in their demonstrations, the handful of Workers found themselves in the company of Communists. Dorothy Day's comment was that the recognition of injustice by Communists should not automatically blind Catholics to the injustice. The young Workers thrilled at the novelty and daring of the work.

The appearance of persecution added zest to their lives, and where was there a more fitting villain than Wall Street itself? Two Workers, Anthony Ullo and Joe Calderon, had been selling the paper and speaking at the corner of Wall and Broad streets, two days a week at the noon hour, on Catholic ethics in business and on Scholastic philosophy. Calderon, who had four years of service with the Stock Exchange, was summarily fired. Then Ullo, in the midst of a noon-hour talk, was checked by a police sergeant. A new ruling had been made: because of the complaints of the Bankers Trust Company and others, there were to be no more talks on economic or social subjects. Speakers on religion would be tolerated, but they would have to have proper ecclesiastical authority.

And there was Maurin, bringing the excitement of his sense of mission into their lives. Using Steve Hergenham as his foil (a role Hergenham had been cajoled into taking), Maurin would set forth the personalist position on the issues of the day as Hergenham took an opposite one. Since Maurin regarded totalitarianism as the chief danger to mankind, Hergenham had frequently to take the villainous role of the Fascist. Dorothy Day related in *The Long Loneliness*

that they discoursed in the evenings at the Worker house, at
Union Square and Columbus Circle, and in Harlem. They
even spoke at a Holy Name meeting, but the men of the
parish thought it was some kind of a comic show with (the
German) Hergenham and (the Frenchman) Maurin, both
with heavy accents, setting forth their arguments with gestures, oratorical flourishes, and striking poses. As their audience laughed they laughed, too, Dorothy Day recounted.
"They thought they were being laughed with. Or perhaps
they pretended not to see."

But the young people around 436 East Fifteenth Street
knew better. Listening to Maurin's ideas, repeated again
and again, they began to sense their meaning. When he
made off for Columbus Circle they followed, reciting an an-
tiphonal chant as they made their way down the street.
When Maurin sang out, "To give and not to take," the less
bashful would respond in chorus, "that is what makes man
human."

For these young, the Worker was good news. Remembering those days, Stanley Vishnewski observed, "It came as a
pleasant surprise to hundreds of enthusiastic men and
women that in the Catholic Worker they could be as radical
and heroic as they pleased." A college student, Bill Gauchat,
was so caught up with the vision that he would in time de-
vote his life to it. "We were seeking something and there
was nothing." Then he heard Peter Maurin give a talk, after
which he subscribed to *The Catholic Worker*. "It was dynamite!" Florence Weinfurter, a Milwaukee Catholic Worker,
recalled the conviction shared by the young that "we were
going to work out the divine plan . . . we were the first to
think in terms of the solidarity of the human race."

No wonder *The Catholic Worker* declared in December,
1933, that "A spiritual revolution is upon us!" "Ah, those
early days," Dorothy Day recalled years later, "that early
zeal, that early romance, that early companionableness.
How strongly they all felt it. . . . It is a permanent revolution, this Catholic Worker movement."

There were others, however, who viewed the new movement with suspicion. A writer for the *American Mercury* saw it "as an officially inspired attempt to win back labor to Catholicism and to make advances among Negroes." It was an "open secret" that Dorothy Day, "ex-Communist, former Greenwich Village habitué and recent convert to the Church" carried on her work "with the approval of the Cardinal. . . ." The Communist *Daily Worker*, too, saw the movement as something perfidiously devious. "Militant Phrases in The Catholic Worker Hide Program of Fascism," ran the headline. "Why do you lie so steadily, Peter Maurin?" the article asked. "You know that you want no 'new' society, you want a society even older than the one we have. You want to go back to medievalism." And Maurin, no doubt, would agree, for the synthesis he had in mind did involve the medieval idea of spirit infused into the life he found around him, to subdue and direct a world already fragmenting.

# 6

## POVERTY

It has been one of the central traditions of Christian history that the free choice of poverty is the most direct road to freedom. The effect of such an action is to bring the universe into harmony with itself. For within history there has always existed that other force toward eccentricity, the sign of which was the bourgeois man—he who had lost the sense of spirit and who would become, as Nikolai Berdyaev said, a "king on the earth."

Peter Maurin taught voluntary poverty. It was, Dorothy Day wrote in the *Worker*, his "most fundamental and necessary plank." It liberated man from fear. It opened his mind to the reality of spirit where thought could be free and where it could produce consequences that related most truthfully to man's concern for community—that concern that was the antithesis of fragmentation and objectivization and that lay over creation as the ultimate promise of its eternal unity. For, as Dorothy Day added, "once we begin not to worry about what kind of house we are living in, what kind of clothes we are wearing—once we give up the stupid recreation of this world—we have time, which is priceless, to remember that we are our brother's keeper and that we must not only care for his needs as far as we are able immediately, but we must try to build a better world."

It was to the poor that the primary concern of the Catholic Worker movement was directed, a position that Dorothy

Day repeatedly emphasized and which Peter Maurin had impressed upon her. As he liked to say, quoting the great seventeenth-century French bishop, "Bossuet says that the poor are the first children of the Church," so "the poor should come first."

In an age when people have been schooled in attitudes of reverential respect for data and planning, Maurin appears as an absurd simplist. It is difficult to understand his teaching of a revolution of self, his insistence that isolation and fragmentation come from pursuing the objectivized goals of bourgeois culture, and that community comes from voluntary poverty and going to the poor. What seems most absurd is the way in which he practiced his convictions. How could he be engaged in revolution by spending a year in Harlem or by taking back to Fifteenth Street for food those wasted and deranged souls that he found on the Bowery? How could a few people, trying to "clarify" thought by discussion and publishing a monthly paper, and otherwise living precariously from day to day, do anything to save the obviously tottering world of the mid-thirties? What was needed, most would think, was exhortation, massive programs, and some striking promise of sustaining the bourgeois world, even to the complete atomization of man in totalitarianism. Looking back, Stanley Vishnewski recognized that the simplicity of the Worker movement had been a stumbling block to many who wanted a high-powered propaganda machine and extensive organization.

When Maurin brought those forgotten men back to Fifteenth Street to give them hospitality, he was, in his view, moving creation into focus. The Worker, he hoped, would set an example for hospitality that the Church and the world would be persuaded to follow. He would instruct those who would listen to him: "We need houses of hospitality to bring the Bishops to the people and the people to the Bishops . . . We need houses of hospitality to show what idealism looks like when it is practiced. . . . We need houses of hospitality to bring social justice to Catholic Action exercised in Catholic institutions." Or, as he would say on other occasions in a phrase typically his own: "We need parish homes as well as parish domes."

So, the barbershop on Fifteenth Street became not only a center for the clarification of thought, but also a house of hospitality. With more young people coming into the movement and a growing number of guests to accommodate, a next-door store was rented, then a dilapidated building and several cheap apartments. On December 11, 1934, the Teresa-Joseph House, a six-room shelter for women, was opened. It had been made possible by the assistance of two priests of the Immaculate Conception parish on Fourteenth Street who collected the money from their working-class parishoners. Meanwhile, at Fifteenth Street, conditions became so crowded that meals had to be served in shifts. Arthur Sheehan recalls that when the telephone rang everyone in the dining area would have to stand up so that the person summoned might get to the phone!

In March, 1935, the Workers moved to 144 Charles Street, a Greenwich Village location almost on the edge of the Hudson. The homes in the area had once been substantial, but most had faded, and this one the Workers had rented especially showed signs of neglect. With its four floors it was large enough to bring the Workers and their guests under one roof, and there was much enthusiasm over what could be done to restore to it a measure of its former dignity. One of Stanley Vishnewski's recollections of the Charles Street house was that it was right across the street from the police station and that a trucking firm was located at a nearby corner, and he was aware of trucks pulling in and out all night long.

The move had been exhausting. In the April *Worker*, Dorothy Day hoped that she would not have to recall for long the confusion and discomfort of trying to arrange furniture and keep warm. For several days there was no heat or warm water. They wore layers of clothes and went to Mass in the morning heavy with grime. She thought it better to remember how hard all of the girls had worked—"with heads bound up and skirts girded about them, they swished

through the tombcold place with brooms and mops and now
. . . we are really clean."

Yet, even as they moved into Charles Street, they were
thinking of a venture into the third part of Maurin's program, that of "agronomic universities." It was a Maurin
phrase, but it covered an idea that has appealed to reformers throughout history—that of an agrarian cooperative
community. The thought of working on the land, naturally
enough, came upon them in the dead of winter. In Maurin's
words, she wrote in the March *Worker* of their hope for the
spring: "We wish to open . . . a farm and school combined,
where scholars can be workers and workers scholars. We
have no money for this venture." This went without saying,
yet she added, in case anyone were listening, that they
would like to have a place on Staten Island so that the fare
into the city would not be too much. There was also the delight of the ferry ride to be considered.

It was Maurin's friend Steve Hergenham, the artisan, who
described in full-blown Victorian prose what the Workers
had in mind for their farm. The farm community idea, he
said, if widely practiced might ultimately "humanize large
hordes of slum dwellers" and "restore to them their natural
heritage—the gift and opportunity to see their hands as well
as their heads and hearts, their ingenuity and love for work,
to build, produce and create." It had been an unnatural and
"lop-sided money economy" that had robbed the modern
factory worker of "the most sublime instincts; and it is the
renascence of a rural economy, upon which we may hope to
sink our foundations for a more rational and better social
order." The Workers got their Staten Island location by
renting a large old house with an acre of land at Huguenot,
just a ferry ride across the harbor from Manhattan. It was
not what Maurin had had in mind, Dorothy Day admitted,
but they could think of it as a training ground for the larger
farm to come.

The gardening was led by Hergenham, who carried
hundreds of boxes of topsoil from the nearby woods to en-
rich the beds he had carefully prepared. Dust storms and

drought prevailed over the great Midwest that spring, but at Staten Island the thundershowers came regularly, and by mid-June the household was eating lettuce, onions, radishes, and string beans. "Soon the tomatoes will be ready," Dorothy Day exulted. "One of the best smells in the world is the smell of tomato plants, or perhaps the wet earth after a rain, or honeysuckle or privet hedge in blossom. The world is full of good smells."

The sense of community that came from a common belief in the radical Christian idea could be increased, Workers thought, by the common physical labor. Work on the land was the leaven that would bring together the intellectual and the laborer. But the idea fell short in practice that summer. There were those whose love of the earth was more academic than real, who found that ideas flowed better while lying in the cool of the shade, rather than hoeing in the heat of the sun. Hergenham was contemptuous of those who would not work but only talked, and he expressed bitter thoughts about them. But Maurin was not dismayed, and standing in the rows of vegetables, he listened to the ideas of those who worked and tried for "clarification."

A tragedy occurred that summer. A Jew from central Europe, "black-haired and black-eyed," heard Dorothy Day speak one day at an East Side meeting, and something stirred in him. He went to the Charles Street house and stood in the middle of the room, reciting the Psalms in Hebrew. Then he sat down to eat, and thereafter he came to the Worker house regularly for his meals. In time he heard about what the Workers had come to call their garden commune, and one day he begged a nickel for the Staten Island ferry and then walked on to Huguenot. All day he worked in the garden barefooted, his sweat-soaked undershirt clinging to his back. Occasionally, he would be seen drawing his toes slowly through the dirt, as if caressing it. When the plants began to come up, he would walk between the rows and look lovingly at the new growth. "I draw them up out the ground with the power of my eyes," he said. He ate with the group, but at night he refused to sleep in the house, perhaps because he wanted to remain close to the garden. He gave his labor to the Workers that summer, Dorothy Day records him as saying, "for the sake of communism, a Holy Communism, comradeship, cooperation, brotherhood, unity." "Christ was in his heart," she believed. "We loved him. . . ."

But one of the "scholars" at the garden commune thought that the Jew was a madman, an opinion he believed to be confirmed by a strange episode. One day at lunch this strange, half-wild person picked up a piece of black bread that had been left on the table and raising it aloft, as a priest does when consecrating the host, said, "I am Lenin, and these are my words: this is my body broken for you." So the scholar told him to begone, threatening him with imprisonment if he remained. He was not seen again.

The house at the garden commune was atop a hill overlooking Raritan Bay. It had eight bedrooms and a wide porch that ran completely around it. More young people came to the Worker that summer, and naturally they liked to have their conferences there. Speakers came from Columbia and other universities, and the young people talked long over subjects that interested them—whether or not it would be better to say Compline, the last prayer of the day, in English or in Latin; machines and the land; organization and freedom; and the rising tide of totalitarianism.

In July, when Jews were being beaten on the streets in German cities, some of the young people at the commune decided to demonstrate in protest. Although they only passed out literature, they became involved in a riot when some Communists, representing themselves as Catholic Workers, tore down the swastika from the German liner *Bremen*, moored at its dock. Dorothy Day, demonstrating with a Marquette University student, Nina Polcyn, was appalled by what she considered extreme brutality by a few of the police who had been sent to break up the demonstration. She wrote a letter to the police commissioner: "I was sitting on the steps of Unity Hall, a building a few doors from the station with a . . . girl from Marquette when two men dragged another man up the steps by the side of us, knocking me over in their haste, and in the darkness of the doorway one man held the victim while the other began smashing his face in. . . ."

But the summer was otherwise peaceable, and some at the commune tried in a personalist way to reshape the world along more human lines. Julia Porcelli, who had told stories to children at Peter Maurin's Harlem house, took the lead in organizing weekend expeditions to the island for children suffering from poverty and crowding. Later, she recalled the terrible conditions in which some of them had lived: "One was from a large family . . . and was terribly overworked. I remember how we had to beg this mother to let this child go out. She was only ten or eleven but she did all the work and errands, and was up five flights, and there were any number of little children. Her name was Santina, and oh my, it was heartbreaking. But we finally got this child out, as well as Negro children . . . that we'd known from Harlem."

Dorothy Day's time was spent moving between the island, where the young hoed, talked, and took care of the children, and Charles Street, where the old were fed and the paper published. One afternoon near the end of summer, she went to the island on a day so hot and heavy that it was hard to breathe. At the island there was time for a swim before supper, so she, Tamar, and several others went down to the bay. The water "was oily calm, with the sky hanging so low over it that you could almost reach up and touch it with your hands. We all crouched in the water, digging for small hardshell clams. . . ." Tamar found the most.

In September Tamar went back to school at St. Patrick's on Staten Island, and Dorothy Day noted in the *Worker* that while parents were "reading all these editorials and notices in the Catholic diocesan papers about sending their children to Catholic schools so that they will not lose their faith," they should also know that "many of our parochial schools are closed to Negro children. . . ." She urged them to use their influence to change that policy so that "we may complement this physical contact by spiritual contact and build up the understanding of the dogma of the Mystical Body."

Christmas came, and ten persons from the Worker house took bundles of the paper down to the Municipal Lodging House at the South Ferry, where twelve thousand men were being fed their Christmas dinner. After distributing the paper, they returned to Charles Street to their own dinner, prepared by the sisters and students of Cathedral High School.

With the end of the holidays, Dorothy Day took Tamar back to school. The ferry ride to the island gave her again those precious uninterrupted moments when she had no call but to absorb the sensations about her. This time it was an atmosphere of winter desolation: the chilled air and the "gulls [which] stood out white against the gray sky," turning and gliding, and "swooping down into the water now and then after fish." The only sounds in the winter stillness were the cries of the gulls and the wash and slap of the water as the boat churned through it.

For Americans, the year 1935 was one of continuing depression, and abroad, new positive signs marked the depravity of Nazism. But on Charles Street, there were those few who talked of turning the world around, and for them at least there were some small signs of progress.

With the May, 1935, issue, the circulation of *The Catholic Worker* went over one hundred thousand. At least, that many papers were printed. Many, of course, were thrust into unwilling hands at union halls and parish meetings, but it was significant that the paper was producing enthusiasts anxious to promote the cause it stood for. From Union Square and Fourteenth Street the *Worker* salesmen moved to more prominent positions in the flow of West Side and upper Manhattan life—in front of Macy's or St. Francis' Church, or in Times Square, or in front of Grand Central Station. It was not an occupation that Dorothy Day enjoyed, especially in the new areas where the outcries that went with paper-selling made "one indeed look the fool."

Sometimes the young salesmen had bad moments. Stanley Vishnewski, the chief *Worker* newsboy of that era, recalled an occasional angry reaction from someone to whom the word "Catholic" registered as an inflammatory challenge. Julia Porcelli was once selling up and down Fourteenth Street when she was threatened with arrest. "This police officer came up—my heart was in my mouth. In those days it wasn't very fashionable to get arrested . . . he said we were littering . . . I thought surely we were going to prison."

In September, 1935, Dorothy Day wrote again in the *Worker* that the paper was for the oppressed and the poor. So that it might always speak free from pressure, it took no advertising, even though its normal financial condition was, as Dorothy Day once said, a part of the holy poverty that they were always talking about. It took up the cause of Tom Mooney, imprisoned for the Preparedness Day bombing of 1916 and long regarded by radicals, and by some others seeking fairly to evaluate the evidence, as a questionable victim of the red scare of the twenties. The only crime he had been guilty of, said the *Worker,* was that of opposing capitalism. There was still the cause of the Scottsboro boys who, guilty or not, were being victimized by race prejudice. And there was Angelo Herndon, arrested in Georgia while leading a demonstration to reopen a New Deal relief station. And what had been his crime? Only that Herndon was a radical—"and worse than that, a 'nigger.'" The state had asked the death penalty for him, but he had been let off with twenty years. What could be worse, asked the *Worker,* than the lot of a "radical 'nigger'" in the worst prison system in the world? Then the paper invoked a vision of ankle chains, a cage crawling with vermin, and beatings and lashings in the hot Georgia sun.

While the passion was justified, the rhetoric reeked of Hollywood. Occasionally, too, a news item sounded as if it had been written for a class struggle publication: "While Andy Mellon fights to hang onto the few million dollars of his $181,000,000 fortune . . . Mrs. Mary Johnson, employed for the last twelve years by the National Biscuit Company, is out on strike because she needs more than the twenty-two and a half cents an hour which is the wage to be paid her by the largest biscuit company factory in the world, in order to take care of herself and her invalid husband. . . ."

These departures from the personalist principle bothered some who were genuinely concerned with the welfare of the movement. Edward Skillin, editor and publisher of *Commonweal*, wrote to Dorothy Day about these lapses, citing particularly a woman who had been upset over something in the *Worker* "about the Morgans etc. rubbing their hands with glee at the prospects of war and blood money."

The year 1935 was one in which the spirit of objectivization made its first challenge to the Worker idea. "There were some," related Stanley Vishnewski "who wanted to throw out the bums, the deadbeats, the derelicts, the freeloaders, and just use the Catholic Worker as a pure propaganda cell." They wanted to systematize operations, possibly to make a move uptown and utilize the techniques of Madison Avenue. Eventually, these people drifted away from the Catholic Worker movement.

"These people," primarily, were those who had organized the activist Campion Propaganda Committees that had branched off from the Worker. For a while the news of their involvements had been carried in the *Worker*, but after 1935 these reports ceased. Looking for a more effective and "relevant" work, they departed for yet another undertaking. It would always be this way. More controversies would develop and rage—pacifism, manual labor and farms, anarchism, and even the nature of the Church would become issues for division and separation. To those who longed for more tangible and exciting signs of community, the Worker inevitably seemed to take the impossible course.

"The poor must come first," Maurin had said, and so the Charles Street house, which had seemed so large, was soon outgrown. On Saturday, April 18, 1936, the Workers moved to 115 Mott Street, and this was to be its headquarters for the next fourteen years. "There must have been twelve loads coming down from the Charles street place on our Ford truck," Dorothy Day wrote in the May *Worker*.

Mott Street runs a mile, north and south, from Houston Street down to Chatham Square. It is a long, gentle curve, descending in its lower part through Chinatown and turning into Chatham Square where the Bowery ends and becomes Park Row. Dorothy Day has described the street as it was in the thirties:

> Mott Street is a slum street in the most thickly populated section of New York. There are factories, little bake shops, livery stables, laundries, fish markets and push carts. . . . Summer and winter people live on the streets, and throughout the day the musical call of the hucksters and pushcart peddlars may be heard singing their wares. The pushcarts make bright splashes of color along the street.

The Mott Street center was two houses, front and rear. The rear house had been built in 1860. The front structure was built sometime later when the area shifted from homes to tenement apartments and storefronts. Initially, the Workers were to have had the rear house free in return for collecting rents from the inhabitants of the front house. But as the tenants left, the Worker itself took over the vacant flats and soon took over that building, too. When expansion had run its course, the Worker had sixteen rooms in the front house and twenty in the rear building.

It was an old woman, lame and half-blind, named Mary Lane who began the succession of events that enabled the Workers to take possession of the Mott Street center. Living on a small pension, she had read the *Worker* and then had begun to collect clothes to allay the poverty she read about. When she met Dorothy Day, she immediately inquired about the latter's "ecstasies and visions." Convinced, probably, that only a person of saintly character could exhibit such a steadfast concern for the poor, she yearned for a firsthand recounting of what she had always been taught to believe were the certain signs of advanced holiness.

It was Mary Lane's friend Gertrude Burke who owned the Mott Street place and who, after Miss Lane's intercession, suggested that the Workers might use the vacant rear building in return for collecting rent from the tenants in the front section. Dorothy Day was indignant at the thought of charging rent for such a place—better that it were torn down. These, at least, were her private thoughts.

But as the need for room became more pressing, she thought again of Mott Street and reopened the subject in a letter to Miss Burke. But she was too late; the place had been given to some Catholic women who ran the House of Calvary, a cancer hospital for the poor of the Bronx. It was these women who made the rear house available to the Workers. They did more. After witnessing the work for a time, they made some costly and needed repairs on the place. Perhaps Miss Burke had been behind it all; the Workers were never sure.

The move to Mott Street had scarcely been made before an operation began that was to become one of the central actions of the Worker house in those Depression years: the breadline. According to Arthur Sheehan, the breadline started in a very innocuous way. "One day as some of the members of the group were coming from Mass, they found some men standing outside, evidently from the Bowery. . . ." Soon over a hundred were coming daily, and by the end of the year the line extended down Mott Street and around the corner almost to Mulberry Street. In August, 1937, when a drying up of New Deal spending put the country into a new recession, the line sometimes had as many as five hundred men.

In the February, 1937, issue of the *Worker*, Dorothy Day recorded an early-morning impression of the breadline:

> The radio is cheerful; the smell of coffee is a good smell, the air of the morning is fresh and not too cold, but my heart bleeds as I pass the lines of men in front of the store which is our headquarters. The place is packed—not another man can get in—so they have to form a line. Always we have hated lines and now our breakfast which we serve

Peter Maurin making a point during a lecture in the 1930s.

Mott Street breadline, New York City Catholic Worker, ca. 1938

of cottage cheese and rye bread and coffee, has brought
about a line. . . . It is hard to say matter-of-factly and
cheerfully, 'Good morning,' as we pass on our way to
Mass. . . .

Worker hospitality knew no bounds. More came to stay
permanently at the house. Some came planning to stay a
year, but dismayed at the poverty they found around them,
they stayed only a night. Others came to spend a weekend
and remained for years.

In her book *Loaves and Fishes,* a series of episodes in the
life of the Catholic Worker movement, Dorothy Day tells
the story of one who stayed, a "Mister Breen"—someone,
she said, that they would not soon forget. Old, alone, and
destitute, he stumbled into the Worker house one morning,
having found it impossible to get along in the city Municipal Lodging House because of his blatant racism. His
talk was filled with words like "kikes," "dinges," and "da-
goes." At the Worker house he encountered a Mr. Rose, a
Black whom he delighted to insult. Rose, for his part, found
a flaw in Breen's armor. When Dorothy Day was away
somewhere, Rose would sit at her desk, lean back in her
chair, and relate to Breen stories about the susceptibility of
white women to black male sexual prowess. Such talk would
cause Breen to erupt in an apoplectic roaring, but when the
others came hastening in to see what the commotion was
about, Rose would pretend to be deep in work at the desk
as the trembling Breen stood above him.

His prejudices also included the Jews. Newspaperman
that he had been, he had the habit of reading all the papers
and dropping them around him. Once, unable to shake out
the flame of his match while lighting a cigarette, he
dropped it on the papers. With a conflagration in the making, a Jew named Freeman began putting out the fire. As he
beat out the flames from around Breen, the latter tried to
fend off Freeman with his cane, calling him a "goddam
Jew." But Freeman saved him anyway.

Irascible and intemperate with age, the old man nonetheless had a feeling for the poor, and he could tell stories

about them, one of which Dorothy Day recorded in her
Journal. He recounted a scene he had witnessed in what
must have been the world's largest bedroom, a dock down
at the South Ferry, where the city had cots for about twelve
hundred men. So vast was the long dim dock at night that
one deranged old·man thought he was in a cathedral, "and
in his night shirt, with his long sticks of legs making him
look like a strange bird, he used to 'make the stations' down
the inner aisle between the double decker beds, pausing at
every seventh bed to pray."

Within and without the Worker, however, there was the
constant criticism from those who felt that charity had been
carried too far and that those who were making a good
thing out of hospitality ought to be sent on their way. But
Dorothy Day steadfastly opposed any attempt to clear their
rolls of the "unworthy poor." It was hard to remake men,
she said; it was not a matter of a few months or even a few
years. In a circular letter sent to the other Worker houses,
sometime in the late thirties, she said that whenever anyone
came into the group, he was to be accepted fully as a
brother. Problems should not be solved by an imposed
order; they should be suffered—"the more we suffer . . . the
more we learn. Infinite patience, suffering is needed. And it
is never-ending." Think of Lazarus at the gate, she advised.
"Read 'The Honest Thief' by Dostoevsky. There is a great
lesson of love here. . . ." As for getting rid of the freeloaders and taking in only the deserving poor, "one may as well
understand that the new batch will be exactly the same as
the last. You cut off the head of the tyrant and two others
spring up."

Stanley Vishnewski tells of how he once became so depressed with all of the poverty and suffering in the Catholic
Worker that he told Dorothy Day that they were "just plain
saps" for putting up with it. Yes, she said, they were nothing
but gutter sweepings, but added if once they started purg-
ing poor people and improving their own lot, there would
be no end to it. They would end up by getting rid of each
other.

Julia Porcelli also remembers the poverty of those early years: "People were shocked when they came down and found we were living in the slums. Every day without fail we had very thin soup, and I always remember people remarking on the food. I was always hungry and whenever I got a little sad looking Dorothy always said somebody should take me out and buy me a steak."

Vishnewski thought that it was the discrepancy between the romantic ideal of poverty and community on the one hand and the reality of the tensions and quarreling that occurred at the Worker house on the other that proved to be a source of scandal to some of the people who came to the Worker. As he explained: "They came expecting saints; they found human beings. And it was a great pity that none of us could measure up to their . . . dreams of us."

There was always the pressure for money and it was sometimes desperate. In September, 1935, Dorothy Day wrote that the Workers had bills of over a thousand dollars "and nothing in the bank to pay them." But they were not worried. This was "the holy poverty we are always talking about. This is the insecurity which we do most firmly believe is good for us to have." Miss Porcelli remembered that they were always out of money. "We'd take turns going over to Church and spending some time, perhaps an hour, praying and begging for money. We were so behind with the butcher, the baker and everyone that we just didn't have a cent in the house." She recalled a time when one of the young men of the house, Jerry Griffin, went up to his room to take a nap, saying as he left that he should be awakened only when someone came in with a hundred dollars. So the others went off to work on the paper, and, as they worked, a stranger did indeed come in. He was shown around and when he left he handed one of the group an envelope to be given to Griffin. They all knew that it had to be the hundred dollars. And so it was.

There were other occasions like this in the life of the Worker, and for the generation of the thirties and forties that had taken on this life, they were always looked upon as

providential interventions. It was not that they hoped or expected Providence to perform the miracle of suddenly ban-
ishing the whole problem of objectivization and fragmentation against which they, as Christians, struggled. For they
understood that if God should banish evil He would no
longer be God, since by that act freedom itself would be destroyed, and freedom was the very mark of God. Nonetheless, they delighted in those small signs, accidental or not,
which they thought gave evidence of spirit.

Small miracles and the most sacrificial poverty could not
house forty or fifty people, feed sometimes a thousand a
day, and underwrite a penny newspaper that took no advertising. Houses of hospitality, as Dorothy Day said, had to be
financed by appeals—"not demands as Peter used to say"—
and decidedly not by state grants. The support of the
Worker movement came as a response to her appeals, which
she periodically wrote for *The Catholic Worker* and which
also were printed separately and sent to subscribers. The
appeals were essays on the subject of love in which, usually,
some Gospel situation was given meaning in terms of those
problems of distress of body and spirit that the Worker confronted daily. They were an instruction in personalist Christianity, and the person who read them came to feel that he
too might share in this revolution of spirit. Among these
who over the years have supported the Worker movement,
most were persons who had little to give—members of religious orders and persons lonely and poor who understood
little about the Worker's social philosophy but believed that
what it said and did was good. "Wrapped in the enclosed
wad of paper you will find two dimes in answer to your appeal," ran one letter. "Wish I could send you a dollar bill instead but am working . . . on the Spokane County Poor
Farm. About the latter part of next month I hope to move
into Spokane to earn my own living again. . . . Will ask you
to pray for my intention of being self-supporting . . . after
more than nine years of ill-health."

The effectiveness of Dorothy Day's appeals came from
their quality of expressing simply and directly the soul of

the Catholic Worker movement. People contributed not because they were sold or conditioned by clever insinuating
words but because they believed in the Worker or wanted
to believe in it. Workers did indeed live in poverty in these
early years, but the movement survived and its ideas were
heard because of the gifts it received.

# 7

# THE SPREAD OF
# MAURIN'S IDEAS

During the years of the Great Depression, as time slowed, the Catholic Worker movement had a remarkable expansion. There always had been those who gladly would have led lives of sacrifice and service for the Church, as they had been taught, but who found such impulses stifled in the routine prescriptions of Catholic observance and the formalisms that structured its life. It was to such as these that Peter Maurin had sought to bring his "clarification" so that the formalisms would not command but serve. Most who heard him, probably, saw his vision only dimly but they knew something was there. They got it when they read *The Catholic Worker* and when they heard Dorothy Day tell of life at the Worker house. Many saw this life as something they would like to try.

New houses appeared almost from the first. In 1935, after Dorothy Day had made a talk to a group in Boston, Jane Marra, a labor union worker, organized a house there. Soon there was another at St. Louis organized by student Don Gallagher. A large expansion occurred during the summer and fall of 1937, and by 1939, in addition to the Mott Street house, there were twenty-two Worker houses of hospitality, two farms, and thirteen "cells," the latter being discussion and action centers. Each of these Worker houses deserves its own history, not because of any notable successes in social reclamation or even because of the sacrificial heroism of those who organized and staffed them, but because each story is the drama of a few people who were convinced that the doomfelt shaking of an increasingly eccentric universe could, through active love, be brought into harmony; that one could begin this reconstruction only in the "little" way of St. Thérèse of Lisieux and with a few of the most woebegotten of men; and that, indeed, to "succeed" would be to fail.

Many of the houses were started after a talk by Peter Maurin or Dorothy Day, and invariably they were examples of Dorothy Day's counsel: begin where you are and with what you have. Llewellyn J. Scott, a Black, wrote of the beginnings of the Blessed Martin De Porres House at 48 I Street, N.E., Washington, D.C. He had heard Dorothy Day talk on the Mystical Body of Christ. "This was . . . new and strange to me, but as she spoke . . . I could see the thing I wanted to do. . . ." When he talked to her about it, she said that he should begin immediately. "Here is five dollars, it is all that I have," she told him.

Another time she received this news from a group organizing a house in Los Angeles: "John . . . wants me to tell you . . . he has found a house at last—and at his price, $25 a month!" It was, in fact, a typical Worker "miracle." Had not "John's" footsteps (through the intensive prayers of some Maryknoll Sisters) been directed to a particular person of Jewish faith, the owner of the house, the miracle would never have happened. For "the persuasive John, after giving the owner a 'heart to heart talk' finally managed to get the rent reduced from $65 to $25," the owner saying that the difference would be his own contribution to the cause.

In Cleveland it was the Black intercessor, Blessed Martin again (a favorite with young Workers), who was "prevailed upon in a Novena by a couple of Jesuits . . . to give Cleveland a House and someone to run it." In the course of the Novena, Blessed Martin "dug up $5 and found an abandoned store front for $5 a month." Likewise, he "fingered" Bill Gauchat as the one to head the work, directing him with his helpers to clean up an enormous amount of rubbish and pigeon dung, since the place had last been used as an aviary. Their perseverance prevailed and, after a hard day's work, "the boys . . . found the floor."

And so it went, from Hamilton, Ontario, to Houma, Louisiana, and from Boston to Butte to Portland. As those at the New York house, the others made their first business that of feeding and sheltering those gaunt, clay-faced men and women who had no place to go. Dorothy Day described her arrival at the Detroit house in May, 1938: "The table is well set, the bowls of soup are rich and steaming, there is plenty of bread and the service is swift and efficient."

There were study and discussion sessions. At the Milwaukee house at 1019 North Fifth Street, study groups met nightly for discussion on Catholic social doctrine, liturgy, peace, labor, and theology. The Houma house announced in March, 1938, that its group would lay "particular stress on the interracial justice part of its schedule, as a result of the shameful exhibition of Hitlerian views on race that some U.S. Senators have been perpetrating in Washington." Many of the houses published a newsletter and some put out a paper. Chicago had two houses, with John Cogley beginning his illustrious career as a journalist and editor by editing *The Chicago Catholic Worker*. The St. Louis house published *The Missouri Catholic Worker*.

Like the New York house, they all had the mark of the Catholic Worker in those colorful and slightly mad characters who drifted in to partake, more or less permanently, of Worker hospitality. The Cleveland house had one in its cook and, when he died, Bill Gauchat wrote a description of him:

> Albert Brady is dead. Late lord of the kitchen, and hero of his own magnificent dreams, he succumbed to the abrasion of daily reality. Broken in body, a hunchback, he cherished a mental picture of himself as a strong, self-sufficient, silent power, a man, not always a cripple, able to cope with the best. Fawning to authority, and domineering to the weak . . . he could only live by lying to himself, for the truth was too bitter to accept.

St. Francis House (Detroit).

When we consider his life, what we know of it, we can only pray for this friendly, little, queer, unhappy man. He used to talk to me often for hours at a time; truth, fantasy . . . vague statements, obviously lies, waved away at a question, followed one another in a mysterious whisper. He loved to get one behind a closed door, and with an air of mystery, expound upon an obvious commonplace. He lived in a world of make-believe, and cooked abominable food.

Factionalism and rivalries festered constantly in Worker houses, and sometimes an aggrieved person would pour out his unhappiness in a letter to Dorothy Day. One disconsolate resident told how he had become the victim of a general uprising because his prayers were "too long." Later, this same person apparently erred again: "Because I dramatized in the streets on the 9th and 10th inst. our Catholic Worker gospel of social and economic good works . . . these persons [other Workers] decided I was insane and needed to be restrained."

How the writer "dramatized" his point of view must have been interesting, but otherwise it was another one of those problems that in a Worker house could take on the proportions of a major crisis, causing the contestants to rush to Dorothy Day, hoping that she would bless the one and excommunicate the other. But she never excommunicated. Sometimes a disaffected resident guest might charge that she was obdurate, stiff-necked, and an unfaithful guardian of the truth by her refusal to eject those whom others might regard as the poisoners of community life. But here she would follow Peter Maurin: eccentricity and madness were marks of suffering, and those who bore them should be cherished even more. Then, either by a visit or a letter, she would try to calm the tempest. In response to some minor problem in the Buffalo house, she counseled that "until people do have all these problems and sufferings the work is really not getting underway." Starting a house was "lots of fun . . . everybody has a grand time getting everything started, everything goes so smoothly, the men are all so nice, everybody cooperates, and then life settles down to a dull, ugly monotony of meals and lodging and nothing at all seems to be done or done right and we seem rather to be contributing to people's delinquencies rather than helping them; and that of course is the charge that is made always against us."

Personality conflicts, boredom, and disenchantment might plague the houses, but Workers seemed to have something in their lives not possessed by ordinary people—or so many thought. Florence Weinfurter remarked on the strength of this feeling in the Milwaukee group—the untroubled conviction that they were right and "that great sense of community" that came from it. Together, they went to daily Mass at Marquette University's Gesu Church at 5:30 in the morning. Jesuit Gerard Smith was there to open the door and then say the Mass. He "led the pack," Miss Weinfurter recalled.

There was, of course, romance. Earnest young ladies from Catholic girls' schools who helped out at the houses subjected themselves to the danger of being swept from their middle-class moorings by the young men who staffed the houses. And many were swept away—into marriages in which the Worker idea remained strong, and where, in some instances, great sacrifice was required and patiently made. Larry Heaney of the Milwaukee house met his wife, Ruth Ann, there; John Cogley met his wife at the Chicago Worker; and the marriage of Lou Murphy and Justine L'Esperance came from their association at the Detroit house.

At the Cleveland house, a student from Notre Dame Academy, Dorothy Schmitt, came to help out, and Bill Gauchat, taken with her zeal and goodness, was soon writing to Dorothy Day about this "young lady . . . whose heart you have won completely"—a heart that he could only think of as "warm and generous." Would Dorothy please write to her ("I know it would make her very happy") and send the letter in care of him?

They were married and had a family, but it is the unusual form taken by their Worker vocation that makes their story remarkable. Having experimented with a farm commune during the war, their principal work began in 1947 when they adopted a child suffering from a brain injury so severe that such care as it got was based on the assumption that it would soon die. The child did indeed die, but not before the Gauchats had come to love it, and it was out of this experience that they were led to take as their particular vocation the care and rearing of infants and children so malformed and handicapped that ordinarily they would have been foredoomed to the most formal of institutionalized existences.

Some marriages that had Worker beginnings did not work out well. It was, perhaps, the element of instability that brought some people to the Worker in the first place that made them a high risk in a marriage venture. Suffering was frequently the lot of one or both partners of these marriages, yet there was demonstrated in some instances a steady faithfulness to their commitment that was unaccompanied by whimpering and bitterness.

One group that began as a Worker house soon took an independent course. In May, 1936, four Pittsburgh priests, Charles Owen Rice, Carl P. Hensler, Tom Lappan, and a professor at Duquesne University, G. Barry O'Toole, organized the Catholic Radical Alliance. While the group maintained a house of hospitality where study sessions were held, the alliance took a more exclusively labor action direction. It sponsored in Pittsburgh the Association of Catholic Trade Unionists, and Rice, especially, became so vocal in the support of the CIO that he was given the title of "labor priest."

The growth in the number of Worker houses caused Dorothy Day to travel more than ever before. Houses importuned her to come and see how the work was progressing, to settle a dispute, or to give a talk. For some in the movement, consigned to remain at home and take care of the routine of feeding the line and getting out the paper, her traveling, with its occasional opportunities to dine and consort with persons in high places, provoked envy and sometimes disgruntled comment. Many times, she was only too glad to assign a visitation or speaking invitation to someone else, but usually it was only she whom persons wanted to hear and see. And she, wanting nothing more than a chance to rest, would nonetheless take off by bus for a round of visits to Worker houses, with here and there a speaking engagement thrown in to pay the cost of the trip.

She came to regard travel as an essential part of her Worker life. Peter Maurin traveled extensively. It was an aspect of his idea of "clarification"—taking the message of personal responsibility abroad as well as to those who came to Mott Street—and she followed his example. Beyond this, traveling was a part of her nature; she had always been a traveler. In traveling alone, as she mostly did, she achieved an anonymity that probably was balm compared to the sometimes intense personal interactions that could occur in a Worker house. Traveling, too, gave her time to read, and books were always a necessary part of her life.

Travel had its price. The bus was her accustomed means of transportation and days and nights of riding it, with layovers in stations, was an exhausting experience. Then, reaching her destination, she was many times immediately confronted with the formality of "arrangements"—social gatherings and dinners—when doubtless she would have preferred something less taxing. Neither did the prospects of speaking exhilarate her. She recorded in her Journal: "Tonight I have to speak . . . and I am so fatigued by a two weeks speaking trip that I was miserable about it. . . . It is only with the greatest effort that I speak. The idea depresses me for a day beforehand. I get physically sick from it. But it must be done."

Distressing though her talks might be for her, they awakened those who heard her. They were simple recitations about the personalist idea as it operated in the Worker experience, as it might operate in life. There was nothing of pose or dramatic contrivance in her manner. Its very simplicity and the directness of her ideas made her effective. "I am so glad that you came," a physician wrote to her after hearing her speak. "You and your work . . . and dignity

Bill and Dorothy Gauchat, Our Lady of the Wayside Farm, Avon, Ohio. 1943. Catholic University Bulletin photo published 11 June 1943.

Dorothy Day speaking in Seattle, February 1940.

won everybody I have talked to—I hope you will always speak of the Mystical Body, because you were the first one who ever really made me think about it—so I want everybody else to—it seems the crux of everything."

After a long trip of speaking and visiting the houses, she was glad to get back to Mott Street and to take up again the routine of life there. Sometimes many problems had accumulated: funds were low and the telephone and lights had been cut off; the cliques in the house were at it again, denouncing one another with a "positive venom" that shocked her. There were charges "of mismanagement of funds, self-glorification, domination, etc. God knows why the whole think does not fall apart."

But even with the complaints there were many times light moments that relieved tension. One morning Dorothy Day opened a note and read a complaint from one of the men who had stood mornings in the coffee line. He did not like the service. "Could you please . . . get rid of that overgrown bum who has charge . . . in the mornings? . . . This big stiff has of late turned down many people for no sane reason whatever. . . . Miss Day I will inform you that I know this big bum from days gone bye [sic] and know that he belongs to the insane."

Sharing in the work and life of the house of the thirties were the young Workers, recent college graduates for the most part, full of idealism and anxious to sacrifice to put Peter Maurin's vision into life. Stanley Vishnewski had been one of the first, then came others like Bill Callahan, Jerry Griffin, Julia Porcelli, and Joe Zarella. Zarella, Julia Porcelli recalled, "was young and he was Italian and I was Italian. They were always trying to start a romance between us. Yes, he was very alive and a very, very hard worker and a good dancer. He and Jerry Griffin were sort of soul-mates."

It was during the winter of 1935–1936 that some of the young Workers began to think again about Maurin's idea of the farm commune. The weather had something to do with it. That winter was an especially hard one in New York: sidewalks glazed with ice, dirty snow piled on the ground, and gray skies. What better to do than to dream of earth, warm sun, and rich harvests? Dorothy Day remembered one especially cold Saturday afternoon when, against the background of a lively discussion of the form their commune would take, she tried to listen to a broadcast of *Aida* from the Metropolitan Opera House. It was the young men, Eddie Priest, Bill Callahan, and Jim Montague, who expanded on the idea with the most enthusiasm, and as they talked the vision took on the character of a new Garden of Eden. They would, they were sure, start a farm commune that would be a model for the thousands of others that would certainly follow. Peter Maurin had taught them a philosophy of work—that the manual labor that represented a cooperation with nature and not a despoiling of it could be ennobling. In a community-sharing of such work—tilling, planting, building—polarizations could be broken down. He had them read not only the ideas of Peter Kropotkin but those of two of Maurin's contemporaries, the English stonecutter and artist Eric Gill and the Italian priest-politician Don Luigi Sturzo. Gill taught a philosophy of work that was like Maurin's, and Don Sturzo, in the spirit of Kropotkin, argued for a cooperative political and social order as against the corporate state.

The young Workers had given a ready assent to Maurin's ideas, but in listening to them that Saturday afternoon, Dorothy Day wondered how they could have forgotten so soon. Did they not remember what kind of people had come to the Staten Island garden commune? They had been the least fit, she thought, to build a solid foundation for the realization of such an idea. They had, in fact, looked upon the garden commune as a refuge from the established world which in their minds had been so inhospitable to what they conceived of as their true worth. She remembered an episode of that summer where a whole group had gone along the beach collecting clay to make dishes, assuring themselves that they were practicing crafts. This, Dorothy Day reflected, could have been viewed as a harmless and tranquilizing occupation, except that they were always washing the clay down the drain of the kitchen sink and stopping up the plumbing.

But the young men talked on, and in the midst of the discussion a letter came from a woman who had heard of the Worker's interest in starting a farm community. She would contribute a thousand dollars toward the venture if the Workers would build her a house on the land with the materials she provided. One phrase in the letter was recognized as an unhappy augury for a future relationship between this person, so captivated with the farm idea, and the Workers. She pointed out that her contribution would not "pauperize" people and further contribute to their delinquency, as might be the case if nothing more than the breadline was provided for them.

Feeling that this prospective doner should be dissuaded, Dorothy Day responded in detail as to the kind of people the Workers were and what they were trying to do. She relates in *Loaves and Fishes* that she explained that Workers were not a community of saints, "but a rather slipshod group of individuals who were trying to work out certain principles—the chief of which was an analysis of man's freedom and what it implied. . . . We were trying to overcome hatred with love, to understand the forces that made men what they are. . . . It was a practice in loving, a learning to love, a paying of the cost of love."

Dorothy Day had tried to explain the harsh reality of Worker life, but for an outsider it was difficult to comprehend, and the offer was not withdrawn. Why, the young ones felt, should they say more and thus frustrate the obvious design of Providence? So with Big Dan Orr driving a borrowed car, they began their search over the icy roads of New Jersey. They searched long, but finally on April 19, three miles out of Easton, Pennsylvania, they found a twenty-eight-acre farm atop of what was called Mammy Morgan's Hill. The view of Easton down in the valley below was so beautiful that all knew the search had ended. Leaping from the car, Big Dan threw himself on the grass, crying, "Back to the land!" The down payment was made and that evening, bearing trophies of dandelion greens and "country" eggs, they returned to Mott Street, envisioning already their twenty-eight acres as richly yielding the substance on which their community would be built.

In such innocence was Maryfarm begun. Jim Montague assumed the position of manager, and using the Worker's old Ford truck, he and an ardent group of helpers closed the Staten Island house at the garden commune and moved its contents to Easton. Five persons moved immediately to the farm, the beginning of a stream that would continue to grow. That summer a retured newspaper editor and his wife took charge of the farmhouse and watched over Tamar. The attic was made into a dormitory for men and two bedrooms were used for women. Shortly guests were spilling into the outbuildings and even into the animal quarters.

When John Cort went to Easton, he was quartered in the pigpen. "It was one of the nicest places I ever slept in my life," he declared. His shelter was a tin tent, open at both ends and with the floor covered with fresh straw. When he awoke on his first morning there, the sun was shining brightly on the straw and made his couch look like gold.

It was an unusual group at the farm that summer—a circumstance that for the Catholic Worker was completely usual. There was a man just out of Sing Sing who planted flowers, a seminarian who brought six pigs, a group of children from Harlem, some striking seamen, and an ex-circus performer who would do cartwheels down the hill in back of the house when the moon was full. Some of the young student Workers who stayed pretty much at the farm were Hazen Ordway, Cy Echele, and Arthur Sheehan. Frank O'Donnell who had been with the Worker since the days of the apartment on Fifteenth Street, planned to live with his family permanently at the farm. John Filliger, one of the striking seamen, had come "to give Miss Day a hand." He found Worker life so much to his taste that the sea never reclaimed him. That fall (as Workers might have viewed it) he had a kind of sign that he was to remain at Easton. While painting the barn he lost his hold and fell some forty feet.

Maryfarm, Easton, Pennsylvania, September 1941.

Fortunately, his guardian angel had "pushed him in the right direction" into a manure pile and he was unhurt.

In time the Maryfarm commune idea would lay bare serious faults in the achievement of the community ideal, but that first year the problem was more one of a lack of experience than of community zeal. One young farmer, thinking that potato vines represented a foreign incursion, pulled them up. Another took asparagus plants to be a noxious weed and laid them low with his hoe. Constructive work was slowed by the lack of adequate equipment. The first plowing was done by towing the plow behind the old truck that ran only when the notion struck it.

It was not long after their arrival at Easton that Workers received a gift of fifty dollars, specified for the purchase of a cow. Dorothy Day, Eddie Priest, and Bill Callahan were members of the purchasing mission, and one sunny May day they set off walking over the hills along the Delaware River to a neighboring farm. They were in a gay mood; dandelions covered the field and once a black snake slithered through the grass beneath their feet. Given their choice from a whole herd of Holsteins, they selected a large-uddered, complacent-looking cow and named her Rosie in honor of the Rosenberg family who had donated her purchase price.

The Workers were inexperienced farmers and they blundered occasionally, but on the whole it appears that the farm was productive enough to go a long way toward feeding the people who lived there and the many more who came as guests. Also, during the summer season there were many times when a car returning to the new house on Mott Street was loaded with produce for its table. When one considers that Maryfarm, like Mott Street, took on the mission of a completely open hospitality, it is recognized how much hard work was accomplished by the few who were dedicated to the purely farming part of the project.

Amidst it all Peter Maurin indoctrinated. John Cort remembers that on his first day at the farm everybody sat around the big dining-room table and listened to Maurin

make a point. There were long discussions about unemployment, the use of leisure, and the survival of the family.
Maurin was happy. He was witnessing, he believed, the
seeding of his most cherished idea. It was during that summer of 1936 that his ideas were put in print and received a
further circulation. In June, Sheed and Ward published a
collection of his *Easy Essays*. Dorothy Day wrote an announcement of the book in the July issue of *The Catholic
Worker*. They were essays, she said, that had been written
in the coffeehouses along the Bowery, in a barn by the light
of a lantern on a farm near Kingston, New York, and on the
benches at Union Square. She had seen him stop in the
picket line in front of the German counsul's office and take
out his notebook to write while his sign, protesting Nazi
anti-Semitism, for the moment ignored, drooped off his
shoulder to trail behind. She had even seen him break a
meditation in church to write down something.

She knew, she said, that Maurin would hate the story she
was writing about him and would withdraw into a shell. But
fortunately, she added, "he also has a quality of humility
and of submission in . . . small things, and if I, who am apt
to be a domineering woman, say very firmly, 'Peter, it is
necessary that we tell our readers about these things . . .'
he will shrug his shoulders with a wry look, and going out
into the streets with a bundle of books and papers in his
pockets, soon forget about it."

# 8

## DEPRESSION YEARS

Thought, in Peter Maurin's view, was primary. It was the idea which, if it were to prevail, must do so because of its final reasonableness and with its truth so exemplified in personalist lives that it required neither force nor emotional appeals to sustain it. For him, to give the personalist example required that he go no further than the Bowery. But Dorothy Day would take the personalist idea into the heart of the economic problem of the thirties. In the explosive expansion of capital that has been one of the primary marks of the modern history of the Western world, it was the workingman in his labor who paid much of the price of that expansion.

In the mid-thirties one could not affirm a personalist position on economics by reference to a well-marked chart. Peter Maurin and Dorothy Day took different positions. "Strikes don't strike me," Maurin would say, meaning that he looked to a cooperative order built within the shell of the old structure, while strikes represented polarization and struggle. But Dorothy Day, who likewise said that she was an anarchist and believed in a cooperative order, supported organized labor, and on many occasions Workers picketed with strikers. In September, 1937, the *Worker* declared that it was the right and duty of the workingman to join a union. "We know that by himself the worker can do very little. He has to join into association with his fellows in order to have the strength to meet with his employer and to bargain collectively." She could justify the strike as a tactic, not primarily as a means of securing better wages and hours, but of securing for workers the right to be treated as human beings. When men struck, she said, they should be fighting also for the right to be considered as partners in the enterprise in which they were engaged. Dorothy Day's justification of Workers participating in some of the labor struggles of the mid-thirties was so directly related to personalist ends that Maurin seemingly came to agree with it. The difference between them was more a reflection of background and temperament than anything else. Maurin was the peasant theorist, and Dorothy Day was the ex-radical and activist.

In January, 1936, when the Workers were still on Charles Street, they involved themselves in a dispute between the Borden Milk Company and its deliverymen. The issue, so *The Catholic Worker* charged, was the company's attempt to force milk wagon drivers out of their Teamster Union affiliate into a company union. The *Worker* called for a boycott of Borden products, to which the company rejoined with an advertisement in the Brooklyn *Tablet*, declaring that its policy toward the workmen was reasonable and just.

The *Worker*, however, saw it all the other way. It supported its position with a tone of crusading righteousness that warmed the emotions of young Workers but affronted some readers who thought Workers ought to confine themselves to passing out old clothes and feeding the hungry. "Catholicism pertains to religion, and has no bearing on industrial and economic life," one reader declared. It was necessary, he believed, that matters "pertaining to business and specific corporations should be avoided. . . . I would consider it an opportunity, if the occasion should arise, to declare that the Church is at its greatest when adhering to thoughts only on religion."

That winter Dorothy Day visited the headquarters of the Southern Tenant Farmers Union in Memphis, Tennessee. In all of American labor, it would have been difficult to have found a group more depressed than the sharecroppers of Arkansas and southern Missouri who worked the rich flatlands on the west bank of the Mississippi and whose miserable hovels sparsely dotted the broad expanse of the cotton fields. The organizers, Protestant clergymen, were few, but they were brave and determined. The so-called headquarters consisted of a few dingy rooms, so bare that some of the organizers slept on the floor. It was at this headquarters that Dorothy Day spent the night before her trip over into Arkansas.

It was very cold when she and the head of the union set out. They crossed the swift-coursing Mississippi on the old Harahan Bridge, passed through West Memphis and then north to Turell. Along back roads of mud and ice they found a company of sharecroppers, recently evicted from their shacks, living in tents. Half were children, and all were cold and hungry. They visited a family in a cabin where lay the body of old man who had died the night before. It was a picture, as she described it, of dumb and hopeless misery.

Deeply concerned, she sent a telegram to Eleanor Roosevelt telling her what she had witnessed. Mrs. Roosevelt responded immediately by getting in touch with the governor of Arkansas who went personally to investigate the situation. But in the report that was given to the press, it was said that nothing was wrong, that the group was a shiftless lot who refused to work. The unfortunate publicity (as *The Catholic Worker* quoted) was "the result of a Catholic woman's report to Mrs. Roosevelt." The explanation for the "Catholic woman's" action was that she was of a type that made "fat salaries off the misery of the people."

The story of Dorothy Day's visit to the tenant farmers was carried in the April *Worker*, which also carried an account of a tragic occurrence several weeks after she left Memphis. A group of masked riders had broken into one of the tenant houses she had visited and murdered the occupant in the presence of his wife. He had had the misfortune of witnessing the shooting of two Tenant Farmers Union organizers.

The most significant involvement of Catholic Workers in the cause of labor began in May, 1936, when seamen in New York left their ships in a spontaneous strike, protesting both the policies of the shipowners and of the International Seamen's Union, headed by Joe Ryan. The ISU was an old and established union that had become corrupt, so the striking seamen charged, with its officials reflecting a company-union mentality and receiving large salaries.

Some of the seamen, with no money and no place to go, drifted to the Worker house. For over a month fifty of them were housed there and many more were fed. When the strike temporarily ended, most of them left, but two, Hans Tunnesen and John Filliger, remained permanently. Filliger became the head farmer in a succession of Worker farms, and Tunnesen became the craftsman and cook. It was not the intellectual dimension that held these two and others like them to the Worker movement. It was the sense of community they found there. There was work to be done which was important to the continuation of the Catholic Worker movement and it was work they could do well.

In the meantime, with the coming of May, Dorothy Day went to Maryfarm to see how the planting was going. As the young men worked with the plowing, she sat beneath a tree to write her column for the *Worker*. Her job was to see that the newly acquired Rosie did not stray from the southeast pasture where the fences were being mended. The Catholic Worker movement had completed its third year.

Back at Mott Street, she took a bus to Washington to interview John L. Lewis. She went favorably disposed toward Lewis because she believed he stood for the ideal of an industrial democracy that went far beyond the traditional wage-hour goals of the unionism of the past. The interview seemed to have been rather perfunctory, since Lewis was not drawn into philosophizing about labor but preferred to talk of the issues immediately confronting the CIO.

From Washington she went to Pittsburgh to see the labor situation there firsthand. She had dinner with Bishop Hugh C. Boyle, after which they talked for another three hours about American labor, the social teachings of the Church, and about community farms.

The next day she toured the factory area with Mary Heaton Vorse. Miss Vorse had been one of the writers for *The Masses*, and she, with John Reed, had written the articles on the labor situation. She had covered the big steel strike of 1919 and she knew some priests in Pittsburgh who on that occasion had turned the basements of their churches into relief centers for the strikers. That afternoon she and Dorothy Day visited the priests, after which they went to an open-air labor meeting and distributed copies of *The Catholic Worker*. It was a pleasant day, especially so because of the renewal of an old association. There had been one diversion. A young Catholic student reader of the *Worker* drove them around to the little towns, in the process of which he insisted on talking about his soul. Miss Vorse was filled with wonder when he began to discuss the penances he practiced, one of which was to go out at night and roll in a briar patch.

When Dorothy Day was not traveling, she spent much time at Maryfarm to be with Tamar. When fall came she was there again, writing for the *Worker* a hymn of joy in the contemplation of Indian summer. She had come down to Easton one warm September evening, finding at Maryfarm a richness of delightful smells that contrasted sharply with those of the city. There was "the warm, sweet smell of the good earth [that] enwraps one like a garment. There is the smell of rotting apples; of alfalfa in the barn; burning leaves; of wood fires in the house; of pickled green tomatoes and baked beans than which there is no better smell, not even apple pie."

There was another moment of joy on one November evening just after she arrived at Maryfarm. Rosie had just had a calf. "The little one was gamboling around, answering to the name of Bess, and actually cavorting with the joy of life that was in her." The barn had been fixed up for the occasion—"new roof, new sides, whitewashed within, lots of bedding on the floor, and everything so snug and bright that it was a pleasure to contemplate the scene. It was dark and the light of the lantern cast long shadows. Never again will I meditate on the third joyful mystery [of the Rosary] without thinking of that scene which brought home so closely the birth of our Savior amidst the kindly beasts of the field. We were all so happy, and it was one of those moments of pure unalloyed joy so rare in this life."

Later, when the weather got cold, there was another delight for her at the farm. "We take hot bricks to bed at night. It was one of the thrills of a life time to feel one's warmth gradually permeating the icy sheets and one's breath making a corner warm for one's nose." It was a pleasure "the inhabitants of steam-heated apartments can never know."

But, as she said, such moments were rare. In November the seamen were striking again. This time the Workers not only made their Mott Street house available, but also rented a large store at 181 Tenth Avenue, just around the corner from the headquarters of the striking seamen. The Tenth Avenue place was constantly thronged. Joe Hughes, a striking seaman himself, took charge, and helped by John Cort, Bill Callahan, and others, kept three five-gallon pots of coffee boiling. Soon they were feeding a thousand a day, in addition to the daily line at Mott Street. "We can only beg from issue to issue of the paper," Dorothy Day wrote.

In January, 1937, the Bishop of Great Falls, Montana, Edwin O'Hara, visited Mott Street to see how the Workers were faring in the strike situation. It was snowing as they walked over to the Tenth Avenue store and the sidewalks were ankle deep in slush. They found the place packed with men. The air was heavy with the odor of wet, dirty clothes, and pools of water were on the floor. The men were eating, and Bishop O'Hara served himself a thick slice of Finnish rye bread spread with cottage cheese. Later he told Dorothy Day that even though she might be called a Communist for her work, she should not worry. There would be many to defend her.

That summer the seamen organized the National Maritime Union, CIO, during a convention headed by Joe Curran. The *Worker* rejoiced at the prospects of a new unity for the seamen and spoke well of Curran. The prospects of unity, though, were not well founded. The emergence of a new union at the expense of an old and established one produced one of the more bitter occasions of labor strife in the years just before World War II. With Joe Ryan and the ISU upheld by conservative and reactionary elements, on the one hand, and Joe Curran and the NMU bidding for the support of radicals and Communists on the other, the lines were drawn.

Down in Louisiana a newly ordained priest, full of the Worker spirit, found the line difficult to cross. When Father Jerome A. Drolet was asked to give the opening prayer at an NMU convention, he was ordered not to do so by the chancellor of the diocese. "I'm having a hard enough time convincing myself that the 'Church' means what she says in the Encyclicals," he wrote to *The Catholic Worker*. "As a priest at the retreat said to me, 'What's the use reading those things, what's the use studying the social philosophy of the Church. The Bishop trips you up as soon as you make a real move to put the d--m things into practice.'"

The bishop was obviously concerned about the charges of Communism in the NMU but the issue did not disturb Dorothy Day. What eventually did disturb her about Curran was what she considered to be his short memory where the Workers' services to his union were concerned. It was in June, 1946. She had been in Washington and there, with Mrs. John Brophy, wife of a CIO official, she had heard Curran testify before Representative Martin Dies' Un-American Activities Committee. When Curran discussed the aid the Communists had given the NMU in its birth struggle, he observed that "there was no one else to help us." Apparently, observed Dorothy Day, "he didn't like . . . to acknowledge any Catholic help. It is in the tradition of the worker to think of the Church as tied up with the shipowner rather than the worker. Of course we admit our help was but a drop in the bucket and the Communists must have poured money in." Even so, the Catholic Worker had housed "many a worker during the early strike of '36 and we spent many thousands of dollars which our kind readers sent us to feed the men." Curran or not, she believed the seamen would "long remember the gallon pots of coffee on the stove night and day . . . and the wooden tubs of peanut butter and cottage cheese and the good pumpernickel bread and the radio going and the piles of literature on social action."

The slight to Dorothy Day and the Workers was perhaps more wounding because, of all those involved in labor strife during the thirties, the Workers felt closest to the seamen. Dorothy Day was especially concerned about three of them who had been arrested on New Year's Day, 1937, for organizing in the territory of Frank Hague, the political boss of Jersey City. She had written to a priest, presumably with access to Hague, asking him to intercede for the men. "A written word from you to the parole board might mean that the men would be freed," she wrote. The priest, however, did not think he could do anything but he would keep the thought in mind.

One of the prisoners, Anthony Panchelli, wrote to Dorothy Day to thank her for her concern. "I am very glad to hear that you are taking such a great interest in the case of we three Brothers here in Trenton N. J. State Prison," he said. "Keep up the good work. Brother John Lewis, the working class needs you and the other organizing officials of the great power The Congress of Industrial Organization." He had received a letter from "one of the Jewish Brethren found in the columns of *The Catholic Worker,* and wish to let him know I appreciate his interest in me. . . . I wish to thank him for his kindness in sending me the dollar for 'smokes.'"

In the spring of 1937 another new CIO affiliate, the United Automobile Workers, introduced the sit-down strike as a means of securing industry recognition. Like the seamen's new union, the UAW was thought well of by the *Worker*. In February, Dorothy Day visited the strikers at

Fr. Jerome Drolet with August 1937 issue of *The Catholic Worker*.

the Fisher Body plant at Flint, Michigan. The doors of the plant were barricaded, but she got in by climbing on top of a box and going through a window. She found the men in high spirits and willing to hold out indefinitely for recognition of their union.

Peter Maurin, having previously expressed dissatisfaction with strikes, approved the sit-down strike because it seemed to be conducted on Gandhi-like lines.

On the Fourth of July, 1937, Dorothy Day and most of the Workers spent the day at the farm where a large group of children, Black and White, had been brought for the weekend. Even with her ten quarts a day, Rosie was hard-pressed to meet the demand. As the children screamed and raced, Dorothy Day wrote an article for the *Worker* on the violence at Republic Steel at Massilon, Ohio, and the situation at Johnstown, Pennsylvania, where the CIO was organizing Bethlehem Steel.

She was off traveling again in August. Governor Frank Murphy of Michigan, who had worked hard and successfully to settle the sit-down-strike issue, was in the hospital and had asked Dorothy Day to visit him. He was reading a book by Hilaire Belloc and listening to the radio when she got there one Sunday afternoon. Murphy was a regular reader of *The Catholic Worker* and had wanted to meet Dorothy Day.

In October she went to the Pacific coast. A priest drove her to San Quentin Prison to see Tom Mooney, now beginning his twenty-second year in jail. She had to wait an unusually long time to see him and was beginning to think that she was being subjected to a persecution by prison officials when Mooney appeared. He explained that the delay was of his own making, for he had been unwilling to leave the bedside of a dying prisoner in the hospital ward where he was an orderly. Dorothy Day found him happy and serene. He said he was glad he could help someone and he did not worry about the future. "I've had to live from day to day," he said. "Right now I look forward to nothing. I expect nothing."

Leaving San Quentin, she took the bus to San Diego. This trip did not provide the atmosphere for the relaxation she was accustomed to getting when she rode the bus. Two men sat talking about President Roosevelt in voices loud enough for everyone to hear. "They called him a yellow coward, with the heart of a louse, a maniac on the verge of total insanity. They talked of their investments and losses. They talked of public utilities. And every minute they cursed him. 'There'll be bloodshed yet,' they concluded, and angrily added that they'd like to take a part in it. Hate was etched into bitter lines of their faces and into their voices." With labor in the process of extensive reformation, such talk was not uncommon at the time, although it was more likely to occur in the parlor cars of trains than on buses.

*The Catholic Worker* had shown obvious enthusiasm for the CIO and its organizing efforts, but Dorothy Day disclaimed any final partisan convictions. Nobody seemed to understand, she said, that when Workers went to strike meetings or picketed, they primarily were trying to bring the social teachings of the Church to the man in the street. Yet many had insisted that "we are participating in the strike or endorsing one faction against another. We do not know the least thing about factions in the various unions. . . . We are out to convert others to our point of view, to work for a pluralist order where Agnostics, as well as Catholics, Protestants and Jews, can work for the common good."

How had the workingman reacted to the presence of the Catholic Workers on his picket line and to the support they gave his cause with material assistance, as in the seaman's strike? Dorothy Day recorded her observations on this point in her Journal. She had found in her travels that some laborers knew about *The Catholic Worker* and approved of it. In talking about the paper, however, they preferred to emphasize its concern with the poor and were unwilling to acknowledge that a religious publication could have anything to say about their concerns. They were grateful for the help they got in the seamen's strike, "but where there is no crisis, they are condescending. We are missionaries. . . . They still

Harlem children at Maryfarm, Easton, Pennsylvania.

think, as they have always thought, that the church . . . and unions cannot be mixed. In other words, they distrust Catholics because of the sins of Catholics. It is not because of a lack of recognition of the need to correlate the material and spiritual."

After 1937 Dorothy Day's and the Workers' involvement in the labor revolution slackened. Major changes that seemed to portend a better day for the worker had been effected, and the acute pangs of the Depression had been somewhat eased. Yet the satisfaction that might have come from the sense of having made economic progress within the nation was dimmed by an awareness that the world was sinking into the tragedy of another war from which would come new testings of spirit, undreamed of in those simple days of the Depression.

# 9

# ISRAEL

By the mid-thirties, as the Fascist polarizations in Europe became more pronounced, there were many American Catholics who came to regard them as the most active agent in the fight against Communism and who thus favored them —in many instances with an enthusiasm that suggested the spirit of a crusade. The Spanish Civil War began in July, 1936, and it was in this event that many American Catholics found a rallying point for their anti-Communism. "Almost to a man," says David O'Brien in *American Catholics and Social Reform,* "the hierarchy and the American Catholic press supported the Franco side, insisting that the Loyalist government was Communist-dominated, did not represent the will of the Spanish people and was bent upon destruction of the Church in Spain." There were, however, a few exceptions to American Catholic support of Franco, and *The Catholic Worker* was the most significant one. When the war began, the paper, voicing Dorothy Day's position, declared that it was pacifist and refused to take sides. Both sides were at fault, the *Worker* thought.

As the war settled into its bitter and sanguinary course, the *Worker* tried to offer a reflective Catholic counteropinion to the "propaganda in favor of Franco and Rebel Spain" which the American Catholic press had been "zealous in spreading." It thought that "Catholics who look at Spain and think Fascism is a good thing because Spanish Fascists are fighting for the Church against Communist persecution should take another look at recent events in Germany to see just how much love the Catholic Church can expect. . . ."

The *Worker* was probably the only Catholic paper that tried to give something of the position of those Catholic intellectuals in Europe who voiced reservations about an emotional abandonment to the cause of Franco. In December, 1936, the *Worker* carried a letter written by a Catholic Spaniard to Emmanuel Mounier, this letter having been published in the November, 1936, issue of *L'Esprit*. The writer felt that the issues that had prompted Franco's action did not justify a violation of the Fifth Commandment. "What are we to think of so-called Catholics who believe themselves free from its observance because their own particular conception of patriotism is at stake?" he asked.

Jacques Maritain gave much distinction to Catholic intellectual life in the thirties, and Dorothy Day made a special effort to get his views on the war for the *Worker*. His was the personalist's position. He was especially concerned over the disposition of some Catholics to make the conflict a holy crusade against Communism. "To intrude the myth of the holy war into the conflicts from which Europe is now suffering would be an irreparable calamity. It is Christianity that would be hardest hit by this myth, since it would create moral wounds and incurable animosities in one of the contending parties, and, in the other, favour an internal alteration, a kind of Islamisation of the religious conscience itself." The holy war idea, as Maritain well knew, was an aspect of an imperial impulse where the spirit of religion would itself become objectivized.

Maritain was the main gadfly to the Catholic imperialist Francophiles, and in the Catholic Worker Papers there is a manuscript copy of "An Interview with Jacques Maritain," which was apparently set up to reveal other aspects of Francophilism. The interviewer began by noting that Franco's Minister of the Interior, Serrano Suñer, had called Maritain "a Jew, a Mason, and a Communist." Acknowledging that he was risking impertinence, the interviewer wanted to know if Maritain was indeed a Jew?

Maritain answered: "Alas, no; I am not a Jew. I regret it, for it is a great privilege to belong to the same race as Jesus Christ and the Blessed Virgin." Suñer had called him that "because I am a Catholic and because I have no faith in a holy war which is ruining Spain with the help of the fascism of Mussolini and the racism of Hitler, let alone the Moors."

Was Maritain a Communist?

"I have no desire to convert all Communists into ashes; I should like them to become converts to God, and I love them as my brothers. I remember that the Pope has said, 'Let us then accept the outstretched hand, but in order to draw them to the divine doctrine of Christ. And how shall we draw them to this doctrine? By teaching it? No. By living it, in all its beneficence. The preaching of truth did not produce many conquests for Our Lord; it led Him to the Cross."

The Jews and the Communists! These were the counter-symbols to the Catholic objectivist-imperialists, too. The interviewer thought he knew why Maritain deviated from the imperial Catholic line. Maritain was a "convert" to Catholicism and "to the ministers of General Franco the word 'convert' is a term of abuse, even of vilification, almost synonymous with 'Jew' and 'free mason.' This was a relic of those happy times when in Spain people were forced into baptism under pain of losing their citizenship. . . . I suppose the same ministers do not much like Saint Paul or Saint Augustine. . . . This is what a certain religious racism describes in curious jargon as being a 'born Catholic.'"

Maritain had given the personalist response to the imperialist spirit, and this was what Dorothy Day tried to do in *The Catholic Worker*. "We do not expect a glittering army to overcome . . . heresy. . . . As long as men trust to the use of force—only a superior, a more savage and brutal force will overcome the enemy. We use his own weapons, and we must make sure our own force is more savage . . . than his own. . . . Today the whole world has turned to the use of force. . . . If we do not . . . emphasize the law of love, we betray our trust, our vocation."

Its stand on the Spanish Civil War brought the strongest reaction to *The Catholic Worker* that it so far had experienced. "You never seem to understand that your Maritainian discordant shouting, 'conciliation and peace above all things' is not conciliation and no peace at all," wrote a stirred-up cleric. "Peace is not peace, which is not based on order, and true order never exists unless based on justice, a virtue, which, sweetened with charity, demands either the extermination of the wicked or their rendering unharmful to the good. Now, if you have eyes and ears, you do not need but to open them to see . . . that justice and charity . . . are . . . exclusively on the side of Franco."

Another priest thought it was "high time" that Dorothy Day left the Spanish question alone. If she could not sympathize with "those Spaniards who, by the shedding of their own blood, are saving the spiritual heritage of future Spanish generations," then the "least you could do would be to keep your hands off a question about which you seem to know next to nothing." The writer noted that the Worker had also featured the opinions of "a Maritain, of a Mauriac . . . and of a Bernanos, the same Bernanos who during his stay of months on the island of Majorca, whose bishop, clergy, and religious of both sexes he is now calumniating, showed himself such a wonderful Catholic that he did not bother to attend Mass on Sundays."

Even one of the Mott Street "Ambassadors" felt that he should let Dorothy Day know that she was making a spectacle of herself. He had been to a "public meeting" where a "leading Catholic" had made "condemning remarks about you." This "leading Catholic" had said "that you are trying to be a better christian than Christ Himself, that you are a great hopocrit [sic] unable to distinguish between true christianity and communistic every day propaganta [sic]. Yes, he had reference to the Spanish question . . ." and he could go right to the heart of the problem, "since I do know you." The Worker "does good work among . . . particular people," but "the fact remains that you are stubborn about your ideas and efforts of doing good amongst the depressed. . . . You go only one straight narrow road, unassissted, unadvised, not listening to anything or anyone else. . . ."

Another Worker critic was one whom more and more Americans were hearing about, the radio priest of Royal Oak, Michigan, Father Charles E. Coughlin. Within the ranting circles of American political activity, there was agitation over the *Worker's* position, including the rising cries of Father Coughlin giving voice to the imperial and objectivized impulses in American Catholicism. In the July 5, 1937, issue of Coughlin's weekly, *Social Justice, The Catholic Worker* was condemned. Knowing little of the personalist ideas of European Catholic intellectuals, *Social Justice* could only invoke an authority image as the basis for its condemnation. Though the *Worker* might appear "most orthodox to the mind of the superficial reader," there was indeed much about it to make it highly suspect. *Social Justice* recalled that "In Nov. of 1936, the Most Rev. Michael J. Gallagher, late Bishop of Detroit . . . read an article in the *Catholic Worker* and commented that, 'despite all the reference to the saints, the Popes and the Encyclicals, its attitude on the Spanish question was enough to make one wonder if the thing were not downright Communism, camouflaged with Catholic paint.' "

The article recalled a meeting of the Catholic Press Association of the previous May, where Peter Maurin and Bill Callahan had urged Catholic editors to remain open-minded and neutral on the Spanish issue. This attitude had "offended the Catholicity of practically every man who attended this convention," yet it was a fact that "hundreds of priests have fallen 'hook, line and sinker' for the *Catholic Worker's* program."

Then there was the Brooklyn *Tablet* which similarly felt that when authority could be invoked there was little use for further argument. Editor Patrick Scanlan was quite disturbed about the *Worker's* position on the war and wrote a letter to Dorothy Day's confessor, Father Joseph McSorley, expressing his concern. He had never taken *The Catholic Worker* "very seriously," but he had become aware of "the dignified and austere position" in which McSorley had placed the Worker movement. Scanlan went on to say that he had held "no antipathy to Dorothy Day and her colleagues. Twice when the late Cardinal Archbishop [Hayes] was about to ban the movement, or at least place severe strictures on its activities, I defended them." McSorley "probably knew that last June the Cardinal took some action after Dorothy Day at Father Ford's Forum had espoused the Spanish Reds' cause. His Eminence then, at St. Joseph's, Sullivan County, said he was shocked after he had publicly prayed for Franco to have a Catholic in a Catholic hall going just the opposite. He used the word 'disloyalty.' "

But there was one prominent Catholic clergyman who supported the *Worker* position and publicly declared it in a letter to the paper. Father Virgil Michel, who had been a friend of the movement from the first, wrote just two months before he died in 1938: "There are few things I have read recently which I enjoyed and which gave me more comfort than your . . . 'On the Use of Force,' in the . . . *Catholic Worker*. It was especially comforting to know that your . . . ideas are taking root in the minds of many young groups. . . . Keep up the good work no matter what slanderous tongues may say. That is the way Christ himself did it."

Once, though, the Workers found themselves aligned with the Catholic majority. When the movie *Blockade* was shown at Radio City Music Hall in June, 1938, Stanley Vishnewski, Joe Zarella, and Bill Callahan went uptown from Mott Street to picket it on the grounds that it was a propaganda film aimed at removing the embargo on arms to Spain. Set upon by pro-Loyalist sympathizers as they picketed, and finding themselves in league with members of the Knights of Columbus, who also objected to the movie, must have made the three picketeers wonder whether they were doing the right thing after all.

It was now a friend from the Left who called Dorothy Day gullible. She had, he wrote, permitted her group "to be taken in by the Tory-cleric bloc in the USA who are fighting for the retention of the embargo against the Spanish Government." She should know that the "entire world labor movement is behind the Spanish government while the entire Fascist world supports Franco." It was a "notorious fact that the Jesuit order in Spain has gotten its properties returned from Franco while all but a few top clerics in this country have remained silent while the unions of Spain were crushed and smashed by the agents of such degenerates as the Duke of Alba and Alfonso the absentee monarch."

But even as this letter was written, the Loyalist cause was crumbling, and as 1939 dawned the Catholic imperialists rejoiced. One wrote Dorothy Day a final five-page letter quoting the Vatican newspaper, *L'Osservatore Romano,* and lesser sources to point out wherein she had erred. Concluding, he declared that he was "grateful to God for raising up another great Catholic hero . . . Spanish chivalry which once saved the western world from the inroads of oriental Mohammedanism, is now saving civilization from communistic atheism." He hoped and prayed that Franco would set up "a great Catholic state in which will begin a Catholic renaissance that will spread to all the world."

Such a pious hope in the dawning months of 1939 could only echo discordantly in the fateful formation of onrushing events. It was inevitable that some of the most ardent imperialists, in their dredging for issues to fuel a crusade, should hit upon that most tragic of aberrations in the history of Christianity—anti-Semitism. That this was a tool handy to the uses of the Catholic imperialists was demonstrated by Father Coughlin. It was he who gave the call to arms for those who would see Communism as the devil-born calamity of modern man and behind it the visage of the Jew— gray, cunning, and inscrutable.

In the early thirties Coughlin had acquired a national

radio audience by persuasively advancing old Populist ideas concerning the cause of the Depression, the "international banker" customarily being put forward as the favorite villain. Responsive to the imperial call, Coughlin seemed to feel that his potential as one able to bring the light to people ought to be channeled into the stream of political action, but such overtures as he made to the newly elected Franklin Roosevelt were coolly received. Thereupon Roosevelt himself was made into an agent of darkness, and in 1936 Father Coughlin helped to organize a third-party attempt to win the 1936 Presidential election. The venture failed ignobly, and restlessly he turned his attention to the "conspiracy of the international, communistic, capitalistic Jew." By the summer of 1939, Coughlinites organized the Christian Front, at whose rallies and lectures execration of the Jew was standard fare.

It was the American middle-class Catholic, his press, and his clergy who had supported Franco, and when Coughlin's *Social Justice* gave the cause its sometimes strident support, it was doing as it was expected to do. But when *Social Justice* began to focus on the Jew for his supposed role in fomenting capitalist depressions on the one hand, and international Communism on the other, the middle-class Catholic was not altogether persuaded, and some important elements of the press and some high clerics disavowed him. In the Christian Front period of the Coughlin crusade, it was mainly the Brooklyn *Tablet* that maintained a friendly and open attitude toward it. Its converts, full of a loud crusading spirit, came largely from the lower class. And thus, as some commentators would have it, the Coughlin phenomenon was largely a Populist phenomenon arising out of economically troubled times. That a class of persons experiencing difficulty and frustration in their concern with obtaining the status and security found within bourgeois life definitions should have accepted Coughlin's delineation of the Jew as the culprit is understandable. But to the Catholic Workers and according to the personalist tradition, an explanation of anti-Semitism based solely on the class principle was a by-pass of the central issue. It was nothing less than a rejection of Christ.

As the Jews moved into the most agonizing phase of their history, Peter Maurin in one of his phrased essays, stated his thoughts on the Jews in a paraphrase of the French person-alist writer, Leon Bloy:

> We forget
>     or rather
>     we do not wish to know
>     that Our Lord made man
>     was a Jew,
>     the Jew par excellence,
>     the Lion of Judah;
>     that his mother was a
>         Jewess,
>     the flower of the Jewish race,
>     that his ancestors were Jews
>     along with all the prophets,
>     finally that our whole
>         sacred liturgy
>     is drawn from Jewish books.
> How then can we express
>     the enormity of the outrage
>     and the blasphemy involved
>     in vilifying the Jewish race . . .?
> The history of the Jews
>     dams the history
>     of the human race
>     as a dike
>     dams a river
>     in order
>     to raise its level.

With the tempo of anti-Semitism quickening in this coun-try in 1938 and 1939, and with the plight of the Jews in Eu-rope becoming even more desperate after the beginning of World War II, Maurin wrote frequently on this evil. In one essay, obviously aimed at allaying one aspect of the anti-Semitic outcries from *Social Justice,* he declared that the intellectual historian, Werner Sombart, had been wrong for blaming bourgeois capitalism on the Jews. The classical economists, he said, were theoreticians of capitalism, and in Germany it had been Bismarck who had fostered its development. "Let's Keep the Jews for Christ's Sake," he urged in a seven-essay group. Their presence "all over the world is a reminder to the world of the coming of Christ. . . ." Repeatedly, he pleaded for the removal of barriers to Jewish immigration into the United States. In the first year of the war, a Worker was asked to write some reflections on Maurin for the paper, and he seemed to have been most impressed by Maurin's concern for the Jews. "Peter believes we should have more Jews than we do in this or any country. He calls them a bulwark against Nationalism. . . . Christians are followers of Christ. Because of this, says Peter, every time a Christian sees a Jew he should be reminded of Christ and love him for being of the race that Christ was a part of."

Arthur Sheehan states that Maurin had a special love for the Jews, and he found many in the nearby East Side to whom he liked to talk. Once, he got a room there, where he hoped to expand contact and discussion, but possibly fearing an attempt at conversion, few Jews came in to talk. But a Miss Weiss, who was a convert, did come frequently. "She felt that the group at Mott Street did not fully appreciate Peter. She liked to take him out to dinner and buy him presents, especially new hats. To her he was a king and perhaps this was her symbolic way of crowning him." Stanley Vishnewski remembered that there always had been heavy pressures from Catholic anti-Semites to turn the *Worker* into a "hysterical red-baiting sheet." They "hinted at promises of increased circulation and large expense accounts." One group was so insistent that Dorthy Day "literally" had to throw it out. Once, a hate group invaded a discussion at St. Francis of Assisi Church in mid-Manhattan. When some Catholic Workers got up to protest the anti-Semitic tirades, they were rushed out of the hall amidst the booing of the anti-Semites.

Oddly, one of the first contacts between Workers and the Coughlin forces came in the first years of the New Deal when Coughlin, citing encyclicals as the basis of his position, was calling for vigorous action against the Depression. Feeling that the *Worker* and Coughlin had similar objectives, one of Coughlin's supporters wrote to Maurin suggesting an alliance. Workers, he said, "are all good at drawing up indictments and pointing out injustice, but I have yet to hear of any program of action. . . . Let us get together and form a Catholic Political Party. . . ."

Maurin rejoined with an essay:

Our Holy Father does not ask us to reconstruct
  the social order through Catholic political action
  but through Catholic social action,
You would like to stop Communism, but a
  Catholic Political Party cannot stop Communism. . . .
There is no substitute for Catholic Social Action
The Catholic Worker Movement fosters Catholic social
  action and not Catholic political action.

Four years later *The Catholic Worker* explicitly stated its difference with *Social Justice*. On August 18, 1938, the Coughlin paper began to publish *The Protocols of the Elders of Zion*, a concocted series of twenty-four lectures supposedly by Jewish leaders on how to take over the world. This fanciful hoax was prepared in France but first published by Russian anti-Semites in 1905. The editors of *Social Justice* apparently thought that they could pass this forgery off upon its readers and thereby accelerate the momentum of the Coughlin crusade. In its December, 1938, issue *The Catholic Worker* denounced the publication of the *Protocols* and went through them one by one to expose their fakery.

In September, Bill Callahan, who had become one of the *Worker* editors, began a column called "The Gadfly," which was, obviously, a column by a young man who wanted to say pointed and direct things about people and the times. His

May, 1939, column was an "Open Letter to Fr. Coughlin on
the Jews." He first derided Coughlin's contention that he
was not anti-Semitic, but that he was only trying to expose
the "bad" Jews. Why then did Coughlin not mention the
"Good" Jews! "Read *Social Justice*," and judge, wrote Callahan. "It makes the point of mentioning the obviously Jewish
names of Communists, and all sorts of undesirables such as
criminals and international bankers." There was no word of
the great Jewish philanthropists, scientists, and artists.

Then Callahan went on to a subject about which Workers
knew a great deal. He wondered about Coughlin's trying to
make heroes out of those salesmen of *Social Justice* because
they were sometimes "insulted." What about the *Worker*
salesmen who had been "insulted by Coughlinites innumer-
able times. We have stood . . . selling or distributing *The
Catholic Worker*, and have been forced to listen to the loud,
coarse gibes of your followers. . . . They stand about yelling
'Communists,' and have, on occasion, torn papers from our
hands and even struck us. Your followers are of that temper,
Father." Callahan concluded: "If a real wave of anti-Semitism sweeps the United States, if in the future Jews are persecuted as they are in Europe, you, Father Coughlin, must
be ready to assume a goodly part of the responsibility. Are
you ready to do that?"

This column brought a flood of letters similar to the outpouring provoked by the *Worker's* position on the Spanish
Civil War. "Why should he not chide the Jews—isn't he a
Priest of God?" asked one reader. A priest wrote to say that
he wanted no more bundles of *Workers* in his church. "If
you presume to send any more . . . the same will be *refused*
and *returned* at your expense." Callahan's criticism of
Coughlin "was out of place and as long as you continue to
print such articles your paper is not good scrap paper in a
Catholic home." Another decided that it was time to tell
Dorothy Day "personally" what he thought of her. "I think
that you are still a dirty Communist parading as a loyal
Catholic . . . a two-faced hypocrite, a wolf in sheep's clothing, serving your Red master, Joseph Stalin, who guides

from his capital at Moscow." Another thought Coughlin "a Prophet sent by God to lead us into the promised land." A letter to Callahan asked if he were "fighting for Christianity or Judaism. What genius tells you that the followers of Father Coughlin are not capable of judging for themselves? I have sprung from the same race as you (if Callahan is your real name)."

Yet there were also those who thought that the anti-Semites were the real enemies of the Church. "I have ceased attending the church in my parish," one *Worker* reader wrote in. "The members seem to have a religion called 'Coughlinism,' I feel it has nothing to do with Catholicism. . . . They have a religion of hate that makes me shudder. . . . Very seriously I think it is high time for the Catholic Church to unfrock this 'Father Coughlin.' . . . ." Another wrote to say how deeply disturbed he was when he walked along New York's streets to hear the hawkers of *Social Justice* cry out the latest revelations of Jewish perfidy.

The Lower East Side Jews of New York lived between two Catholic voices, the Brooklyn *Tablet* and *The Catholic Worker*, and the fact that the *Tablet* dismayed them with its support of Coughlin and the paper's own disposition to see the conspiratorial Jew behind Communism was a matter of concern for the *Worker*. For Dorothy Day, the concern was heightened by the fact that as a young Socialist she had lived on the Lower East Side, had come to know the richness of Jewish life and the Jewish concern for justice. Thus, when Coughlin in an especially offensive radio broadcast had adverted more directly to the presumed link between Jews and Communism, and when he was warmly seconded in this view by Patrick Scanlan in the *Tablet*, Dorothy Day reacted. Sometime in December, 1938, she sent a statement to several New York newspapers and the *New Republic*. It read:

> Inept and untimely was the radio broadcast of Father Coughlin in which he admonished the Jews on Communism, and equally inept and untimely was its pugnacious

defense by Mr. Patrick Scanlan, editor of the Brooklyn *Tablet*. It is to be hoped the Jews of America will consider both cases not in the light of anti-Semitism but rather as two cases of extraordinarily bad manners.

While Jews probably recognized that "manners" was not the issue involved in the statement, Scanlan was aghast that he should be called into question and immediately wrote to Father Joseph McSorley. If he were not mistaken, Scanlan said, "Canon Law prohibits Catholics writing for anti-Catholic publications without permission," and it was obvious that the "attack on me was sent to publications which are anti-Catholic and take glory in attacking Catholics." Moreover, he continued, the article in the *Tablet* supporting Coughlin "was not written by me" but by "a pastor, a cultured priest of great standing in this Diocese. . . ." McSorley informed Scanlan that he had talked to Dorothy Day. "I believe she's going to call upon you soon. . . ." But Scanlan was not mollified. "Needless to say, I do not want to see Miss Day."

These were the days of rapidly mounting terror for Jews in Germany, gathering on November 17, 1938, to even greater excesses by the desperate act of a seventeen-year-old Jewish youth who shot a Nazi official in Paris. When the latter died two days later, there occurred a Nazi reaction of looting and burning Jewish stores throughout Germany, of burning synagogues, and of beating and killing.

This *Krystallnacht*, as the episode was called, revealed the destructive madness of Nazism, and those around the world who were not mad should have been sobered and revulsed. But the year 1939 found anti-Semitism reaching a crescendo in the United States, with a reported 121 anti-Semitic organizations active at the time. Most of them were presumably inconsequential, so obviously made up of lunatics that their meetings, resolutions, and hate literature left most untouched. But to millions of American Catholics, a priest spoke with authority, and many American Jews must have wondered if a *Krystallnacht* might not be in the making for them as well. Not many read or knew of the *Worker*, but those who did found some comfort in it. One wrote to say that while walking along Forty-second Street he had been "shocked to see the number of Father Coughlin followers selling *Social Justice*. Fortunately, however, for every man selling the Father's yellow sheet there was a representative of . . . your publication. Your paper reveals fortunately that not all Catholics are as bigoted and illogical as the father would have us believe and thus offers the Jews some solace. . . ." Another wondered about Coughlin, "who has . . . been preaching anti-Semitism contrary to the teachings of the Church, the Pope and destroying the principles of the Prince of Peace and the universal brotherhood of men." He found it "very discouraging."

In order to focus attention on the person and thinking of those Catholics who viewed the Coughlin phenomenon with dismay, Dorothy Day took another action. Sometime around the first of May, 1939, she helped to organize the Committee of Catholics to Fight Anti-Semitism. Professor Emmanuel Chapman, the Jewish convert who was then teaching philosophy at Fordham, was the committee's first executive secretary. In Chicago, a companion committee was organized by John Cogley. His associates were Edward Marciniak, active in Catholic action, Marie Antoinette Roulet, a worker in the labor movement, the Jesuit Martin Carrabine, and Professor Herbert Rattner of the University of Chicago. Around these core organizers the committee shortly came to have a lengthy list of distinguished sponsors. A paper, *The Voice*, was published, and *Worker* salesmen, heeding Dorothy Day's request that they "exert greater efforts in the 'street apostolate,'" sold *The Voice* in direct confrontation with *Social Justice* salesmen.

Shortly after the committee was formed, Bill Gauchat of the Cleveland Worker wrote to Chapman to assure him "that everything I . . . can do to fight anti-semitism will be done." A *Worker* reader wrote that he would "be glad to cooperate with the 'Committee' . . . having been fighting it myself on a small scale for the past year or so." Whatever else the committee accomplished, the fact that it existed and that *The Voice* was sold on the streets of New York must have lessened for some Jews the despair they felt over the rising wave of anti-Semitism.

# 10

# PACIFISM

The years 1938 and 1939 were the last ones of an old world, for the war would loose new and accelerating forces of whirl. This was the last of the time of immediate expectations that marked the early years of the Catholic Worker movement. Thereafter, the war and then whirl would blur those expectations.

On the first day of 1938 Dorothy Day awakened at Maryfarm after nine hours' sound sleep. The house was stone cold, but in the kitchen there was a clatter of stove lids being removed as someone stuffed wood into the range, and shortly she caught the fragrance of the smoke that escaped. Outside, a new snow lay so deep on the ground that getting to Mass was perilous.

For the next two days the weather confined her to the house, but it was no hardship. She was reading George Bernanos' *The Diary of a Country Priest*. She told *Worker* readers that she had found it "tremendously moving"—so "overwhelming on first reading" that she read parts of it over and over. She added that since Peter Maurin was always making lists of books for others to read, she would make a list of her own and in it she would include *The Diary of a Country Priest*. The others which she liked were François Mauriac's *Life of Jesus*, Ignazio Silone's *Bread and Wine*, and Maritain's *Freedom in the Modern World*.

Before anything else, though, she placed the Bible and *The Brothers Karamazov.*

Her own book, *House of Hospitality,* was published in 1938. It was a collection of the columns she had written for the *Worker* that described life at Mott Street. In January, 1939, her autobiographical *From Union Square to Rome* came out. This story of her conversion began with her earliest memories and carried through to the Washington hunger march and her meeting with Peter Maurin. It was simple and straightforward, with vivid and interesting sections that dealt with her girlhood in Chicago and later her days at the University of Illinois.

The year 1938 was one of even more traveling. Under the pressure of encyclicals on the one hand and the social ferment caused by the Depression on the other, a number of Catholics came to seek more understanding of what was occurring. For some of them the name of Dorothy Day had become familiar. Schools, pastors, and bishops sought her for conferences and speaking engagements. A high point in her travel-speaking activities occurred in Milwaukee when, in May, 1938, she spoke to ten thousand at the conclusion of a Catholic Action conference that had been called by Archbishop Samuel Stritch.

In some respects this period was a high point for *The Catholic Worker.* It was filled with the reporting of the scribes of the various houses and in the July–August, 1939, issue the "Ben Joe Labray" series began. The articles, written by different persons under the pseudonym of "Ben Joe Labray" were accounts of aspects of the life of a poor man, a bum—his encounters with the police—looking for a place to sleep in vacant tombs in a graveyard—experiences in a New York City poorhouse. The articles were written by persons who had experienced what they wrote about and therefore had a special kind of realism. Carl Sandburg is said to have thought highly of them. Possibly it was the Ben Joe Labray articles that prompted him about this time to send a dollar to the *Worker* requesting a four-year subscription.

Dorothy Day has related how the articles began. She and

Margaret Bingham, a Worker friend, were sitting down by
the docks, waiting for a seaman to come off a ship. Why
not, she thought, get a number of the people around the
Worker house to write articles about their experiences
"which would show in some small way a new character in
history, a new kind of saint for our times, the kind of saint
we need, the saint-revolutionist who would not only use
spiritual weapons of prayer, poverty and penance, but
would try to begin, here and now, that kind of social order
which would indicate his sincere belief in the doctrine of
brotherhood. And I remembered St. Benedict Joseph Labre,
who was a bum, who reacted against the effete delicacy of
his time . . . by going unwashed in rags, who rebelled
against the luxury and wealth and hoggishness of his time
by asking nothing for himself (like our own Peter Maurin)
who did penance for the world and died in a gutter." The
articles continued for several years but were stopped because "a priest in Brooklyn, whose church was named after
Labre, objected, feeling that the Workers were 'casting dis-
honor' on his patron."

It was in 1939 the *Worker* noted the appearance of two
new Church leaders. In the March issue, observing that it
had critics who had questioned its Catholicism, it pledged
its "unqualified support and allegiance" to the new pope,
Pius XII. "Thou Art Peter," it declared, an affirmation it
thought should be sufficient answer to these critics. In June
the paper took the occasion "to felicitate Archbishop Francis J. Spellman on his elevation to the head of the New York
Archdiocese, and to pledge him its loyalty and devotion."

Dorothy Day's father died that year. She wrote in the
June issue of the *Worker* that he had worked right to the
day before he died, and that was some little consolation.

Mr. Breen, the choleric old journalist who had appointed
himself the official greeter at the house, died about the same
time. Someone had been with him through the long afternoon before he died, dropping in to pray. Dorothy Day recalled the scene: "Outside the children were playing in the
yard, calling out joyously to each other. On the rear of the

front house the sun shone and the shadows of pigeons
flecked the walls as they wheeled in the sun." Mr. Breen
died quietly that evening just as the dinner bell rang.

Despite his prejudices and his irascibility, Mr. Breen had
had his good points. He had tried in every way he could to
help out at the house, and, whenever he got any money for
writing a book review, he would give it to the house fund.
"He left only his cane," Dorothy Day wrote, "that cane he
used to shake at people in arguments. Many a time he had
threatened to wrap it around the neck of one or another
around the house. That cane is now mine. And when I use it
on the hills around the farm, I shall think of Mr. Breen, part
of our family who is now gone."

Mr. Breen also left a poem he had recently written:

Red Fox, step lightly
On the crisp, gray moss;
St. Francis said his prayers here.
Look where his cross
Is sunk in the stone!
On the bracken and briar,
Let four feet and two
Seek the shortest trail
    homeward
Through moon-filtered dew.
And each in innocence
Folded in night,
Lie on the heart of God
Safe until light.

One September evening shortly after nightfall, Dorothy
Day sat out in front of the house to watch the Italians of the
neighborhood celebrate for the fourth night the feast of San
Gennaro. Every day bands had been parading through the
streets. Now there was to be a dance in the little playground across the street. Japanese lanterns hung every-
where and a loudspeaker was blaring forth swing music.
Soon the playground was full and young people were jitter-

bugging in the street. The old people sat in front of the doors and watched.

One of the Workers made a pot of coffee and brought Dorothy Day a cup. Inside, Bill Callahan and Joe Zarella worked on the paper. Julia Porcelli and some of the others had walked down the street to watch the celebrating. It was the first cool night of fall; the stars could be seen, the air was so clear; and for a long while the half moon, brilliant even against the streetlights, hung above the middle of the street. After a while, Kichi Harada, a Japanese woman who stayed at the house, came up. She had been walking on the East Side and was much taken by the Jewish observance of the Day of Atonement. "I passed the synagogues, there were lights in all of them and the doors stood wide open. There was music, queer music, so I went upstairs and asked if strangers could come in. The man at the door told me I could go upstairs to the gallery and I went there and sat with all the women . . . who sat and wept, the tears running down their faces. They were so devoted, I never saw people so devoted." When she had finished telling her story, the moon had passed behind the tall tenements, but the stars still shone with sparkling brilliance. Dorothy Day reflected that most of the world had become engulfed in war, but there on Mott Street the traditions continued.

As the war began, Peter Maurin made a judgment about it. "We are witnessing," he said, "the historical liquidation of Jean Jacques Rousseau's world." It was true. Something of the spirit of that Enlightenment universe, that had seemed so new and so hopeful for so long, would fade—the belief that rational man, identifying, sorting, and rearranging the data of the object world could program an inevitable progress for himself. True, the forms of Rousseau's world would linger after the war, but the conflict would go far to diminish the sources of nourishment on which those forms had for so long derived their life.

Maurin was completely a man of peace, but he never reached the point of making his pacifism a pronouncement. Perhaps to have gone this far even on the subject of peace would have offended his personalist sense. Peace was of the spirit, and a preoccupation with identifying and battling the evils of the object world could delay the quest for spirit. Yet, as he taught, it was the object world that must be directed by spirit, an ideal that brought a direct confrontation with the problem of attitudes and institutional forms. These were questions which throughout history had been plagued with the most confusing perplexities, and war was the ultimate question. Here man would have to make his decision, directed by a reason animated by that spirit of peace that lay at the heart of the Gospels.

*The Catholic Worker* emphasized its pacifism from the first. In October, 1933, it stated that its "delegates" would "be among those present at the United States Congress Against War" and that they would be representing "Catholic Pacifism." That they represented scarcely more than themselves they well knew. In December, 1935, Bill Callahan gave a talk to the Catholic Social Club of Brooklyn, entitled "Catholics Should be Conscientious Objectors in Time of War." Then, in October, 1936, the *Worker* announced "the formation of a Catholic organization of conscientious objectors." The reason for organizing was that "when the next war comes along, and it will, Catholic conscientious objectors will have no standing with or recognition by the authorities unless they act now to build up in the public mind a recognition of the fact that Catholics MAY [the *Worker's* emphasis] be conscientious objectors and do not have to place themselves at the beck and call of whatever group of politicians that happens to have control of affairs at the time. Conscience is still more important to Catholics than a misguided loyalty to specious ideals."

The organization was announced four months later as the Pax group. Callahan, Joe Zarella, and the others promised that "we shall make no concessions to public demand." The principles upon which they stood were that there could be no justifiable war in modern times; that a person had the right to judge for himself the morality of war; and that he need not accept the judgment of the state. Their program was one of "refusing unqualifiedly to bear arms or otherwise assist in the carrying on of a war." They would support "good neutrality legislation" and also "a strong international body to settle . . . disputes between nations." They would engage in a "vigorous defense of civil rights," and they would expose "the acts of munition makers, warmongers, and military supporters. . . ." Above all, they would "by prayer, and through word and example" follow "a technique of love for the technique of class war as now practiced by left groups and the defenders of the status quo. . . ."

The weakness of the Pax position (and that of *The Catholic Worker*) was in the argument that it used to justify its position. For a Catholic, the completely acceptable position on which to base one's pacifism was that the war in question was not "just." Like a lot of other people in the world, Workers took the position that what was happening in Europe in the thirties was just a rerun of the bad business of 1914–1918. In 1934, the *Worker* quoted retired Marine Corps General Smedley D. Butler as saying that wars were a "racket," and if their profits were taken away they could cease. Also quoted was the Paulist orator and columnist, James Gillis: "Wars nowadays are to protect bankers' investments in foreign lands." Citing a 1935 book on agrobiology called *Nations Can Live at Home* by O. W. Willcox, it said that the United States might well abandon the doctrine of neutral rights at sea since "we would still have a surplus of food and material goods with which to help feed nations which had been made gaunt by war." In January, 1938, the *Worker* reacted to the Japanese sinking of the United States gunboat *Panay* and three Standard Oil tankers in the Yangtze River by exclaiming, "Here We Go Again!" It asked if American taxpayers were obligated to protect Standard Oil's "private little navy" and its "miserable coolie labor."

The *Worker* refrain that wars were the work of the big capitalists was one frequently heard in the thirties, stated and restated by America Firsters, Coughlinites, Bundists, and a considerable company of educated Americans who, like the *Worker*, believed that this argument was a completely sound one on which to base opposition to another war. In taking the position that the brewing war was a conspiracy of high finance, the *Worker* was joined by a notable member of the American hierarchy who added to it the proposition that it was also of Communist inspiration, with a further admixture of New Deal intrigue. In April, 1938, the *Worker* carried a letter by Archbishop John T. McNicholas of Cincinnati which was read in all the churches of his diocese. In a bold front-page declaration, the *Worker* proclaimed that the "Archbishop Urges League of C.O.s." It quoted McNicholas' letter at length: "Our 'war-makers' are . . . the materialistic capitalists and industrialists who wish to stuff their own pockets, the Communists and other deluded visionaries who would welcome war as a means of overthrowing the present set-up and the short-sighted politicians who wish to advance the ends of their own present system. . . ."

When the war did break out, the *Worker* continued to insist that it was a repetition of 1914. It gave its position in a front-page statement: "We Are to Blame for New War in Europe."

We can confidently expect more and more propaganda designed to inflame the passions of the American people. Our newsreels and papers have started some time ago. In advance, the minds of the people have been formed to the belief that Hitler is responsible for it, that he is an enemy of the world, that, somehow, he is personally responsible. . . .

*The Catholic Worker* views the present conflict as an unjust war. We believe that Hitler is no more personally responsible than is Chamberlain or Daladier or any other leader. The blame rests on the peoples of the entire world, for their materialism, their greed, their idolatrous nationalism, for their refusal to believe in a just peace, for their ruthless subjection of a noble country. Capitalism's betrayal came more quickly in Germany because of the Versailles Treaty, and Nazism flowered as a logical result.

. . . Hitler is incidental; the war must have come sooner or later under the circumstances. . . .

Let us not be smug. The responsibility for the war is no

less fixed on the United States than on the warring countries. Let us realize that we are responsible as much as
Hitler.

With the assurance of hindsight, it is easy enough to say
that this desperate backward looking that Dorothy Day and
many others engaged in ignored the fact that the disease
was already epidemic and that a lament over the circumstances of its inception helped nothing. Recognizing the obvious, the well-disposed of the world should then have fore-
gone the breast-beating and taken what strong action they
could to limit the war and, especially, to save the Jews.

Whatever the fault of Dorothy Day in this matter, it was
not a fault of spirit but of a bad reading of history. And here
she could scarcely be blamed for echoing the positions of
those whose profession was history and who, with much
conviction and a spectacular array of factual evidence, had
concluded that if another world war came it would be because the "lessons" of the first one had been forgotten.

The pacifist-neutralist position of the *Worker* was not
without a partisan spirit, especially in the early months of
the war. In that period, as the French kept guard behind
the great concrete-domed turrets of the Maginot Line, the
*Worker* continued to insinuate that the British, as usual,
were up to something. In October it addressed an appeal to
the workingman—"you whose sweat and labor is the life-
blood of our country, you whose blood must flow if the United
States engages in another imperialist war, you whose fellow
workers are now dying for capitalist gain and imperialist
ambition in Europe. . . ." Refuse, it urged him, to manufacture or transport any articles of war, no matter to whom
they were consigned.

In November, Bill Callahan, in his "Gadfly" column, said
that the United States was already in the war and that it
ought to be honest and admit that it was fighting for British
imperialism and American profiteering. "Mighty mother England has again cajoled her sometimes wayward children

into defending the old homestead on which the sun never sets, and international financiers gleefully watch the crucible in which blood will turn to gold."

The war-involved issue that concerned the *Worker* more than anything else at this time was the draft. It loomed when the war began, and after the fall of France it took on considerable urgency. The *Worker*, of course, opposed it and supported its position by enlisting the opinions of the Right Reverend G. Barry O'Toole of the philosophy department of Catholic University in Washington, D.C. O'Toole called conscription one of the disastrous brood of evils spawned by the French Revolution. It was all right when used to support an offensive war that was just, but if a potential draftee was not certain about this, he should become a conscientious objector. Otherwise, he would be committing a mortal sin.

In June, 1940, Monsignor O'Toole, Dorothy Day, and Joe Zarella went to Washington to register their opposition to the Burke-Wadsworth Compulsory Military Training Law before the Senate Military Affairs Committee. Dorothy Day spoke to the committee of the Catholic Worker movement and of its opposition to conscription—"because we believe that Christianity is the only practical solution to the world's problems, a solution which has not been practiced, we are committed to this stand. . . . And because we believe that the counsels of Christ must be kept alive in the world, voices must still be raised in spite of the inevitable, immediate failure to accomplish our purpose; because we are thinking of the future, of life for the coming generations of men, we must continue to protest."

In opposing conscription, the *Worker* presumed the support of one of its old friends and apparently presumed too much. Writing to Dorothy Day in April, 1941, John A. Ryan declared that he had been incorrectly interpreted when the *Worker* referred to some parts of his book, *Modern War and Basic Ethics*, as representing an opposition to conscription. He was not talking about conscription but about excessive

armaments, he said. Shortly after this he felt again that he
had been presumed upon by the *Worker*. It had not printed
a correction to the statement made by a contributor who
had referred to Ryan as saying that modern war was irra-
tional and therefore sinful, and that Catholics ought not to
take part in it. "I do not hold, nor have I ever held or expressed such doctrine," said Ryan.

Where Catholics were concerned, the fundamental question involved in the draft issue was finally that of their own
conscience. "How many Catholics know what the teaching
of the Church is in regard to peace?" the *Worker* asked as
the war descended on Europe. Most Catholics probably
thought that the question was pointless. The ancient arms-
bearing traditions of European states had become so invested with approving sacerdotal rites that war and the instruments of war appeared to have a divine stamp. When
the state gave the call to arms, Catholics, as much as anyone, gave themselves in complete peace of mind to that
pious and comforting thought that they might save their
souls by killing their brother in Christ provided he was on
the other side of some mythical line. If anything, American
Catholics, wanting desperately to be thought of as patriotic,
gave themselves even more extravagantly to this mood.

*The Catholic Worker*'s answer to this tradition was to say
that no matter how many priests had blessed tanks and bat-
tleships, the true mind of the Church was peace, and it provided many references to the statements of Church Fathers
and of Pius XII to document this point. Further, it supported its position by featuring the writings of priests like
Barry O'Toole and John J. Hugo. Hugo was a young Pittsburgh cleric who would have a long association with Dorothy Day and *The Catholic Worker*. He was a theologian
with a clear, original mind, and much of his writing in the
*Worker* had to do with the use of what he called "weapons
of spirit" in what he, like Workers, thought of as the real
war against history's movement toward a spiritless objectivization and violence. Among his first writings in the *Worker*,
appearing in 1941 shortly after he met Dorothy Day, were

Fr. John Hugo, at Maryfarm, early 1940s.

treatments of the primacy of conscience in the face of the call to war by the state.

Yet most of the Church establishment stood against the pacifists within its ranks. One *Worker* reader thought that Catholic C.O.s would probably suffer for their pacifist convictions, but the real test would come from "our rationalizing theologians" who "will probably be more hard on us than the military authorities."

Catholic Workers tried to give form to their antiwar position through an organization. "We urge . . . the formation of a 'mighty league of conscientious objectors,'" the *Worker* declared in the opening days of the war. "We must prepare now for the struggle to come." But there were few with whom to start such a league. The Pax group had had its ups and downs. In 1940, Callahan left the Worker house, and with the draft law imminent, there was an obvious need for a reorganization of those who held pacifist views. The new group gave itself the self-explanatory title of the Association of Catholic Conscientious Objectors.

The Selective Service Act became law in October, 1940, immediately creating the problem of what to do with those who had declared themselves Catholic conscientious objectors. The resolution of this matter was given to the National Service Board for Religious Objectors, an agency that had been formed by the Brethren, Friends, and Mennonites to take care of their own C.O.s. When the draft law was enacted, Selective Service officials met with the National Service Board and worked out a system of Civilian Public Service camps, organized as counterparts to the old Civilian Conservation Corps camps. The government paid nothing toward their operation, an obligation that fell on the National Service Board.

It was, then, with the National Service Board that the new group of Catholic C.O.s planned its future. Arthur Sheehan had taken on the job of directing the new group, and it was his idea that the Catholic C.O.s should have their own camp which would operate under the supervision of the National Service Board. His request was met, and the Catholic C.O.s were given a forestry camp at Stoddard, New Hampshire, that would accommodate forty-five men. In June, 1941, three objectors began their residence at Civilian Service Camp No. 15, and on August 15 the camp opened with sixteen men. It continued to grow and on March 5, 1942, some of the men of the Stoddard Camp were sent to another operation at the Alexian Brothers hospital in Chicago. In the fall of 1942, the Stoddard camp was closed and the men were moved to a larger forestry camp at Warner, New Hampshire. By March, 1943, Warner had sixty-three C.O.s, forty-seven of whom were Catholic.

But the Warner camp did not survive long. Within two months of the time it was opened, Selective Service officials began to look critically at its operation, the reason for which is obvious in Sheehan's explanation of what went on at the camp. There was an "encouragement of personalism at the expense of military precision, of neatness, and, at times, of property. . . ." Thereafter, Catholic C.O.s served at Friends' camps and subsequently at the Rosewood Training School for retarded children at Owings Mills, Maryland.

As the *Worker* began to stiffen its resistance to the war mood, the priest upon whom Dorothy Day increasingly relied for spiritual direction, Father John Hugo, sent her a note: "No doubt [pacifism] is all clear to you; but then you have not tried to work it out doctrinally. If you knew no theology, it would probably be simpler to make a solution. Yet the decision must be based on doctrine. Pacifism must proceed from truth, or it cannot exist at all. And of course this attack on conscription is the most extreme form of pacifism."

Whatever the fault Hugo detected in Dorothy Day's pacifism, she had, through 1939, used history-based arguments to justify Worker pacifism. By 1940, it became clear to her that those arguments from history had little direct meaning for the European situation. Nazi Germany was not the Weimar Republic, and to continue to base her pacifism on the points made by the revisionist historians on the causes of World War I was obviously not a position that would sustain her. Hugo was right; her pacifism must proceed from truth, and if the lessons drawn from an observation of recent history were false, then good riddance.

There was that truth of spirit that should shape history, and it was to this point that she moved as the root of certainty for her convictions. It was the personalist response to the ultimate problem of objectivization—that the object world when loosed from spirit had no end to its action but violence. Her position was that nothing—neither political forms, economic forms, nor even that final mysterious fusion of spirit and matter that was life—was equal to that act of love that looked only to God's love as its example. And such love, being so contrary to those drives that would compel man to become "king of the earth," as Berdyaev had said, was hard and bore with it the promise of suffering. It could not be otherwise, for a love that sought to transcend the world of form and time and ignore its requirements could only produce discordancies in the time-form state that would mean hardship and even tragedy. But for those "fools" who had an intimation of the reality of love, there could be no choice but to reach out to it. To go with the mood of the object world was to move in the time-form stream where spirit was lost and the end was nothingness. How infinitely better to go the straight way of bringing heaven on earth than to follow those illusions and empty promises of the object world.

Few understood. The world is real, they said. We must deal now with the situation so that the future can be better. Many thought that Dorothy Day had gone far afield. "I have always felt that your work of feeding the poor and harboring the harborless was really the work of Christ. . . . Now, however, you seem to have entered another field of action," wrote a reader. Another declared that while she was "in sympathy with the general outlines of your social reforms," she was nonetheless convinced that "the pacifism you preach is *false, unpatriotic* and *dangerous.*" Before she would make another contribution to the movement, would Dorothy Day assure her that "*not one cent* of what I send

you will be spent for pacifistic propaganda?" Dorothy Day
would so assure her. A notation on the margin of the letter
read: "Yes, we'll buy beans for soup."

A reader in England made a point that would be made
many times against Worker pacifism. "If you have still the
space in America to discuss whether a christian can fight or
not it is primarily because . . . the Atlantic is wide and because the people of Britain and her allies are prepared to
risk their own mortal and immortal safety for the sake of
their fellows, the men and women Nazism tortured and betrayed."

The issue caused dissension in the houses. In June, 1940,
Dorothy Day sent a letter to all of them concerning the
issue of pacifism. "We know that there are those who are
members of "Catholic Worker' groups throughout the country who do not stand with us in this issue. We have not
been able to change their views through what we have written in the paper, or by letters, or by personal conversation.
They wish still to be associated with us, to perform the cor-
poral works of mercy." And that, she said, was all right. But
there had been other cases when some associated with the
movement had taken it on themselves to suppress the paper.
In such instances she felt it would be necessary for those
persons to disassociate themselves from the movement. The
disassociation statement was directed at the St. Francis
House in Seattle, for as that house's correspondent explained
some time later, "the New York 'Catholic Worker' was not
distributed at the House—simply because it was filled almost entirely with 'pacifism' and tended to arouse the 'pacifists' to new outbursts that were far from pacific." Instead,
the Seattle group distributed the Cogley-edited *Chicago
Catholic Worker*.

Father H. A. Reinhold of the Seattle house wrote to Dorothy Day to protest her letter. "I do not approve of this at
all and I think that others should be heard, and your letter
should have shown if a majority, or at least a leading minority, stand behind you." He was aware that she and Peter
Maurin were the founders of the movement, "but I wonder

if you can take the name of the whole movement, which stands for far more things than conscription, and tag it on this one issue, throwing out all these who do not agree with you." He did not think that she wanted to "adopt dictator's methods, lay down party lines, purge dissenters," but "the practical result is a purge."

From Louisiana the young priest Jerome Drolet, who had supported the activities of the National Maritime Union there and who had had an association with the Worker house at Houma, was distressed. "I've been wanting to write you this for days now . . . and urge you with all my heart to change your stand if you can—otherwise whether you wish to or not, you will find yourself in the awful company of Father Coughlin's *Social Justice,* and the anti-semitic party-line followers." The war was "a question of taking every legitimate means to preserve our civilization—or what's left of it—so it will not be set back a couple of centuries by the rule of the pagan brute force—by the Nazi Iron Heel."

With all of the debate and rising tension over the war, life at Mott Street went its ordinary way, seemingly reluctant to become involved. It was in the Lenten season of 1940 that the Workers there decided to do something out of the ordinary for the men who came daily for food. They would give them a religious retreat. Much preparation went into the affair—a reception room was set up, a lounge room, and a coffee room. In the front building, the glass storefront was enclosed with white sheeting which formed the background for an altar made from a wooden sideboard covered with purple-dyed lace curtains and a white tablecloth.

The retreat went on for two days, Holy Thursday and Good Friday, and over a hundred men participated. At the end of the first day some of the Workers wondered if the men had come for spiritual nourishment or for the sandwiches that some of the young men made. The next day, however, their questions were removed. The men went through the Good Friday fast with such attention and devotion that Dorothy Day was convinced that not even in St. Patrick's Cathedral "was there a congregation which entered more earnestly into the passion of Him who gave His life that all might live."

Eight months later the war brushed on the group at Mott Street. In January, 1941, Joe Zarella and Jerry Griffin received their questionnaires from the draft board. By April, four of the young men at the house were taking their physicals and two were already in camp. May came and Workers again went out on the streets to sell *The Catholic Worker*. This began the ninth year of the movement.

In October, the Workers opened a women's house, a rear building at 104 Bayard Street. Julia Porcelli managed it. With this matter settled, Dorothy Day and Peter Maurin took a bus trip through the golden fall days to Newport, Rhode Island, for the wedding of Dorothy Schmitt and Bill Gauchat. Miss Schmitt was the young lady with the "warm and generous" heart who had helped Gauchat start the Cleveland house. Now, after a year at Ade Bethune's craft studio, she would return with Bill to the Worker farm at Avon, Ohio. Dorothy Day wrote of the trip as relaxing. The weather was beautiful and it had been a happy occasion.

---

# 11

# WAR

After Pearl Harbor, Catholic Worker pacifism was confronted with a test of a new dimension. For the United States, the Japanese action of December 7 brought everything into focus. Doubt and hesitation were dispelled; the debate was ended. The old noninterventionist arguments based on the ancient history of World War I no longer meant anything. The Japanese had acted with a perfidiousness that to all seemed to reveal the stamp of the devil as the chief mark of their national character, and it was this revelation of the devil in the visible form of a nation that represented an escape for the American people. Now community could be recaptured. The symbols of the community of nationhood were alive with a reborn meaning. Patriotism flamed anew. Sacrifices could be made and even life given for this community. Men were brought together again.

How would Dorothy Day and her friends react? While affirming the good of peace, would she not, many hoped, admit at last that the Japanese had acted with a treachery that affronted the most fundamental principles of international decency? Would she not now become a part of that unity so desperately required to turn back the threatened aggression? She might have done so, laying aside for the moment her "ideals," which, after all, could not function in the real world, and make the breakthrough to the higher reality of a recognition that the nation, with all of its imperfections, stood as man's only hope against inhuman forces. There would have been applause, more contributions to the movement, and people could have pointed to Dorothy Day as that saintly character who rose to new heights because when the chips were down she saw the light and rallied to the cause.

Thus it was probably with dismay that many read the headlines of the January, 1942, *Worker:* "We Continue Our Christian Pacifist Stand." Seventy-five thousand *Workers* went out every month, Dorothy Day wrote. What should they print? she asked. "We will print the words of Christ who is with us always . . . 'Love your enemies, do good to those who hate you, and pray for those who persecute and calumniate you. . . . We are at war . . . with Japan, Germany, and Italy. But still we can repeat Christ's words, each day, holding them close in our hearts, each month printing them in the paper. . . . We are still pacifists."

One reaction to this statement came from the Communist *Daily Worker.* "I just can't ever believe the mystic who says he 'loves his enemy,'" wrote Mike Gold. It was "the most difficult of all tenets in Christian theology and some of the noblest of human beings have spent unhappy lives trying to practice it. But who ever succeeded?" He was thinking of his "old friend, Dorothy Day," and her "earnest little paper." He recalled that she had always been an honest person, but in this instance he would be much more respectful of her pacifism if she had been a pacifist during the Spanish Civil War. She had been on Franco's side then and had not had a word of reproach for the Fascist massacres of whole cities. He concluded sadly that Dorothy Day had been more affected than she knew by the politics of the Fascists in the Catholic Church.

Gold's statement was absolutely false, as he should have known, but many Catholics had a reaction that was little different from his. A pastor wrote to tell of a "rather unfortunate thing" that had happened in his church that made it advisable for him to ask Dorothy Day to discontinue sending him *The Catholic Worker*. The problem was his assistant, who "very strenuously objected to the article on pacifism and conscientious objectors in your last edition saying it was against the teaching of Moral theologians and against the Archbishops and Bishops of the country who sent word to our president telling him they were in utter cooperation with him in the present crisis." The really difficult aspect of the matter was "that my assistant is a very close friend of our Bishop's secretary and if I would continue giving out the paper . . . it could easily be interpreted that I was against episcopal authority, so you can see my position in the matter."

Her critics said she was a sentimentalist and talked about the necessity of her giving up her pacifism in face of the transcendent obligation to fight for decent human values. She answered by saying that the Catholic Worker movement had been fighting for decent human values for ten years, a war which the majority of the middle class did not recognize and in respect to which *they* had been the pacifists. "They even pretend," she said, that there had been no need for a war against poverty and discrimination because such things did not exist. She had repeatedly been counseled to treat the national war in the same way they had treated the Worker's personalist war. She had been told not to write about it. One of her readers had urged her to "Keep silence with a bleeding heart." *He* was not a sentimentalist? she asked.

What of Pearl Harbor? There were Pearl Harbors continually occurring the world over. She recalled that it had only been weeks ago that in America a Black was shot and dragged by a mob through the streets behind a car. Still alive, he had been drenched with kerosene, set fire to, and then, when he had died, his body was left lying in the street until a city garbage truck had removed it. "What of the Negroes?" she asked. Were they supposed to "Remember Pearl Harbor and take to arms to avenge this cruel wrong?" No, the Blacks were supposed to be pacifists in the face of the aggressions committed against them.

But all in the Worker movement were not as convinced of the absolute nature of pacifism as was Dorothy Day. In Pittsburgh, Father Charles Owen Rice disassociated his Catholic Radical Alliance from the Worker movement over the peace issue. In Chicago, John Cogley, preparing to encamp in St. Louis in the Signal Corps, wrote Dorothy Day telling her that "The Catholic Worker is gone." At the New Haven house, a house member, told of feelings there that were running high because "many of our friends disagree with the stand which we have taken." In the May, 1942, *Worker*, Dorothy Day noted that she had been accused of splitting the Worker movement from top to bottom by "her" pacifism.

Some of the houses may have closed because of the issue of pacifism, but others closed because of a shortage of manpower. From South Bend, Julian Pleasants, head of the Worker house there, wrote to say that he doubted he could carry on. Not many people were coming to the house and he thought he would soon be drafted, anyway. It was the same elsewhere. By the end of 1942 sixteen houses, or one-half of them, had closed, and by the end of the war there were only ten left. With the press for manpower, the breadlines dwindled. At Mott Street there were changes and a slowing of tempo. The line that had once numbered over a thousand dwindled to several hundred.

It was the limbo-like state of things at Mott Street and the turmoil in the houses that prompted Dorothy Day to begin a long journey in April, 1942, that would take two months and carry her across the country to the West Coast and back. It was no time to travel, she knew, but if there was the work of the war, there was also her own work. The trip was exhausting, as her comments in the *Worker* on her traveling indicate. She wrote part of her column in the Albuquerque bus station "so weary that I could almost say with Odysseus: 'Than roaming naught else is more evil for mortals.'" She noted the crowds around her, soldiers, wives and children following them, workers and their families moving to new war industry centers. She quoted St. Teresa's remark that " 'Life is but a night spent in an uncomfortable inn.' " For the moment, her inn was the bus, with weary travelers sleeping on one another's shoulders. Only the Lord knew when she would be home, she said.

A month later she was writing from Seattle, preparing to return home by way of Butte and Minneapolis. This was the time of the great Japanese offensive aimed at Midway and the Aleutians, and she found Seattle full of rumors—that Japanese aircraft carriers were on their way to the Pacific coast and that invasion was imminent. She dismissed the rumors. Otherwise, she observed, few seemed to realize that a war was in progress "except as a gigantic adventure and a great prosperity suddenly descending upon us. There is more money than anyone has seen for a long time and people are stocking up. . . . There are evidences of boondoggling on a large scale, at big salaries, and when I think of the men on WPA accused of leaning on their shovels (in the face of the tremendous public works they accomplished) and at the miserable salaries the public complained of I could weep."

She wrote a part of her column in Seattle, sitting on top of a hill in a garden outside of a church where she was sharing a day of spiritual reflection with friends. Down in one valley she could see the Boeing aircraft plant and in another the homes of the workers. Continuing her description of the scene, she innocently gave an account of the military installations around her: "In the field on the other side of the church within 100 feet of me as I write . . . a huge monster of a barrage balloon shaped like a fish, is tethered to the ground, and around it are tents and huts for soldiers." On the other side of the church was "a lovely little monastery garden" where there had been set up "a machine gun nest and an antiaircraft nest . . . all camouflaged, surrounded with sandbags, and covered with branches." This made her think of Spain and how the priests had been accused of setting up machine guns in the turrets of their bell towers. Then across the bay, over Bremerton, she described the air as filled with barrage balloons, "all tethered in the fields

looking like . . . grotesque idols, deities of the state, served
by a uniformed priesthood who put their trust in all these
works of their hands, to save them from the wrath of the
Lord." She thought of a line in Scripture: "His eyes look
searchingly upon the nations."

In an article on the West Coast Japanese, she said that
she had seen something of the atmosphere of the concentration camp there, where the Japanese-Americans were being
held before their resettlement in inland areas. She stated
her abhorrence of the relocation policy, declaring that it
was an injustice she was bound to protest, otherwise she
would be failing in the works of mercy.

Later, when she was back at Mott Street, she got a letter
from the U.S. Office of Censorship whose contents were predictable. Her story on the location of antiaircraft batteries
violated the principle of voluntary censorship that had been
established for the war. The office also objected to the story
on the Japanese, feeling possibly that Dorothy Day's insistence on invoking the works of mercy in the face of the exigencies of war was being obtuse.

From time to time FBI men visited Mott Street, checking
on those who had declared themselves Catholic C.O.s. They
were polite, but Dorothy Day thought they were lacking in
sensitivity to the Gospel position on the question of war,
one agent even professing a lack of familiarity with the Sermon on the Mount.

One day, though, they came with serious purpose. Sometime in the fall of 1942, two agents appeared looking for
David Mason. Mason, who had been a proofreader for one
of the Philadelphia papers, had worked at the Philadelphia
Worker house. Upon coming to Mott Street he did everything: attended to the mail, shopped, distributed clothing,
cooked, and did much of the work of getting out the paper.
When the agents asked where Mason was, someone directed
them upstairs, and there they found him preparing supper.
He was taken to the West Street Federal Detention Center,
there to be charged with having refused to register for the

draft. Mason was within the draft age by only a few months so he was held only a week.

These were the few instances where the federal government intruded into the life of the Catholic Worker during the war. The state, which Dorothy Day and the Workers believed had become the focus of so many problems for modern man and the main agent by which he was being deprived of his freedom, scarcely told her nay when she opposed it in what was assumed to be a life-and-death struggle. The government probably did not take the Catholic Worker movement very seriously, but had it ever approached the point of being a real threat to the war effort, the authorities might have dealt with it more vigorously. As it was, the Worker movement could be pointed to as an example of the benign way in which dissent could be accepted, even in wartime. After a sign so clear and striking as Pearl Harbor, there were, after all, very few who doubted that the war was right. The very few who believed otherwise could be tolerated.

The war claimed one of the Workers early in 1942. The body of James McGovern, a merchantman, was found off the coast of Panama. His ship had been torpedoed, and adrift at sea, he and his shipmates had died of thirst. McGovern was a graduate of Marquette University, but his attitude toward religion had been one of near indifference until he heard Monsignor Fulton J. Sheen preach an Easter Sunday sermon at St. Patrick's Cathedral. Sheen had spoken of author Paul Claudel and had so aroused McGovern's interest that he read Claudel and from him found new sources for belief.

McGovern and Frank O'Donnell were the first business managers for the *Worker*. Both had a taste for roaming around New York and liked to go to out-of-the-way taverns and cafés to distribute *Workers*. During the Christmas holiday of 1934, McGovern fell in love with a girl visiting the Worker house, and his proposal, soon offered, was accepted. "I can remember his wedding day," Dorothy Day wrote, "when he came over to Charles Street . . . to clutch my hand and stammer happily, 'I hold you responsible for this, so you've got to pray for me.' "

In the *Worker* of January, 1943, Dorothy Day wrote a summation of her activities for the previous year, observing that much of 1942 had been spent in traveling—five months all told. Yet even as 1943 began, she announced that she was away again to take her ailing mother to Miami and to visit friends of the Workers in Southern states. In the meanwhile, affairs at Mott Street had been going well. Nina Polcyn of the Milwaukee house and Justine L'Esperance of the Detroit group had helped at Mott Street during the summer of 1942. Maurin had spent that summer teaching at Bill and Dorothy Gauchat's farm at Avon, but he was now at Mott Street. Dave Mason was at work again after his week's sabbatical at the Federal Detention Center, and there was also Smokey Joe who did his share, although he strongly disagreed with the pacifism that surrounded him, calling the movement the "Catholic Shirker."

Dorothy Day stayed in Miami briefly, then by bus headed in balmy weather across the Everglades up to Sarasota and Tampa. After a brief meeting with friends in Tampa, she boarded the bus for an eight-hour night ride north to Tallahassee. It was a painful trip. The weather had turned very cold and the bus was jammed. She got to Tallahassee at five in the morning, stiff and chilled to the bone. The station was a compaction of the misery that many times went with bus travel during the war. Even at that hour of the morning it was so crowded that every bit of floor space was taken by people sitting on their suitcases. A roaring stove kept the atmosphere stifling, but, when the doors to the room were opened, blasts of cold air swept through. Everyone there was in a stupor of fatigue, Dorothy Day wrote.

That afternoon she was in Columbus, Georgia, from which point she went over the state line into the rural regions of Alabama to see the work that was being carried on by some members of a religious order, the Missionary Servants of the Most Holy Trinity. In that socially desolated

area of plantations and Black poverty, she found that the
priest whom she was visiting had his chapel in an old Black's
cabin and that the bed upon which he slept was a slab of
wood.

She had known well the poverty of the city, but there in
the pine woods of Alabama it was made more hideous, sustained as it was by those time-hallowed mythic formations
relating to race that leechlike would suck every humanizing
potential from the Black man's life to lay them as tribute at
the feet of his White overlords. The first family she visited
numbered twenty-two people, all in two rooms, although
most of the families had ten or twelve in them, but always
in two rooms. Frequently she saw little children scarred
with burns they had gotten from falling into fireplaces. She
traveled over one plantation of five thousand acres where
sixty Black families lived and whose houses were the worst
of all. The houses sagged, the porches were rotten, and the
cracks in the roof were large enough to see the sky through
them.

In one house lived an old woman named Neecy. She was
alone and had rheumatism so bad she could scarcely move.
There was no food in the house but everything was clean
and in place, and Neecy proudly showed her the "kivvers"
on her bed. Down the road lived Bee with nine children
and no man to support her. She made fifty cents a day but
was docked five cents every time she took time off to nurse
her baby.

Dorothy Day noted that race feeling was running high in
the area and that she would probably get her share of the
blame for it by publishing the article she was writing. Local
residents were also blaming Northerners and the Army, encamped across the river at Fort Benning, for giving Blacks
higher pay and "taking him out of his place." She must have
wondered what "his place" had availed him. On that trip
she had heard of a White man who had killed seven Blacks
for such things as not getting out of his way on the road and
behaving insolently. One was killed for marrying a mulatto
of whom he was enamored. One of the brothers in the reli-

gious order that worked there told her of a young, grotesquely crippled Black man he had seen. This pitiable person had offended a White man at the age of twelve and had been seized and his arms and legs broken as a consequence.

"Are not these sins crying to heaven for vengeance?" she asked. "And how can we do anything but howl over these sins in which we share? They are our sins. Just as we believe in the communion of the saints—that we share in the merits of the saints, so we must believe that we share in the guilt of such cruelty and injustice. . . . Oh, the suffering, the poverty of these poor of Christ, and the indifference of Christians."

She had begun her trip by saying that "God willing," she would be back in February and she was. Affairs at Mott Street had settled into a subdued temper. The city had condemned the Bayard Street house for women, so, since the number of guests was declining, the women were moved to the top floor at Mott Street and all were under one roof again. By now the war had claimed most of the young men. Lou Murphy and Joe Zarella had recently left for duty with the American Field Service, and the rest were in the service or C.O. camps.

Some years later Dorothy Day would refer to some visitors she had had in the fall of 1943. A party of several young men in uniform came to Mott Street wanting to talk with her about her work and ideas. The house that night provided a poor atmosphere for discussion, so they went to an all-night restaurant on Canal Street and talked until the early hours of the morning. Two of the young men were Kennedys, Joseph and John. She recalled that the talk was of war and peace and man and the state.

Even though the Mott Street operations were slowed down during this period, The Catholic Worker showed strength. Because of its pacifism it had lost over a hundred thousand in circulation, but this was due, it was explained, to bundle cancellation. Individual subscribers were again on the increase by 1943. J. F. Powers, still to make a name as a writer, sent in accounts of the prison life he experienced after having been jailed for noncompliance with the draft law. His "A Night in the County Jail" in the May, 1943, issue of the *Worker* was reminiscent of the earlier "Ben Joe Labray" stories.

Robert Ludlow, a penetrating and controversial writer for the *Worker* in the decade of the fifties, began to send in contributions during this period. In the war years he served as a C.O. among the retarded children at the Rosewood Training School at Owings Mills, Maryland. Saving his weekend leaves, he would monthly go to Mott Street for a four-day visit to help with the work there. Gordon Zahn, also at Rosewood, wrote of the work of the C.O.s there. In the spring of 1944, when the government released information about Japanese atrocities, he wrote a pacifist's response to these revelations, making the point that such things were the nearly inevitable consequences of the calculated organization of hate that war was, and that the Americans were as subject to brutalization as were the Japanese. In 1944, such commonplaces were uncommon.

Arthur Sheehan's role in getting out the paper in this period was evidence in his "Interviews with Peter Maurin," a feature that ran through several months' issues. A Maurin touch was given to the paper by the use of a double page headed "Cult, Culture, and Cultivation" under which was placed those essays that dealt with any one of what Maurin regarded as the three necessary aspects of an integrated life. Ade Bethune contributed much to this feature, discussing arts and crafts in a Maurin reference.

The paper was filled with letters and reports in these years from those young men in C.O. camps and those others in the service scattered across the earth. Most scarcely mentioned the war, only their longing to be back at the Worker house. The C.O.s wrote accounts of their work and of their dismay at the increasing fury of the war, as mass bombing raids became increasingly a feature of the news. When one C.O. was asked what he would do about Pearl Harbor, he wrote his answer in a statement to the *Worker:* "Forget Pearl Harbor." Beyond that he would recommend that the

United States repeal all discrimination against Orientals in its immigration policy; remove all trade barriers with Japan; relinquish all claims to special possessions and police power in the Orient; and then apologize to the Japanese for all the military action that had been taken against them.

The enormity of the tragedy of the Jews weighted the minds of Workers in these days. Father Clarence Duffy, a priest who lived at the Worker house, wrote on the subject for the *Worker*, and another priest who was becoming a leading figure as a scholarly advocate of Jewish-Christian reconciliation, John Oesterreicher, also contributed. In the May, 1943, issue the *Worker* featured a talk made by Jessie Hugham, secretary of the War Resisters League, in which the point was made that if the war continued to be pressed unconditionally "we shall be signing the death sentence of the remnant of the Jews still alive. If, on the contrary, we demand the release of all Jews from the ghettos of occupied Europe and work for a peace without victory . . . there is a chance of saving the Jews."

A month later Dorothy Day reported an experience she had had relating to the Jews. She told of a meeting at which she had recently spoken where a member of the audience got up to say that the Jews needed no defending and that she did not believe the stories of atrocities. She gave a harangue on the subject, and, when finally she concluded, she was applauded by a considerable number there. Dorothy Day said that she was stunned by the response and then cited an article by Jacques Maritain that had appeared in the June 4 issue of *Commonweal* which gave a documented survey of instances where Jews had been subjected to wholesale slaughter. She wondered why there had not been more haste by governments in implementing the recommendations of the Bermuda Refugee Conference, which had been held in April. There it had been advocated that as many Jews as possible be speedily resettled in friendly areas, especially in an area that could become a homeland of their own.

Peter Maurin, as always, was concerned, and even in

those desperate years of the war, he wrote of the Jews with
hope. They were an "imperishable people . . . protected by
God" and "preserved as the apple of His eyes." He added:

The very abjection of this
race
is a divine sign,
the very manifest sign
of the permanence of the
    Holy Spirit
over men so despised
who are to appear
in the glory of the Consoler
at the end of time.

With war's separations and suffering, the *Worker* spoke
more of spirit and the Church in these years. John Hugo's
long (difficult, too, some readers thought) articles filled page
after page of the paper. "We Do Not War According to the
Flesh," a long article in the December, 1942, issue, dealt
with the subject that Dorothy Day liked to talk about, "the
weapons of the spirit." In May, 1943, he began his long development of a theological framework for his "Catholics Can
be Conscientious Objectors," and then in November, 1944,
the paper carried ten full pages of his "The Immorality of
Conscription."

Such weighty fare turned many readers aside, but Dorothy Day was concerned that those Catholics who insisted
that every question be put to the test of close theological
analysis also be given reasons for the *Worker's* position. And
Father Hugo was a hard reasoner who, like Jonathan Ed-
wards, found theology sweet to his taste. When once in the
*Worker* he asked the rhetorical question why others in the
clergy had not reached conclusions similar to his own, he
answered by saying that they had not thought enough
about the subject.

Dorothy Day was sustained in her pacifism by relatively
few of the clergy, but in the person and pronouncements of
the pope she believed that she found evidence that the

*Worker's* position on war represented the true mind of the Church. Papal calls for peace at Christmas and Easter were written up in detail by Father John A. O'Brien, and in many cases were commented on by Dorothy Day in editorials and in her column. She was especially approving of the Easter message of Pius XII in 1942, and she wondered why the diocesan papers had been so indifferent to it. Once in an editorial she referred to the pope as "Our Dear Sweet Christ on Earth," saying that it was by such tender words that St. Catherine of Siena addressed the Holy Father in her time and that it was in such words Catholics should think of him now.

The heightened spiritual emphasis found in *The Catholic Worker* during the war years was ultimately a reflection of what was occurring in Dorothy Day's own spiritual life. And what was occurring there in that period was surely the critical juncture in the history of the Catholic Worker movement. She had made her life into a spiritual quest. Peter Maurin, the teacher, had shown her a way and she believed him. But she also believed that in the pursuit of spirit there was no standing still. The way required constant effort, reflection, and prayer.

The war almost seemed to suggest a redirection to her life. Worker houses had closed; the line at Mott Street had shrunk to one-tenth the size it had been in the Depression days. Peter Maurin was getting old, and the fire had left him. The old days had passed of talking through the night at Union Square, when the atmosphere was charged with the freshness of a new idea and the sense of community was strong. Might she not, then, move toward a quieter and more contemplative life? In the war years it was this question that represented the interior history of the Catholic Worker movement.

# 12

# THE RETREATS

Unlike much of the world, the war years for Dorothy Day were a time of arming herself with those weapons of the spirit that she wrote about. It was in this period that the Catholic Worker retreats were held and which, curiously, brought her joy at a time when so many in the world suffered the cruelty of madness and war. "Those were beautiful days," she wrote in *The Long Loneliness*. "It was as though we were listening to the gospel for the first time. We saw all things new. There was a freshness about everything as though we were in love, as indeed we were."

From time to time since then she has referred to the experience, stating in 1963 that she wished, before she died, to write one more book that would be about a spiritual adventure, the retreats that "influenced my life and gave me the courage to persevere, and so filled my heart with joy that 'this joy no man can take from me.'" Again, in her Journal she referred to the role of the retreat in sustaining her through times of tribulation. They had opened for her, she said, a new vision of human and divine love which, had it not been for them, "I would never have a glimpse of this mystery, an understanding of it. I could never have endured the sufferings involved, could never have persevered." In *The Catholic Worker* she wrote of them as "a foretaste of heaven."

In writing of the retreats in *The Long Loneliness*, she began by observing that her first retreat had occurred

shortly after the first issue of *The Catholic Worker* had
come out. But rather than giving her strength, the experience had been "a hard time." She left feeling that it had
been an ordeal.

Then in 1938 her friend Maisie Ward, wife of publisher
Frank Sheed, told her of an evangelical retreat given for
workingmen by a French-Canadian, Abbé Saey. Mrs. Sheed
planned to make this retreat, but Dorothy Day, not able to
understand French, decided against it. A little later she
heard of Abbé Saey again, this time from another friend, Sister Peter Claver of Baltimore. A Canadian Jesuit who had
been influenced by him, Father Onesimus Lacouture, had
given a retreat for priests in Baltimore which, said Sister
Peter Claver, had changed their lives entirely.

A year later Sister Peter Claver visited Mott Street and
brought with her a Josephite priest, Pacifique Roy. Father
Roy, stationed in Baltimore, knew Father Lacouture and
had attended his retreats. Father Roy's impact on Dorothy
Day was immediate. She relates in *The Long Loneliness:*

> We were sitting in the dining room having our morning
> coffee when Father Roy started to talk to us about the love
> of God and what it should mean in our lives. He began
> with the Sermon on the Mount, holding us spellbound, so
> glowing was his talk, so heartfelt. People came and went,
> we were called to the telephone again and again but still
> Father Roy went on talking to all who would listen. The
> men came in from the soup kettles in the kitchen which
> were being prepared for the soup line and stayed to listen,
> tables were set around us and the people came in and were
> fed and went out again, and still Father talked. . . . It was
> like the story in the Gospels, when the two apostles were
> talking on the way to Emmaus, grieving and fearful and
> lamenting over the death of their Leader; suddenly a fellow
> traveler came along and began to explain the Scriptures,
> going as far as the town with them and even going to an inn
> to break bread with them. They knew Him then in the break-
> ing of bread. They had said to each other, "Was not our
> heart burning within us, while he spoke in that way?"

So moved was Dorothy Day by Father Roy's preaching that she and some of the others at Mott Street took to going to Baltimore on weekends to hear his sermons. In his free time he would go to the Catholic Worker waterfront house in Baltimore and talk to them in the big front assembly room where his auditors listened amid the scattered forms of snoring guests. And Father Roy, she said, talked on, in his gently appealing way, of the one thing necessary—love.

But Father Roy was not satisfied with his talks, days of recollections, and little retreats that he gave the Workers. He informed Dorothy Day that the man best qualified to give a full retreat was Father John J. Hugo. It was he who had the best understanding of Father Lacouture's message and methods. So she immediately set out to find Father Hugo, a mission she accomplished in July, 1941, when on her return from her circle of visitations to the Midwestern houses, she stopped off at Cleveland for the five-day retreat then being given by Father Hugo. He consented to go to Maryfarm in August to give a retreat for the Workers. It was thus that Hugo became the master of the Catholic Worker retreats and also the *Worker*'s principal theological reference for its position on war and conscription.

Already, she had directed her own enthusiasm for the retreat to the Catholic Workers. In August, 1940, there had been a retreat at Maryfarm, to which she had sent out a call to the houses, reminding them that "Again and again Christ had to get away from the multitudes who were thronging about Him to be healed, to be fed, and to hear His words" and that they now were invited to follow Christ's example. Seventy-five came, and when the retreat ended, she concluded that it had been decidedly worthwhile. Until then Worker gatherings had been pretty much discussion sessions and when they were over everyone seemed glad to get away from each other. But after the retreat she felt such a new sense of unity among all that there was no need for discussion. "When we separated, it was with pain, we hated to leave each other, we loved each other more truly than ever before, and felt that sense of comradeship, that sense of

Christian solidarity which will strengthen us for the work."

So a year later, in August, 1941, the first retreat was given by Father Hugo according to the principles established by Father Lacouture. The houses were notified on July 22. All Catholic Workers, she said, should come. There could be no valid excuses—"we have taken a wife . . . we have bought a farm . . . we have a new yoke of oxen"—would not do. "We must drop everything and spend one week listening to the Lord, who will speak only if we keep silence," she wrote.

From several viewpoints this retreat can be regarded as the high tide of the Worker movement. It was then that Worker houses were most numerous and Worker belief in a Church-centered social reformation strongest. One hundred and twenty-five persons were there, a figure that probably still stands as the largest get-together of Workers in the history of the movement.

The most characteristic feature of these Lacouture-inspired retreats was their rigor, and in this particular instance to the requirements of silence and fasting was added the additional penance of continual downpours of rain. Some of the young may have chafed at the austerity of the week-long retreat, but Dorothy Day found it good. "We were on a high hill," she wrote in the September *Worker*, "overlooking a flowing river, but down below we could see the smoke and grime of Easton and Phillipsburg. It is a constant reminder to us of our fellow workers, a reminder that God will say to us when we approach Him: 'Where are the others?' " She concluded: "God bless Father Lacouture and his fellow priests who have made such a retreat possible."

The practice of holding retreats went on for seven years. What had the retreats meant to Dorothy Day? She gave what she felt was the answer in the *Worker* of December, 1951. The retreats, she believed, had given her a new meaning for what Peter Maurin had taught. Maurin had emphasized man's worth and had made her understand that the realization of this worth was bound up with the social process. But not before had she had so clearly that transcendent sense of the worth of man's nature. She explained: "For too

long too little had been expected of us. . . . When we listened to Father Lacouture's retreat, we began to understand the distinction between nature and the supernatural
. . . and we saw for the first time the incomparable heights
to which man is called. We saw for the first time man's spiritual capacities raised as he is to be a child of God. We saw
the basis of our dignity."

It was not a matter of ignoring the world for "pie in the
sky." It was, to the contrary, giving the world its highest
due by living in it and using it as man should when he became aware of what God had planned for him and sought to
live in conformity with that plan. She had, she said, known
all of this before. She knew well the scriptural admonition
to "Seek ye first the Kingdom of God." She had known it,
but the retreats involved her knowing in a personal experience. It made clear for her the Worker mission and the position of her person in it. After one of the retreats she wrote:
"Living as we do in the midst of thousands . . . I am often
reminded of our quest:

'I will arise and go about the city: in the streets and
    broad ways
I will seek Him whom my soul loveth.
I sought Him and I found Him not . . . But, when
I had a little passed by them, I found Him whom my
soul loveth: I held Him and I will not let Him go.'

The retreat lifted her vision more fixedly on the supernatural and with a new strength it revivified for her the meaning of love. She wrote of Father Roy: "He made us know
what love meant, and what the inevitable suffering of love
meant. He taught us that when there were hatreds and rivalries among us, and bitterness and resentments, we were
undergoing purifications, prunings, in order to bear a
greater fruit of love."

The retreats seemed to have settled Dorothy Day more securely in some of her positions with respect to the Catholic
Worker movement. She had always subjected her motives to
a strict accounting of *why* she lived among the poor, pro-

vided them with food and clothing, and pleaded their cause. Was there not something a bit phony about it, this pandering to the weaknesses of others in order to build up one's own holiness? Father Louis Farina, an associate of Father Hugo's, had answered that question for her, she said. It was a matter of motive. If the charity of the Workers was through supernatural love—the love of God—then all natural motives, all vainglory, would be weeded out and only then would the object of the charity be truly influenced toward good. To an outside world it might seem that Workers, by striving toward an absolute charity, were actually contributing to the delinquency of those who became the object of their charity. To the contrary, thought Dorothy Day, they were trying to do for others something more than any charitable agency or common sense could achieve. They were trying to change people, and they recognized that they might have to pay for this change with their own suffering.

It was in the course of the retreats that she came to see Christ not primarily as a social reformer but as the exemplar of all-sufficient love. In the January, 1944, issue of the *Worker,* she pondered certain questions about Christ. "When St. John was put in prison by Herod, did our Lord protest? Did He form a defense committee? Did He collect funds, stir up public opinion? Did He try to get him out?" No, she said. He had done none of these things. His mission was not primarily concerned with the world and its forms but with the Kingdom of God.

In September, 1943, *Worker* readers were startled when they read in Dorothy Day's column that she planned to leave the movement for a year. She had come to that decision that summer in a retreat. She would continue to write for the paper, she said, but otherwise she would go someplace where she could read, think, and pray. She did not say it, but she wanted to be free of the obligation she had to the Catholic Worker movement so that she could face more squarely another one—the one she had to Tamar.

With Tamar with her, she began her retreat in September

at the Grail, a school of Catholic Action for girls, at Love-
land, Ohio. There she lived in "much silence, much prayer"
but it proved not to be the situation that was suitable for
both of them, and in October she and Tamar went to Farm-
ingdale, Long Island, where there was an agricultural
school that Tamar was interested in. Here, Tamar was en-
rolled and Dorothy Day took up an abode in an abandoned
orphanage adjacent to a Dominican convent. For six months
she lived in a room filled with sinks and stoves that had
been used for teaching home economics. She cooked her
own meals there and supported herself, as she had done at
other times in the past, by reviewing books and writing articles.

It was, she later concluded, a hard six months. Tamar was
so interested in her schoolwork that she did not see much of
her, although every afternoon Tamar and her roommate ran
over for a cup of coffee or chocolate. Once a week Dorothy
Day was able to visit her own mother who lived not too far
away. Every Friday afternoon she walked a mile to the village, took the train, got off a few stops along the line,
walked another mile, and then sat and sewed and chatted
with her mother.

Otherwise she tried to live in the spirit of the retreat she
had laid out for herself. She got up at 6:30 for an early Mass
and then went back to her room for breakfast. After breakfast it was back to the chapel for two hours of praying and
spiritual reading. It was difficult work. "Mostly I labored at
watering the garden of my soul with much toil," she wrote
in her Journal. Sometimes she prayed "with joy and delight," but other times "each bead of my rosary was heavy
as lead, my steps dragged, my lips were numb. I felt a dead
weight. I could do nothing but make an act of will and sit
or kneel, and sigh in an agony of boredom."

In the evenings she read and wrote her column for the
*Worker*. "Here in the country seven o'clock in the evening
seems very late. It is pitch black outside and there is not a
sound to be heard save the far-off whistle of a train, or perhaps some airplanes. . . . Some nights the wind is high and

the maples outside my window bend in the blast." She
thought of Catholic Workers scattered abroad, Joe Zarella
and Jerry Griffin in North Africa . . . "Jim O'Gara and Tom
Sullivan may be on the Gilbert Islands now . . . Arthur
Ronz in India . . . Jack English on a bomber (we have not
heard from him for months) . . . Ossie Bondy of the Wind-
sor House in England." She thought of the C.O.s., Dwight
and Jim Rogan, John Doebele, Ray Pierchalski, and the
many others. She prayed for them she said. That was one of
the reasons she had withdrawn from the work—"to have
time to gather and hold in my prayers all those members of
our family, all those dear to us."

She gave up her retreat in March. "I came to the conclusion," she wrote in her Journal, "that such a hermit's life for
a woman was impossible. Man is not meant to live alone.
. . . To cook for one's self, to eat by one's self, to sew, wash,
clean for one's self is a sterile joy. Community, whether of
the family, or convent, or boarding house, is absolutely necessary." Then, too, there was a matter developing that
would soon cause her to abandon her retreat. Tamar was
getting married. The man was David Hennessy. He had
been at Maryfarm since 1941. Dorothy Day described him
in the *Worker* as a "bibliophile, roofer and farmer." He was
interested in Eric Gill and communitarian ventures, and he
tried for a while to develop a business through a mail-order
circulation of books and pamphlets dealing with communitarian economics.

With all of the demands on her time and energy of the
Catholic Worker movement, Dorothy Day still reserved a
part of her life for her daughter. Tamar had been the gift
from heaven, the occasion of such joy that in gratitude she
had her baptized and had left off what hold she had had on
the elements of an easier existence—a man, home, and
friends—and herself had become a Catholic. When the
Worker movement began, Tamar was brought into that life
as naturally as the daughter of a house is brought into any
life followed by her parents. She had gone at first to a
public grade school, then when she was eleven she went to a

Catholic boarding school on Staten Island. On weekends she came home. In the summers of the Worker movement's first years, she had spent most of her time at the Staten Island garden commune, enjoying those things she liked most —walking, collecting, making things, and gardening. After the acquisition of Maryfarm, she spent a lot of her time there, and it must have been a place of contentment for her. There were always children visiting with whom she could play; there were the animals that she loved; and there were those older members of the community who made a pet of her—one irascible old man, "Mr. O'Connell," even built her a small house that she could live in and have as her own.

Dorothy Day, as a mother, always lovingly and gladly recognized the claim that Tamar had on her, although she was not a doting or oversolicitous mother. Nor did Tamar seem ever to want that sort of attention. To the contrary, she had her own independent approach to things which she began to show early. It was her pleasure to live close to the creative principle of nature, to build and to grow. By the time she reached high-school age, this trait was so set in her that the requirements of a traditional curriculum seemed pointless for her.

Tamar matured early. Her mother recounted that when she was fourteen she began to show an interest in the young men who came to the house. When she was fifteen she had a proposal—and then another one. When her mother returned from her long West Coast trip in the summer of 1942, she found Tamar in love again and this time she was determined to marry. But her mother would not consent and persuaded Tamar to live with Ade Bethune for a year as one of her apprentices in the household arts. She returned, still wanting to be married, but she was still too young her mother insisted. She should wait, at least until her seventeenth birthday. That date occurred on March 3, 1944, and her resolution to marry was still unshaken.

The wedding Mass occurred at eight o'clock in the morning, April 19, at the Easton church. It was a Worker wed-

ding. The party went to the church in a car lent by a friend
in Easton; John Filliger cooked the wedding breakfast; and
Peter Maurin made a talk. Tamar's first concern after the
wedding was to hurry home to feed her goats, since wild
dogs had killed the parent goats a few days previous.
"Home" for the couple would be some spot on the farm
where they might start to build a house and, in time, Dorothy Day hoped, make their way into the satisfaction of a life
that came from a marriage that would root and grow. Later,
she recalled with a pang how stark had been Tamar's wedding. "On her wedding eve she planted a rose bush. There
was neither mirror nor bath to prepare her for her wedding.
She bathed in a pail the night before, and never did see
how lovely she looked in her wedding dress. . . ."

So Tamar was married. Dorothy Day's second concern
was those young men in the war and at the C.O. centers. In
January, 1944, she got the news that Jack English had been
shot down over Romania and wounded. He had been in a
hospital and was now in a prison camp. A letter came from
Sergeant Arthur Ronz, formerly of the Sacramento house,
now in India. He had heard Dorothy Day was leaving the
Worker for a year. She should have stayed with the work,
he said. What would have happened to Christianity if
Christ had decided to take a year off? he asked. Tom Sullivan of the Chicago house wrote from the Pacific. "I often
think of you, Peter and the gang" while "perspiring on a
plane" or "lying on a cot at night staring at the top of the
tent." He had become friendly with "a very intelligent person" who knew of Dorothy Day and admired her, but who
"fears for you because you seem so sure of the faith." The
friend was also disturbed by the certainty of Raissa Maritain's faith, but he nonetheless read her because of the
"sheer beauty" of the ideas she expressed. His friend's spiritual convictions, Sullivan concluded, "aren't very comforting."

In April, Lou Murphy, in the American Field Service, was
home on furlough. One day he and Arthur Sheehan, taking
a walk on some Worker business, stopped for a soft drink at

a stand just off the Bowery. Sheehan related that "We laid down our folder with its bulge of letters on the stand. A rather seedy-looking man eyed it and said: 'I see you are an artist. I hope you are a good artist.'

'No,' we replied, 'we edit a paper.'

'So,' he said, 'I was an editor once myself in a kind of way.' He mentioned a famous magazine. . . . 'What is the name of your paper?'

'*The Catholic Worker*,' we replied.

He looked at us sharply . . . and said, 'My God, your editor, Dorothy Day, Eugene O'Neill, myself, and another used to drink beer together. . . .'" Then he walked off. It could have been Maxwell Bodenheim, one member of the Worker group later conjectured.

In August, Dorthy Day announced that she was back again as editor of the paper and was taking up again her duties as "mother" to the large Worker family. The retreat, as usual, was held in September and with it came an announcement of a change. Maryfarm would become a center of work and prayer. Every month or two a work course would be offered which would begin with a six-day retreat, during which time there would be silence, prayer, and work. There would be conferences for men in tree planting and grafting, agriculture, animal husbandry, and carpentry; for women, in baking, canning, cooking, homemaking, carding, washing and spinning, and knitting and weaving wool. These retreat-work sessions would be organized by Jane O'Donnell from the Grail, whom Dorothy Day described as "beautiful" and "always undefeated in her opinion." The purpose of the new venture was to try to build a training center for Catholic Workers, "for apostles, for followers of our Lord."

What, then, would become of the farm commune, so excitedly contemplated when Big Dan Orr fell to the ground in a worshipful gesture and exulted over the prospect? It would be given up. "We must confess to failure," Dorothy Day wrote. "Farming communes are not possible without interior discipline, without a philosophy of labor. We should really have grouped ourselves around a religious community so that we could have partaken of their spiritual life; so that we could have been influenced by them, taught by them, as the lay people were taught by the monasteries of old." And what about the families that were living at Maryfarm? Some would move, others would get a deed to three acres of the land and with that they would have to fend for themselves.

The new life at Maryfarm was begun with enthusiasm. Three girls from the Grail were sent to Maryfarm to help out. Father Roy had been relieved of his parish duties and given permission to act as chaplain for the retreat center. He was truly the Worker priest. He built, he dug, he all but started a lumber mill. Hans Tunnesen, the seaman who remained at Maryfarm, worked with him, even as Tunnesen continued to bake and cook.

Father Roy's presence on the farm brought for the Workers gathered there a new sense of community. Worker life then, said Dorothy Day, was beautiful with work, with song, with worship, with feastings and fastings. The priest heard their Confessions and said Mass daily, and made it—even on the coldest days when the water froze in the cruets and his hands were numb—a worshipful and beautiful thing.

In all of this activity Peter Maurin took a lessening role. After Tamar's wedding his thinking and vitality seemed to come under a shadow. When he talked he sometimes repeated himself and would falter in organizing his thoughts. For some time Dorothy Day had been mentioning the possibility of writing a biography of Maurin, and in the October issue of the *Worker* she included the first chapter of it. But she did not carry through with the project inasmuch as her plans for writing always outran the time that she could put to it. Arthur Sheehan eventually took over the job and she was content for him to do so.

One day in January, 1945, she took some time to eat lunch with Maurin. They met at St. Andrew's Church and then walked along the Bowery to the Eclipse Restaurant where he usually had his breakfast. The Eclipse was a large square room with dull, dark-green walls. On the walls were mirrors, some of them broken, and on the broken pieces the day's menu was painted with white signboard paint. That day it was "Pig ears, spaghetti, bread and tea, 15¢ . . . Fried mush, one egg, coffee, 15¢." The standard dish was lamb stew, which Maurin ordered. It came immediately, a huge bowl of it, with three slices of bread and a large cup of coffee. It was the deluxe meal and cost twenty cents. Dorothy Day decided to have the egg and fried mush, but, when she gave her order to the waiter, he shook his head and said, "Lamb stew." That was what she got. Two sailors shared the table with them and said little while Maurin talked about the American labor situation.

The twelfth anniversary issue of the *Worker* came out as Germany surrendered. She wrote an editorial, "Again It Is May," and thanked God for everything—"ploughing and planting and tending new things—all of them samples of heaven, all of them portents of that new heaven and earth wherein justice dwelleth." The world had been on the path to complete destruction, but at least in Europe it had stopped. That was reason to rejoice.

Some of the boys were coming back. Jim O'Gara of the Chicago House had already returned from three years in the Pacific to recuperate from malaria in a Miami hospital. The Russians had freed Jack English from his Romanian prison camp, and after hospitalization in Cleveland he went to Mott Street and helped with the spring house cleaning. Dwight Larrowe was back from Germany. He had begun the war as the spokesman for the Catholic C.O.s but had changed his position and joined the Armed Forces. Tim O'Brien, who had written many of the Ben Joe Labray stories, stopped in for a visit, as did Martie Rooney of the Rochester house. Rooney had just been released from a German prison camp.

In the Pacific the war continued, and the *Worker* demanded that it be ended. "Peace Now with Japan," wrote Father Duffy. Must we, he asked, "beat them and their industries and cities to the ground, burn and destroy everything and everybody in Japan!" The nation was at least prepared to try it. When the news came of the dropping of the atom bomb, Dorothy Day was at Easton. When the war began, she had with outrage denied that mankind could be polarized into segments of good and evil, determined by national boundaries. Now, with the bomb having been dropped, she wrote again with outrage. "We Go on Record," her statement was headed. She had read that President Harry Truman was jubilant. "He went from table to table on the cruiser which was bringing him home from the Big Three conference, telling the great news, 'jubilant' the newspapers said. *Jubilate Deo.* We have killed 318,000 Japanese. That is, we hope we have killed them, the Associated Press, page one, column one, of the *Herald Tribune* says."

It was further to be hoped, she presumed, that "they are vaporized, our Japanese brothers, scattered, men and women and babies, to the four winds, over the seven seas. Perhaps we will breathe their dust in our nostrils, feel them in the fog of New York on our faces, feel them in the rain on the hills of Easton." Could she thank God for this victory? No, because "to thank God for victory is to claim God's approval of the victory. It is to assert that He willed the victory, not only permissively, as He wills evil, but positively and directly as He wills good." It would mean, therefore, that God had approved of all of the means to victory: saturation bombings, and, finally, this.

She wrote bitterly of that "tribal morality" that justified the use of the bomb "because the enemy was so bad we had to do it to them." She criticized *The New York Times* for invoking this morality, and she criticized the Catholic editor who "settled the matter in his own mind, and for his readers, by the observation that critics of the atomic bomb seemed to forget that it was used in a just cause!" Such morality required Americans "to consider it a crime (as indeed it was) when the Germans bombed London, and all the American press showed their righteous horror and indignation at that time. But when the Allied airmen obliterated

Hamburg and Berlin, and dozens of other German and Japanese cities, this was part of a great crusade, morally justified and supremely heroic." It all added up to "What you believe in the matter of war morality depends on what tribe you happen to belong to." She thought what "a fearfully ironical commentary it is on the trials of war criminals!—one set of criminals executing another!"

The bomb, she continued, was created "in the best Nazi tradition, the abuse of scientific truth. We were horrified at the way in which the Nazis bought out scientists and perverted science to serve their ends. Yet we did not fail to learn from them, even to out-Nazi them. And how proud we are (the tribal morality again) of the scientific learning and coordinated research on our side that produced this horror."

She and the Workers sent a telegram to the President: "We are horrified at your jubilation over the havoc inflicted upon Japan. . . . We beg you in the name of Christ crucified to do all in your power to cause this abomination of desolation, this new discovery to be buried forever. Far better to be destroyed ourselves than to destroy others with such fiendish and inhuman ingenuity. . . . When St. John and James suggested that Jesus call down fire from heaven on a hostile people, he said, 'You know not of what spirit you are. The Son of man came not to destroy souls but to save.'"

From Jorhat, Assam, Sergeant Arthur Ronz wrote a troubled letter to Dorothy Day. He had just heard the news of the bomb and it was his opinion that "this creation . . . is far from reflecting the glory of God, but rather it has made a prostitute of science." He knew that "if the powers that be" were to read his thoughts, they would be "misinterpreted." He wanted to express them nonetheless "with the purpose of uniting myself closer to you for I know and realize that you will agree with me that this thing is of no good."

But in the neighborhood around Mott Street most were jubilant, and the festivities went on for several weeks. Then it was September again, four years later. The Italians, who had not celebrated the feast of San Gennaro during the war, were in the streets again, dancing and parading. Farther over on the East Side, the Jews were keeping their time of Atonement.

---

# 13

# THE DEATH OF MAURIN

"Now Peter has gotten suddenly old," Dorothy Day wrote in her Journal in the winter of 1945. His constant sitting by the fire irritated a priest who stayed at the Worker house. "Peter's love is the stove," he would say critically. But Maurin never answered. He never justified himself. He remained silent. Arthur Sheehan remembered that throughout the summer and fall of 1944 Maurin had been making his "essays" from the writings of Eric Gill. Eight loose-leaf volumes of these had been completed when one day he handed them over with the remark, "I have written enough. It is up to the young people now." After that he gave up his "indoctrination." He could not think, he explained. He would live this way for four more years, in and out of bed, but managing every Sunday with the help of Joe Hughes to go to Mass, even on the coldest days.

The decline of Maurin was the loss of a sustaining spirit to Dorothy Day. He had never taken a vigorous personal role in managing the House—"man proposes, woman disposes," he would say. Yet when crises occurred, she found his mind and spirit a source of strength. He gave her good counsel, and she took comfort from his serenity and simple assurance that the tempests in which she found herself were, after all, a sign that her course was well charted. Now this was gone, and it was at a time when she was beginning a period of stress in her life. She was forty-seven when the war

ended, and to the difficulties of such a time there was added
the problem of disruptions and personal conflicts within the
movement.

The Catholic Worker seemed always to have held a special attraction for persons who, streaked with madness,
sought to use it for the purpose of elevating themselves to a
sacerdotal role within the company of its society. Such fan-
tasies, when exercised, brought disruption into the Worker
household and, when reined, frequently resulted in abuse,
directed toward Dorothy Day. The burden of having such
persons around became especially heavy during and after
the war period and finally resulted in the ending of the Easton episode of the Worker's history.

The trouble was rooted in the problem of the families that
had settled on the farm. In 1944 the farm consisted of two
adjoining tracts, the "upper" farm and the "lower" farm, the
latter having been acquired at a later time than the original
1936 purchase. Families had come on the farm, stayed
awhile and then, despairing of prospects, had moved on.
After Tamar's marriage there were three families, each of
which had been assigned three acres to do with as they
pleased. As it turned out, this arrangement was not to their
liking, especially after the fall of 1944 when Dorothy Day
had decided that the agrarian communitarian venture was
not working out and that the farm should be used as a retreat center. But the families, deciding that they were the
foundation for a Christian community, insisted that all be
developed around them and that using the resources of the
farm to hold retreats and succor the poor was a perversion
of Maurin's idea.

A cabal developed against Dorothy Day, the leader of
which was the head of one family that lived on the upper
farm. He had come to Maryfarm in the early period of the
war, at which time, Dorothy Day related, he had reminded
her of Dostoevsky's "Idiot" in his simplicity and frankness.
But the man turned out to be no Prince Myshkin, and Dorothy Day felt that he was guilty of some odd deviations
where the traditional Worker ideas of community were con-

cerned. Emphasizing "the priesthood of the laity," he gathered about him a group of which his family was the center. This man designated one of the group its "spiritual adviser," and then proceeded to bedeck his person with symbols of authority, insisting on the performance of solemn obeisances from the others—bowing, kneeling, and the like—and when they ran afoul of his edicts, penances were imposed.

The head of the group took an extreme attitude toward women, even in those unenlightened times. They were to be the stalwart women of the Old Testament, hewers of wood and drawers of water, as well as mothers of the family. This position was carried to such an extreme . . . that the women were forbidden to speak unless spoken to, and were compelled to knock on the doors of even their own kitchens if men were present.

From the upper farm the dissidents poured down the hill to where the retreats were being held, raiding furniture and food, "explaining" to those there for the retreat that they were the true Catholic Workers and that the retreat movement was a perversion of the Worker idea as conceived by Peter Maurin. When Dorothy Day attempted to admonish them, she was furiously set upon. She was a thief and a hypocrite, lacking in hospitality, charity, and brotherly love. Seeking advice, she wrote to a friend, the Cistercian abbot at Gethsemane, Kentucky, of her difficulties. "Let your charity embrace these evil-doers in your prayers," he counseled. To him, the matters about which she wrote were "truly almost of a nature as to make one wonder if the evil spirit has not a hand in the whole affair."

The situation could not continue. In October, 1945, the upper farmland was given to the head of the dissidents, and in late 1947 the lower tract was sold to a neighboring farmer. It sold for $4,000—the amount they had paid for it. They asked for no down payment and charged no interest on the capital.

In departing from Easton, Dorothy Day recorded her reflections: "We are distressed to say that the type of people we have attracted to this idea have often been the anarchistic type in the wrong sense, those who submit to no authority, talk of property as community property when it concerns someone else and as private property when it concerns them." They were persons "who wanted to be priest and judge, and not worker; to indoctrinate rather than to toil by the sweat of their brows; to live off the earnings of others, in a system which they excoriate."

There was tension at Mott Street. One person, recently released from a mental hospital where he had been confined for having tried to kill his brother, wanted Dorothy Day to get him into a seminary so that he could become a priest. She wrote in her Journal that "He would come in and stand over me and with a livid face—sweat rolling down his face, call down curses from heaven upon me, damning my soul to the lowest hell, for interfering, as he said, with his vocation."

Once, in the midst of the raging turmoil at the farm, she wondered why the parishes had not assisted the Workers with the problems they had had to face. "It was not right nor fair," she wrote in the *Worker* "that we should bear so large a burden; that we should face long lines of hungry, sick and aged people in the morning and the evening. It could well have been distributed through the parishes, the parish halls, the parish properties, the parish societies; and if the old societies are too stodgy to take care of these new needs in a changing world, then new societies . . . should be formed." Why, she asked, "should a priest in Brooklyn call us at ten o'clock at night to take in a girl who would probably shudder at the sight of Mott Street at that hour?"

The crises waxed and waned, and meanwhile in her life and that of Mott Street there were deaths that registered again the sign that in time there could be no completion of community. Her mother died in October, 1945. "I had prayed so constantly that I would be beside her when she died; for years I had offered up that prayer. And God granted it quite literally," she wrote in the *Worker*.

In the following year there were three deaths at Mott Street. Kichi Harada died. She had come to Mott Street in

1937, unemployed and homeless. Because she was Japanese, she had been insulted many times during the war, and even at the table at Mott Street, there were those who told her that with the dropping of the atom bomb the Japanese had gotten only what they deserved. It was true, Dorothy Day commented, that Kichi had argued back vehemently "in a high shrill trembling voice, and she could shout anyone down, but there are few among us who practice holy silence."

Then there was Isabel Conlon, whose married life had seemed unusually beautiful. Her husband had been a physician who had chosen poverty as the condition of his life and when he died there was no estate. She lived in a little tenement apartment near the Mott Street house and made her living cleaning office buildings. Her husband, however, had left her something else, the ability to live with dignity, peace, and grace—qualities that all recognized in her. When Mrs. Conlon got cancer and could no longer work, she sat in her small kitchen at the center table and answered letters that had come in to *The Catholic Worker*. She wrote these notes up until the time she went to St. Rose's cancer home. She died six months later, after great suffering.

Mary Sheehan died that year. She had been among the first to move in with the Workers back in 1933 when they had lived on Charles Street. She had cooked and then joined the rest in selling the Worker on the streets. She died, Dorothy Day supposed, probably feeling unused and unappreciated, but for years her volubility and her wit had brought her prominently into the daily life of the Worker house.

After her mother's funeral, Dorothy Day made one of her visitation trips through the Midwest, aiming for the Catholic Rural Life Conference at Green Bay, Wisconsin. She especially had wanted to see there an exhibit of rural arts. But things did not work out too well. The nun in charge of the exhibit had been told by one of the priests who helped to arrange the conference that the space for the exhibit had been sold for advertising by a television manufacturing company. The last Dorothy Day saw of the "rural arts" corner was "the enthralled backs of half a dozen sisters, watching the high kicking of some Flora Dora girls, which was shown on a screen." She thought of St. Francis' comment as he dwelled on the recollection of having been thrown out of his own home—"This then is perfect joy."

Returning through Milwaukee, she visited Larry and Ruth Ann Heaney. The Heaneys had been active in the Milwaukee house and then, later, lived for a time at Maryfarm. In Milwaukee, she found Heaney working to save enough money to begin another community farm venture. Down in Chicago she saw the two Reser families, founders of the Chicago House, and had lunch with Tom Sullivan, John Cogley, Jim O'Gara, and Father Martin Carrabine. Going back through Cleveland, she visited the Gauchats, who had a new baby. There were three children now, and she stayed over long enough for the birthday party of the oldest, Anita Marie.

There was more to the trip than having a pleasant sojourn. Because of internal dissension, the Boston house had been closed in February, and her trip was in order to take an inventory of the house situation. At least at Harrisburg things were in good order. There Mary Frecon continued her work of eight years at the Blessed Martin de Porres house. Living among blacks in the worst of slums, she remarked sadly to Dorothy Day that she did not seem to be getting anywhere. But Dorothy Day thought she had gone a long way. For eight years, she said, Mary Frecon had been loving her brothers faithfully and unfailingly.

The decline in the number of houses caused some to believe that the movement had had its day. Two expressions of this sort got into print, and to them Dorothy Day took exception. In the summer of 1948 John Cogley wrote an article for *America* in which, Dorothy Day said, he had seemed to say that the Catholic Worker movement was a thing of the past. A year previous, Don Gallagher, founder of the St. Louis house, had written an article for a St. Louis University publication "in which he had spoken too much of the movement in terms of the past."

What had they expected, she wanted to know—"What Dream Did They Dream?" The success of the Catholic Worker movement could not be judged in terms of the number of houses it sustained or the new ones it spawned. Referring back to Cogley's statements, she admitted that "a great many have left the running." Yet house counting was not the basis on which the Worker movement should be judged. "We are still trying to work out a theory of love, a study of the problem of love so that the revolution of love instead of that of hate may come about and we will have a new heaven and a new earth wherein justice dwelleth." The problem of the poor was greater now than it ever had been, she said. There were too many groups studying the problem, working out organizational approaches to it. There were still "too few who will consider themselves servants, who will give up their lives to serve others."

Home a month from her Midwestern trip, she went to Montreal in December, 1946, to visit Father Roy, confined there in a mental hospital. The onset of his illness had occurred at Maryfarm, first noticed one morning when, as he said Mass, he seemed to have lost his memory. Taken home to Montreal, he had wandered away and was eventually found in a small village in northern Quebec. Since he was dressed in old clothing over a pair of pajamas, he had been taken in as a vagrant and was living with a priest for whom he served as an altar boy.

When she saw him in the hospital he remembered her. She relates in *Loaves and Fishes* that he "cried a little when he showed me the bruises on his face where one of the other patients, another priest, had struck him. He told me how an attendant, while changing his bed, had called him a dirty pig. He wept like a child and then suddenly smiled and said 'Rejoice!' I was crying too, and in our shared tears I felt free to ask him something I would never have . . . otherwise, . . . 'Have you offered yourself,' I asked, 'as a victim?' It was then that he said to me, 'We are always saying to God things we don't really mean, and He takes us at our word. He really loves and believes us.'"

For Dorothy Day, Father Roy had been one of the central figures in that time at Maryfarm when the retreats had filled her life and she had thought that she would make the farm into a retreat center. When Maryfarm was given up, she did not, however, give up the idea of a retreat center, and looking toward the purchase of a new place, she sent out an appeal for funds. "Miraculously," she wrote in *The Long Loneliness*, "we were given $10,000 by friends to continue our retreat house work, all the money coming in within a month from a half dozen of our readers." That ten thousand dollars could be raised in a month might have been a miracle, but it was also a testimony to Dorothy Day's unparalleled gifts as a beggar. However desperate the financial circumstances of the Workers might become, an "Appeal" would relieve the drought.

The new farm, called Maryfarm Retreat House, cost $16,000 and was five miles west of Newburgh, New York. They got it in the spring of 1947, in time for the men to put in a crop of vegetables. Most of the old crew were there, Jerry Griffin, Jack Thornton, Hans Tunnesen, Joe Cotter, one of the older workers, and, of course, the head farmer, John Filliger. By August they were harvesting cabbages, tomatoes, rutabagas, potatoes, and corn in such abundance that they were able to take weekly station wagon loads of produce to Mott Street. But Maurin was no longer in the rows of vegetables "indoctrinating." He sat on the stone porch of the farmhouse where he could smell the fragrance of the three huge Norwegian pines that stood in the front yard.

The winter of 1948 brought an abundance of snow, but when spring came again there was the familiar sight of John Filliger with his team plowing far off at the end of the field with his hound dog trailing along behind. Maurin had been taken to Mott Street for the winter, but when the crab-

John Filliger, Maryfarm, Newburgh, NY, 1955.
Vivian Cherry photo.

apples blossomed he was brought back to the farm. When the first bright warm days came, his chair was put in the yard so that he might sit and enjoy the budding spring.

As planned, the farm became a center for retreats, conferences, and family gatherings. Jane O'Donnell continued her work of organizing retreats, and as the *Worker* noted in the summer of 1948, they were going on at full tempo. Lest there be any future misunderstanding on the function of the Newburgh acquisition, Dorothy Day sent a circular letter to all who were associated with the movement. First, she dealt with the question that occasionally had come up, especially with the rise of the retreat movement, of the Catholic Worker becoming a religious order. It was, perhaps, inevitable that some should have made that assumption. But, she said, neither Peter Maurin nor she had ever thought of the movement as anything but a lay group. It was a vocation, and for one committed to its ideal, it was a vocation whose mark was poverty and chastity, too, if one lived in the single state. But vows were never taken, or even thought of, so she wanted to affirm once and for all that neither Peter Maurin nor she had had any intention of turning the work into a religious order.

Having dispelled what concern existed on that score, she moved to the issue that had so disrupted life at Easton—the problem of the families. There had, she said, been a long history to this problem—where the authority lay, what share of the money was their due—with the families usually insisting that their interest should be the first served. She disagreed. Any Worker who married and then had children should recognize that his status in the lay apostolate had changed, that his first obligation was to take care of his own, and that he was not to expect others to take care of them. The first concern of the Catholic Worker, she said, was to feed the poor. If young Workers were going to get married, they could not settle at Newburgh and expect others to support them. No one should ever forget, she added emphatically, that the movement was supported by money from people who lived in the world. Workers, therefore, could not become too self-satisfied about having left the world.

During that summer of 1948, as the retreats and conferences went on, Peter Maurin sat quietly beneath the pines, attended by Hans Tunnesen. The failure of his mental processes was becoming more noticeable. In April of the previous year he had frightened everyone by suddenly disappearing from Mott Street. Thinking that he had perhaps wandered off to his old haunts, a search was made along the Bowery. The police were notified. The Trappists and the Maryknoll sisters were telephoned and asked to pray for his safe return. At night they slept fitfully, dreaming of hearing his cough and his footstep on the stair. But there was no sign of him.

On the fourth day he walked in at noon. He had been lost but had somehow, without help, made his way back to Mott Street. After that, they decided that they would put a note in his pocket: "I am Peter Maurin, founder of the Catholic Worker Movement."

In the closing days of March, 1949, the people at Mott Street got a letter from Marty Paul, who, with his family and the Heaney family, was striving to build a community farm at Rhineland, Missouri—the Holy Family Farm, they called it. Paul noted that their effort was a day-to-day struggle, but that progress was being made. Their gardens had been started and logs for a new home had been cut and were soon to be hauled to the sawmill. He was concerned about Heaney, though. Larry was still in the hospital, where he had been for eight weeks. Now there was talk of a lung abscess and surgery.

Heaney died in that surgery, and the news of his death reached Mott Street at the same time Paul's letter came. Dorothy Day wrote of his death in the June issue of the *Worker*, along with an account of Heaney's life in the Worker movement. He had been head of Milwaukee's Holy Family House, and when that house closed, he and his wife, Ruth Ann, had joined the group at Easton. When the time came to make a choice on the issue of his participation in the war, he became a conscientious objector and did his service at the Keene, New Hampshire, camp. In 1947 the Heaneys and the Pauls began their venture in community farming. When Heaney died, his sixth child was two months old.

Dorothy Day recognized Heaney as a special kind of person. There had been talk of his being a saint, she said, and she did not think it was light talk. One did not live together in a community like the Worker's for too long without one's faults becoming obvious, and she had known Heaney a long time. Gradually, as she had seen, he had pared from his life all superfluous attachments. He practiced voluntary poverty, but he suffered from it, too. At the Holy Family Farm there was no washing machine, no electricity, no bath and toilet, and no kitchen sink. The Heaney family was, nonetheless, a close family. At night the children knelt around their mother and father and prayed for all the children in the world who were orphans and who were cold and hungry. Dorothy Day believed that all who would remember the family would remember how they loved one another. She knew, too, that John Filliger would think of how many times he had seen Ruth Ann and Larry at Easton, walking down the hill, hand in hand, on their way to church, three miles distant. Heaney was buried in a small cemetery near the farm. The Requiem Mass was sung by neighbors and his own family. After the Mass, neighbors carried the coffin a quarter of a mile across a field and through a woods to the grave that they had dug.

Before going to Heaney's funeral, Dorothy Day had paused to tell Peter Maurin good-bye. When she asked him if he remembered Heaney, he said yes. "Now you will have someone waiting for you in heaven," she said, and Maurin smiled. "He had not smiled for months," she added. "There had been only a look of endurance, even pain, on his face."

Returning from the funeral, she stopped off at the Gauchats' at Avon, Ohio, for the night and was sleeping when the telephone call came that Maurin had died. When she had hung up, Bill Gauchat suggested that they say Vespers or the Office of the Dead for Maurin, so they knelt on the living-room floor and said the prayers. For Maurin, Dorothy Day realized, death could be viewed as a happy release, but what she felt was a gigantic sense of loss.

Maurin's death occurred on May 15. It was Sunday and he had had his usual day. Michael Kovalak dressed him in the morning, took him to Mass in the chapel, and then out to sit in the afternoon sun. That night at eleven o'clock Hans Tunnesen heard him coughing and, looking in, saw him struggle to rise, then fall back on his pillow, breathing heavily. Father John Faley, the chaplain at Newburgh who had given Maurin such devoted attention, was called, and, as he and the others of the house said prayers for the dying, Maurin passed away.

He was laid out in a suit that had been sent in for the poor, and after a Requiem Mass at Newburgh, sung by members of the household, he was taken to Mott Street and his coffin placed in the office where Tom Sullivan worked. All that day people came in to view him, and at nine the next morning his funeral was held at the Salesian Transfiguration Church on Mott Street. Priests and seminarians came, Workers were there from all over the country, a group came from Easton, and Mott Street neighbors came. Everyone sang the Mass together, and afterward a procession followed the body to St. John's Cemetery, Queens, to a grave given by Domincan Father Pierre Conway.

Like everyone after the death of a loved one, Dorothy Day was caught in the pathos of his suffering in his last years. One night she had looked in to see how he was before she went to bed. Someone had taken the blanket off him, and he lay there in the icy cold room covered with only a sheet. What was especially hard to bear was the recollection of how he had been shouted at by visitors who thought he was deaf, who talked to him condescendingly as one talked to a child. Silent, he had dragged himself around, stripped of everything. He had stripped himself, she thought, but God had stripped him more. "We are pruned as the vine is pruned so that it can bear fruit, and this we cannot do our-

selves. God did it for him. He took from him his mind, the
one thing he had left."

Peter Maurin's active live with the Worker movement
had spanned a decade. When he died he would have regarded Dorothy Day as well "indoctrinated." She knew his
ideas and she had come to know him "in the breaking of
bread," as she might have said. Knowing him, she believed
that his vision and his revolution were the only ones worthy
of the value she attached to man. For the Catholic Worker
movement, time could bring no new directions or basic reap-
praisals, for Maurin's revolution enveloped time and was not
borne by it. What had he meant to her? She could answer
simply that "he taught us what it meant to be sons of God,
and restored to us our sense of responsibility in a chaotic
world. Yes, he was . . . holier than anyone we ever knew."

Death was always a presence in the Worker movement,
but never more than just before and after Maurin's death.
Few issues of the paper came out in this era that did not
carry a notice of the passing of someone in the movement or
of one with whom the Worker had close ties of spirit. In the
February, 1948, issue, the paper mourned the death of Gandhi. Robert Ludlow, who personally found in Gandhi's life a
compelling spiritual example, wrote a tender and moving
requiem. In April, Emmanuel Chapman's name was added
to the list. A noted teacher, he had with Dorothy Day back
in the thirties helped found the Committee of Catholics to
Fight Anti-Semitism. In May, 1950, the paper noted the
passing of Emmanuel Mounier, the personalist philosopher
whose *Personalist Manifesto* Maurin had so approvingly recommended to the first Worker generation.

The Worker movement lost three other friends during
that period. Sigrid Undset died in late 1950. Dorothy Day
commented in the *Worker* of November, 1950, that she had
read Miss Undset's books before becoming a Catholic and
little thought then that they would become friends. Gertrude Burke, who had helped the Workers get the Mott
Street house, died in January, 1951. Father Onesimus Lacouture, the originator of the retreat that Dorothy Day had

found so meaningful, died in November, 1951. She went to his funeral with the psychiatrist, Karl Stern. In the *Worker* she wrote that she would like to see on Father Lacouture's gravestone the words, " 'He made all things new,' because his teaching of the love of God so aroused our love in turn."

Then came the deaths of three Workers. In September, 1949, Dorothy Day returned to Mott Street from a week's visit to Tamar and her growing family, then living on a farm at Berkeley Springs, West Virginia, to find John Curran critically ill. Curran, who lived with his wife Cecilia in the rear house at Mott Street, had been one of Maurin's dedicated followers. John Bowers, of the old Chicago house, died in January, 1950. Tom Sullivan wrote of his work among needy children and how he had christened the Chicago Taylor Street house the "Holy Child House." Every Monday night, Bowers would prepare a dinner for his friends, and as they ate someone read from the works of Jacques Maritain. When Sullivan had first known him, Bowers had affected a somewhat dandified dress, but over the years he came to wear clothes that were as ragged as any worn by his poor neighbors.

Sullivan lost another friend that summer. One morning, Charlie O'Rourke, the *Worker* circulation manager, got up, had a gala breakfast with his friends, and headed up to Newburgh for a rest at the farm. That night he had a heart attack and died several hours later. A capable construction engineer, he had occasionally gone out on jobs, but when things got into a mess with the paper he would reappear and put them in order, bringing up to date the cancellations and new subscriptions. He loved opera and, knowing that Dorothy Day did, too, he took her to a performance once each winter.

In February, 1952, occurred the death of old Maurice O'Connell, well known to all who had ever been at the Easton farm. In the hoped-for tranquillity of that pastoral setting, he had roared, demanded, intimidated, and threatened violence with his fists, if need be, to back up his demands. He was a carpenter and made a coffin for Dorothy Day (which Tamar took to store clothes in) and varnished it. Writing a decent obituary for him caused Dorothy Day some difficulty, for, as she said, she always had to write all of the truth, lest she be guilty of distorting by telling only part of it. This also involved writing about the past, for there was no present truth unrelated to the past. When she thought about Maurice O'Connell, "The truth was that . . . Mr. O'Connell was a terror."

## 14

---

## ANXIOUS YEARS

For those who hoped for the breath of a new life in the spirit of religion, the years after the war produced hopeful signs. In the intellectual world, the faith in the ultimate power of science to save was becoming hedged with doubt, for it was the atom bomb that was infusing the postwar years with the "anxiety" that poets and historians saw dominating life. Relativism, which so recently had gaily bedded with the ebullient liberal faith of the age of John Dewey, seemed now to promise nothing but disorder, and voices arose to invoke some principle of past stability to apply to a situation that showed signs of gathering a chaotic momentum.

In 1947 Arnold Toynbee's *A Study of History* appeared. It was a multivolumed work that tried to extract from the history of civilizations certain enduring laws—somewhat in the manner of Herbert Spencer, who nearly a hundred years before had tried to do the same for the history of creation. The substance of Toynbee's massive work was that civilizations rose as they produced creative elites, and when purposiveness was lost, civilizations fell. In the twentieth century, the world needed a recovery of purpose, which could be found by seeing anew the vitality of Christian values and ideals. The call to orthodoxy that seemed implicit in Toynbee's study was explicitly made by the theologian Reinhold Niebuhr, who effectively challenged the naturalistic-liberal faith.

For Catholics, the time just after the war was one of seeming progress. The revival of Thomistic philosophy, begun in the twenties, reached a high level of scholarly circulation and acceptance, due in large measure to the brilliant mind and writing style of Jacques Maritain and to some of his American and Canadian counterparts—Anton Pegis; the Jesuit, Gerard Smith, Emmanuel Chapman, and others. It was also a rich time for convert literature, with Thomas Merton's *The Seven Storey Mountain* and Karl Stern's *Pillar of Fire* experiencing a wide circulation in the postwar years.

The relationship of the Worker movement to this new spirit of confidence in the American Catholic Church was indicated in part by the new publications begun by persons who had once been associated with the movement. In 1943, Edward Marciniak, who with Al Reser had started the first Chicago Worker house, began a new journal called *Work*, published monthly by the Catholic Labor Alliance. In July, 1946, John Cogley and some of his Chicago Worker associates put out the first issue of *Today*, a social action journal for young Catholics.

But undoubtedly the most striking and brilliantly executed of the new publications that reflected the spirit and concern of lay Catholics who held a Worker-type social concern was *Integrity*, first appearing in October, 1946, and running thereafter for a decade. A monthly, it offered commentary on the times that was thoughtful, acidulous, and witty. Its creators were Carol Jackson, Dorothy Dohen, and Ed Willock. Miss Jackson and Miss Dohen were students, intellectuals, and Willock, young, too, but with a growing family, was an artist-worker-intellectual who had spent his fledgling years with the Boston Workers on Tremont Street in the days before the war.

A frail person consumed with a passion for work, Willock's mature years covered a brief span. As he wrote and drew brilliant cartoons for *Integrity*, he painted billboards for a living, and then induced some Catholic laymen to buy a tract of land at Nyack, New York, where he began a community-living project, Marycrest. "I count myself as a . . . spiritual god-child of you and Peter," he once wrote to Dorothy Day, and his life witnessed to the truth of this declaration.

*The Catholic Worker* ran in the full tide of this period. In the decade, 1945–1955, it was never better. As usual, the paper was built around the column and articles of Dorothy Day. In February, 1946, she changed the name of her column. Thereafter, "Day by Day" became "On Pilgrimage," for as she explained it, there were already too many columns with "Day" or "Days" in their title, and besides, "We should always be thinking of ourselves as pilgrims."

Her contributions did not, however, dominate the paper as was sometimes the case when talent was scarce. There was Doris Ann Doran, who wrote articles about the poor in Europe after the war, and Irene Naughton, writing about strikes and thoughtful pieces on the relationship between economics and community. Dorothy Day recalled that Miss Naughton had bright red hair, a warm laugh, and that she could write nothing that did not have a poetic quality about it—even when she was writing on economic subjects. Julia Porcelli, who had cared for the children at the Worker place on Staten Island during the summers of the thirities, contributed an occasional article, as did Ade Bethune on the subject of arts and crafts.

Some of the men who had written before and during the war continued to make good contributions to the paper. John Cogley, along with his other journalistic tasks, wrote an occasional article and reviews of books and films. Gordon Zahn, fresh from his experience at the Rosewood Training School, produced some articles on mentally retarded children. Ammon Hennacy, the pacifist-anarchist, wrote of his "Life at Hard Labor" among the Indians and farmers of the West. There were new writers. After 1950 Michael Harrington, a resident Worker, contributed regularly. Tony Aratari, a wartime bomber crewman, who lived at the Worker house and attended Fordham, wrote many good articles.

But the mainstays of *The Catholic Worker*, especially from 1948 to 1955, were Tom Sullivan and Robert Ludlow. Sullivan, a friend of John Cogley's, had been with the Chicago Worker group before the war, had gone into the service during the war, and then, afterward, had joined the Mott Street group. Taking over the management of the house, he began writing a column, "Mott Street," which was something of a successor to the Ben Joe Labray stories that had run during the forties. It was a chronicle of life at the house, done with understanding and humor.

Ludlow, who had occasionally written for the *Worker* during the war, was one of the most thoughtful of that group that wrote in the postwar decade. Raised in Scranton, Pennsylvania, he had become a Catholic from reading Newman. Employed in some nondescript laboring job there, he was delighted when he got the opportunity to leave by taking a job in the library at Catholic University. But even there the prospect of spending an indefinite time in shelving books struck him as exceedingly dull, and, after six months, he wrote to Dorothy Day to ask if he could not join the Workers at Mott Street.

"Joining" the Catholic Worker movement was not complicated. There were no forms to fill out. One simply went to the house and, after a while, through a haphazard process of filtration, found a job that became his own. But first, Ludlow had to confront the prospect of fighting in a war and this he chose not to do. As a conscientious objector, he took his place along with Gordon Zahn and some of the other Catholic C.O.s at the Rosewood Training School. When the war was over, and he was free to do as he chose, he went to Mott Street to remain with the Workers for a decade.

He wrote on a variety of subjects, but tended to concentrate on pacifism, anarchism, and psychiatry and mental dysfunction. There were many times when what he said was over the heads of *Worker* readers. "I personally stand in back of everything Bob Ludlow writes," Dorothy Day once stated, "though his way of expressing himself is at times peculiar, to say the least. I don't think the majority of our readers know what he is talking about when he says, 'The compulsion to revolt is explained as a manifestation of the libido.'"

Dorothy Day's attitude toward psychiatry was not that of an enthusiastic devotee, but Ludlow referred to it out of his experiences with the patients at Rosewood. In writing about the problems of mental retardation and illness, he felt that he was fulfilling an obligation he had to those persons among whom he had lived and worked during the war years. One of his main themes was the growing irrationality of modern society which was becoming fragmented by a rapidly expanding technology. It was, he said, the growing and enveloping monism of our times. Increasingly, "we are confronted with compelling evidence of the futility of the pacifist and libertarian positions. The triumph of the concrete, of the external world, of popular materialism, makes any appeal to transcendental values incomprehensible to the majority." He appeared to be pessimistic: "We proceed in violence, we end in violence . . . we cannot conceive of it otherwise." His conclusion was that if affairs continued on their present course, madness would triumph. This course was making the way of the true pacifist progressively more difficult. It was the Christian pacifist who would be considered abnormal or psychotic. But for Ludlow it was the only course worthwhile—"Even though death come to us all today it is still worthwhile."

Ludlow's contributions to the *Worker* in this era helped much to make it a distinguished paper. Yet to many who have come to know *The Catholic Worker*, no one person, excepting Dorothy Day, stands out as having given the paper its characteristic mark during this era as does the Quaker artist Fritz Eichenberg. His woodcuts began appearing in the *Worker* in 1950, and it was not long before they became the paper's most arresting feature. One re-

quired no schooling or sensitivity to the hidden nuances of
art to comprehend the peace and joy that the presence of
the Christ child brought to man and nature as depicted in a
Christmastime, full-front-page reproduction of the infant
Jesus among the animals.

*The Catholic Worker* began its fifteenth year in May,
1947. On the front page of the paper, prominently boxed,
was the much quoted statement of Pius XI: "Let us thank
God that He makes us live among the present problems. It
is no longer permitted to anyone to be mediocre." Dorothy
Day added the personalist injunction: "The coat which
hangs in your closet belongs to the poor. . . . It is you yourself who must perform the works of mercy."

At the conclusion of that year, some of the old-timers
wrote in, expressing their affection for Dorothy Day and declaring again that in view of the movement's consistent refusal to practice any of the laws of survival in the object
world the fact that it lived was proof of God's personal in-
tervention in its affairs. "I feel more strongly now than ever
before that God is . . . very much with you," wrote Father
D. L. Hessler, who as a young seminarian had been inspired
by the movement. Elizabeth Burrows, a writer, who had a
Worker "cell" at Ozark, Arkansas, said that the Worker was
right, no matter how wild it sometimes became at the
fringes. Just recently she and some of the others who had
been in the movement before the war had gotten together,
"having the sort of bull session . . . John Cogley always
loved" and had reminisced about their experiences. John
Cogley told how he had been deeply affected by the Workers and that he wanted to express full gratitude to the Providence that had directed them.

Jesuit Wilfrid Parsons, exercising the prerogative of his
years, fell to reminiscing about the heroic days. He remembered a lecture he had given that first year on Fifteenth
Street on one of the bitterest February days that New York
had ever had. Just before the lecture Dorothy Day had appeared ("she said she had been in bed because it was the

only warm place") and had informed him that the usual procedure with lecturers was reversed at the Worker house.
The speaker was expected to drop a five-dollar bill in a
cigar box on the shelf in the kitchen. Father Parsons recalled a lady in furs, "a violent sort of person," who "heckled each of the lecturers and we had to be smuggled out
the upstairs doorway to escape her." He recalled that Parker
Moon "once had to take it on the run."

Tom Sullivan, writing in his "Mott Street" column, recalled how he and John Cogley had run across the Worker
movement in a small store on Chicago's West Side. It would
take a book, he said, to give a complete picture of the Catholic Worker movement in that city, but he hoped that someday someone would write that book as well as one about
each of the other Catholic Worker groups.

Completing fifteen years brought no new level of sophistication either to the paper or to the movement. The paper,
with all of its intellectual depth, could still make those egregious blunders that caused readers to groan. In the April,
1947, edition it reported that seven million Sudeten Germans had been uprooted from Czechoslovakia to be resettled in Germany. An aghast reader pointed out that there
were only three million Germans in Czechoslovakia.

Neither, seemingly, had Catholic Workers grown into
that larger appreciation of the realities of economic and political life that governed high Church officials in the conduct of Church business. In the matter of the Calvary Cemetery strike of February, 1949, Workers were found drawn
in battle array against Cardinal Spellman himself. It began
when the gravediggers of Calvary Cemetery, members, by
some higher and obscure logic, of Local 293 of the International Food, Tobacco and Agricultural Workers Union,
CIO, voted to go on strike for what they considered to be
just demands against their employers, the trustees of St. Patrick's Cathedral. That the Calvary strikers were all Catholic seemed not to have impressed the trustees and the cardinal, who were reported as believing that as members of a

CIO union, the strikers were using Communist tactics and that the strike was Communist inspired.

When the strikers learned that the possibility of taint was hurting their cause, they "swore a solemn public oath that they were not communist inspired, were not communists, and abhorred communist philosophy." To this the cardinal was quoted as saying, "I am gratified, but they are getting repentant kind of late." It was also suggested that the strikers, as Catholics, were committing a sin because burying the dead was a work of mercy. "In the name of God," one striker retorted, "how can they keep saying that burying the dead is a work of mercy and we should be satisfied to take less and I've got seven kids to feed? Feeding my kids is work of mercy enough for me and it takes more than what they're giving me to do it on."

As the strike went into several weeks' running, strikers started going to the Worker house for assistance. The Workers, having decided that the strike was eminently justified, gave what relief they could, and otherwise helped the strikers maintain their picket line. It was those "shamefaced seminarians in buses, surrounded by heavy police guards, who drove through the picket line to help break the strike" that Dorothy Day remembered.

In the end the strike was broken, and the gravediggers were forced to terminate their CIO affiliation and join an American Federation of Labor union. Throughout the strike, *The Daily Worker* had jeered at the spectacle of the cardinal standing off a handful of low-income gravediggers. It was the spectacle of this kind of thing that fed the fires of anticlericalism. It was a temptation of the devil, Dorothy Day said in summing up the affair, "to that most awful of all wars, the war between the clergy and the laity."

As a result of the Workers' stand on the strike, rumors grew that the cardinal would take some drastic action against them. One person wrote to the Mott Street group to inform it that he had observed that anyone who expressed approval of Dorothy Day was "being told that Cardinal

Spellman forbids any of his priests to go to her House of Hospitality . . . the inference being that she is a contumacious person who affronted the cardinal and created a public example of disobedience. . . ."

But the rumors overreached their mark. Julia Porcelli, recalling the strike, thought that the best thing in Cardinal Spellman's history was that "he didn't persecute the Catholic Worker. He allowed us to live . . . and, as John Curran used to say, he'd even buy [*The Catholic Worker*] when he'd see them on Fifth Avenue. . . . He was always very pleasant even when we criticized him during the cemetery strike." That he never took oppressive action against the Worker movement was, she thought, the action that "will get him in heaven if nothing else will. . . ."

The fundamental concern of Catholic Workers—indeed of mankind generally—in those postwar years was the persistence of a mood that bespoke the possibility of another war, this time with Russia. It was a mood that was preoccupied with the menace of Communism, and there were aspects of it that reached hysterical proportions. Even before the war ended, Father Duffy at the Worker house commented on talk that he was hearing— "Our Christian civilization of the West is menaced . . . In fact Christianity itself is threatened and may succumb to the onslaught of barbaric hordes. . . ." Such talk was absolute nonsense, he said.

There was the atom bomb, giving a new dimension of horror to war talk. What would the *Worker* do about the bomb? "One thing—destroy the two billion dollars' worth of equipment that was built up to make the atomic bomb . . . put on sack cloth and ashes, weep and repent. And God will not forget to show mercy. If others go to work to build again and prepare, let them. It is given to men but once to die."

In 1946, as the government prepared to test the bomb further, the *Worker* protested again. It was not concerned primarily because of the possibility of a tidal wave or the poisoning of the water and air by radiation, ghastly as these things were to contemplate. It was protesting the tests be-

cause they were a demonstration of power calculated to in-
timidate. They were violence implied. Later, when President Truman announced that he was sanctioning the
production of the H-bomb, Ludlow declared that "The
whole thing has become unreal and fantastic." If nothing
else would bring man to "the conclusion that absolute pacifism is the only answer," this development certainly should.
"We live in a world of hate and we can only oppose it by
going to the opposite extreme."

The talk of war with Russia amidst the frightfulness of
bomb testing brought Dorothy Day to a reemphasis of those
positions she had taken during the war. On the thirteenth
anniversary of *The Catholic Worker,* she wrote a passionate
denunciation of war in which she referred to an event in her
life which must have registered deeply with her because she
would refer to it on other occasions. "Once I had a terrible
dream," she said. This dream, so it seemed to her, was in
reference to the Spanish Civil War and it had something to
do with protecting the Church by the sword. "News had
come . . . of the murder of brothers, priests and nuns, and
the Catholic press was bitter. And we were repeating issue
after issue of *The Catholic Worker* that love and truth could
not be defended by the use of force; that we must begin to
practice and to use the spiritual weapons of the works of
mercy . . . to heal the ills of the world." The dream was
about revolution and conflict—conflicting philosophies.
Somehow these themes were brought into a poem of many
stanzas, and at the last line of each stanza a sardonic voice
would cry out, " 'Be kind, Cain!' with a burst of terrible
laughter. It was like the laughter of hell itself."

What had this dream meant to her? That it was the devil
himself who belittled love as a weapon; who, rather, delighted
in the principle that violence had its legitimate uses, especially when such things as "honor" and "right" were at
stake. Look at the war just ended, she said, and already it
could be seen that the injustices it had sought to repair had
been increased a thousandfold throughout the world. Never,
she thought, had noble words been more vainly used than

in relation to war. The devil himself seemed to have inspired them.

She urged support of the Russian proposal for disarmament, currently before the United Nations. If the United States refused it, afraid of being taken in by the Communists, nothing would be gained anyway. "For we have nothing to look forward to but pulverization." As for the Catholic press, it had "become unbalanced on the whole subject of Russia." It had portrayed the Russian as a beast, devoid of all honesty and never to be trusted. As far as she was concerned, the Russians were like all men, "made in the image of God," and she did not believe they would attack an unarmed people.

A year later, in 1947, she returned again to the presumed menace of the Russians. "Is it Soviet Russia who is the threat to the world? Is it indeed?" What nation had all of the atom bombs? What nation had a navy larger than all other navies combined? It was the United States, she said. She was especially depressed over the attitude of Catholic students. She said that Workers had been going to colleges, distributing leaflets against the draft. And most everyone to whom they gave their leaflets had accepted the draft and thought of it as a good thing. There was a sense of the inevitable, that war was to come, that morality had nothing to do with it, that it was a question of defeating Russia before it got the atom bomb.

She noted that around the local churches they were asking the Italian parishoners to write their relatives in Italy, asking them not to vote Communist. She thought it would be interesting to know why the Communists were presumably such a threat in Italy. She felt that had Catholic leaders there been as much concerned for worker ownership of the means of production and distribution, for decentralization, and for a peaceful liquidation of the acquisitive classes as they had been in establishing a modus vivendi with Fascism, the issue of Communism might not appear so large.

As a course of action, the *Worker*, as it had in World War

II, tried to encourage an opposition to the draft. Ludlow regularly wrote the "Pax" column and an occasional report on Catholic conscientious objectors. Once, he thought it necessary to make it clear that Worker conscientious objectors had nothing to do with Coughlinite C.O.s. He had known many of the latter, and there were none, in his opinion, who were not anti-Semitic. They were not true pacifists. "They cannot object to modern war on moral grounds because they defended the Spanish murderer, Francisco Franco. They have done everything in their power to prepare the people for a 'holy war' against Russia—in which conflict they must, if there is any logic in their position at all, participate as soldiers. . . ."

In April, 1948, the paper carried again the full text of Father Hugo's "The Immorality of Conscription," with seventy-five thousand additional copies printed for handout distribution. It was explained that it was universal military conscription that lay at the root of modern wars. If young men would refuse to be drafted, wars could not be waged. Later came the suggestion that in time would bring considerable publicity to the movement. Those who were interested in a campaign against conscription by destroying their draft cards should organize their actions. Then followed a list of instructions on how to deal with draft boards.

In one instance, however *The Catholic Worker's* program of frustrating the system was considered not to be as imaginative as it might. One young man of the Worker's acquaintance decided to go to the heart of the matter and wrote to Dorothy Day of a plan he was putting into effect. There was a reason, he said, "why I did not refuse to register or go to the Induction Center. First I felt the Army *needs* pacifists *in* it and not outside in prisons and Conscientious Objectors Camps. . . ." The officers and men in the Army "for the most part are decent and attracted by the truth. . . . It is easy to make draftees Pacifists. . . . I told the officers I will not shoot a rifle and they were horrified and sent me to the Catholic Chaplain who was a very pleasant man who believes he is doing right and that negroes have a definite body odor and should be segregated in the army. . . ."

The following day Dorothy Day got another letter. "Have just been *court marshalled*. . . . They brought me before the troops and accused me of subverting discipline. . . . I quoted all of them what Christ had said. . . . They were stunned [and] now I am under arrest here in the Barraks until I am taken to the stockade. . . . But I feel I have done my duty before God to *wittness* for Christ before these men. . . ."

Suddenly, almost within the period of a year, the atom bomb and the presumed menace of Russia became the background for a series of startling events that fueled a national psychosis on the subject of Communist subversion. During the period from September, 1949, to June, 1950, China fell to the Communists, the Soviets exploded their first atomic bomb, the trial of Alger Hiss began, and the Korean invasion was launched. Amidst these events came the revelation in February, 1950, that an atomic spy ring, headed by German-born scientist Klaus Fuchs, had presumably provided Russia with the technical information that enabled it to produce the bomb. It was at that moment that Senator Joseph McCarthy put himself at the forefront of a mounting public concern and from thereon, in a display of crude demagoguery, he took the lead in transforming concern into a witch hunt.

On most of these developments *The Catholic Worker* said little, even ignoring McCarthy except at the height of the hysteria in 1953 when Aratari and Ludlow commented on the baleful oppressiveness to which so many were being subjected as the result of the senator's activities. Dorothy Day was silent, trying to follow, probably, Maurin's principle that Workers should be "announcers" and not "denouncers." Yet Dorothy Day and *The Catholic Worker* took a stand on the particular aspects of the storms that swirled around the Communist issue and were denounced for it.

One of the strongest positions taken by the *Worker* was

its opposition to the anti-Communist Smith and McCarran acts. The former, passed by Congress in 1940, made it a crime to teach or advocate the violent overthrow of any government in the United States, or to be a member in any organization that held such views. The McCarran Internal Security Act denied entrance into the United States of persons whose history had been radical, authorized the deportation of alien Communists, and created a subversive control board. These measures, so the *Worker* believed, represented another movement away from freedom toward the same totalitarianism that they were supposed to be against.

Part of the affront offered by the *Worker* to the public, but especially to the Catholic public, was its disposition to make common cause with Communists against those actions they mutually opposed, even to the point of speaking of Communists as "brothers," and always insisting, when recognizing the shortcomings of Communism, that those of capitalism were as obvious. "I have spoken," wrote Dorothy Day, "at Carnegie Hall against the Smith and McCarran acts, with Communists, and fellow travelers, others of us have walked on picket lines protesting the payment of income tax . . . in Peter Maurin's words, 'we have no party line, neither Communist nor Catholic.' "

It was about this same time that Dorothy Day, Irene Naughton, and Robert Ludlow published a statement on anti-Communism: "Although we disagree with our Marxist brothers on the question of the means to use to achieve social justice, rejecting atheism and materialism in Marxist thought and in bourgeois thought, we respect their freedom as a minority group in this country. . . . We protest the imprisonment of our Communist brothers and extend to them our sympathy and admiration for having followed their conscience even in persecution."

Writing on the Smith Act, John McKeown observed in the November, 1949, issue that that piece of legislation, cheered by so many Catholics, was in reality another in a long series of defeats suffered by the Church "every time it has allowed itself to be dragged into the ideological arena against the Communists on the side of Capitalism." The July–August, 1949, issue was almost entirely given over to the subject of Communism, but which turned out, in part, to contain some critical comment on capitalism. A quotation from the April 10, 1949, issue of *L'Osservatore Romano* was prominently featured: "Communism, considered as an economic system apart from its philosophy, is not as much the antithesis, the opposite and the contradiction of Christianity as capitalism is."

That Dorothy Day should on occasion accept an invitation to appear at some public rally, known by all to have been planned by Communists, struck many Catholics, long taught to think in terms of the "scandal" that might be caused in injudicious associations, as a willful case of publicly consorting with the devil. When Workers had made common cause with the Communists in several instances in the thirties, the outcry was small, but in the fifties, as Senator McCarthy drove his crusade to higher levels of expectations of forthcoming revelations of Communist hellishness, the reaction was sometimes choleric. It became a matter of such moment that Joseph Brieg, a columnist for a number of diocesan papers, took it up in his "As Matters Stand." He said that he revered Dorothy Day for her great charity but he could not say the same for her common sense, a statement he was "sorry" to have to make. "It was silly beyond words for her to consent to be among the speakers at the recent New York meeting of the Communist-front 'National Council of Arts, Sciences, and Professions.'" It was nothing less than a "monumental blunder." Did her heart bleed only for the poor she could see? What about those who suffered from "the blasphemies, the sacrileges, the horrible lies" of the Communists, or did this "leave her cold?" "How can I consort with these enemies?" she asked. "But I have felt the absence of God in many another milieu in my life."

A priest wrote in to charge that the Workers were not Catholics at all. "Why don't you come out in the open, de-

clare yourselves Bolshevik Communists and fight the
Church like men?" He deemed it "One of the frustrating
evils of living in our American democracy" to have "to sit by
almost defenseless while ungrateful parasites like you bite
the hand of the country that feeds you." It was too bad that
there was "no effective police action taken against a publication like *The Catholic Worker* which boasts of and en-
courages the way of life of loafers, draft dodgers, traitors to
their country and sensational publicity-hungry psychotics."

In July, 1949, those Catholics who yearned for a tighten-
ing of battle lines against the Communist menace, prefera-
bly effected by some striking exercise of Church authority,
felt that the Vatican had at last come to see the wisdom of
their vision. On Wednesday, July 27, *The New York Times,*
extracting from *L'Osservatore Romano,* gave the substance
of a Holy Office excommunication decree against Communists. This office, which deals with all questions of faith and
morals, presented its decree in two parts: the first was concerned with "forbidden actions that give direct or indirect
support to anti-religious doctrine and policy, even if those
who promote them do not practice that [communist] doctrine." The second part dealt with those who "profess and
defend materialistic and anti-Christian doctrine of communism," and who are "without question excommunicated."

*The Times* judged that for most Westerners the first part
of the decree was more important than the second in that
many Catholics had been "fooled" by the promises of the
Communists on the issue of social reform. These persons "do
not incur excommunication, but the Holy See places before
them the grave responsibilities they incur by supporting the
arch-enemies of the Christian religion."

In essence the decree changed little. It apparently excommunicated those who had already excommunicated themselves, and, as for those Catholics who collaborated with the
Communists, they were not excommunicated but abjured to
recognize their grave responsibility in giving support to
Communist causes. Yet the Sunday following the decree's

appearance, a sermon was given at St. Patrick's Cathedral in which its application was made to include an extensive company of "duped" Catholics, including, most pointedly, the Catholic Workers. It was the Reverend B. Broderick, of the staff of the cathedral who, in the presence of Cardinal Spellman, interpreted the decree. A Catholic, he said, "may not flirt with Communism . . . nor can he tune in on the party line by reading for information, professional reasons or curiosity, Communist publications. . . ." Reaching for a more dramatic impact, he declared that the decree had turned the "clock to midnight on the masquerade party—the fifth columnist is unmasked, the fellow traveler, for all of his protestations of progressive Christianity, and for all of his attachment to the so-called idealist Christian Left, must declare his proper loyalty. The toying parlor pink must show his true color—red or not red. . . . There's no place in the Church of Christ for religious centaurs, for collaborators, equivocators, appeasers, temporizers, straddlers, deluded professional liberals, carpetbaggers. . . ."

This soaring, florid rhetoric had a quality of gauche humor about it, but it apparently stung Dorothy Day, for she clipped the item and underlined the part condemning "the so-called idealist Christian Left." In the July–August issue of the *Worker*, she said that it was "hard to love those who speak scornfully of progressive Christianity, the so-called idealist left, religious centaurs . . . it is hardest to love and live in peace with those of one's own family. . . . The worse enemy will be those of one's own household."

Nonetheless, she took the decree seriously, as evidenced by a memorandum she wrote concerning her speech at the meeting of the Communist-front National Council of Arts, Sciences, and Professions. She noted that Cardinal Suhard, the Archbishop of Paris, "approved collaboration even with the Communist Party for 'limited and specific ends.'" But Cardinal Suhard's formula hardly applied to her. She communicated with Communists, and attended their meetings at times not to "collaborate," but to bring to them a message of spirit. It was not more polarization that was needed. "We

must seek concordances," she would say, and the journeys
she made into the world of Communism, whether in Union
Square, as on the first day of the Worker movement, or in
Cuba as in a later time, were made looking for the "concordances" of which she spoke.

There were many who, wearing the label of Communist,
felt as she, a call to community and justice, and who responded to her with trust and warmth. In 1952, amidst the
full crescendo baying of those who would uproot from mob
and community all whose views were suspect, Dorothy Day
met with that longtime journalist-spokesman for revolutionary causes Anna Louise Strong. Miss Strong had, since the
days of the Soviet Revolution, been writing sympathetically
of revolutionary struggles around the world, and her meeting with Dorothy Day resulted in a letter to her that produced some reflections on her own life. She herself had had
religious inclinations, she said. When she was young she
had spent many hours lying under the stars in what seemed
communion with God. But then had come the time "when I
knew clearly that if I continued in the social causes that
claimed me, I should gradually lose this vision. . . . I made
my choice, remembering how St. Francis turned to the beg-
gar, yet found the vision in the end of the day. And now
that I have spent my life in the service of a movement
which I still love . . . I sometimes wonder whether—and by
what route—older values are returning. I am not in urgency; I shall not disown any values I have found, but I am
testing them slowly." Miss Strong died in China in 1970,
where she had spent the last decade of her life interpreting
events in that country in a newsletter which she sent to her
friends abroad, among whom was Dorothy Day.

One quality above all that must have reassured Dorothy
Day's friends of the Left was her indisposition to elevate to
immediate sainthood the Communist convert. When Louis
Budenz, an American Communist leader of the thirties, be-
came a Catholic in 1945, the *Worker* greeted him with
"Welcome Home, Louis Budenz," adding immediately that
"We hope now that Mr. Budenz is not going to fight com-

munism." It was a remark that gave pause to an old ex-Leftist, poet Claude McKay. "I was a little bewildered . . . by your "Welcome Home, Louis Budenz," he wrote to Dorothy Day.

There was yet one more event to take place in the sick spectacle of anti-Communist hysteria that many Americans would witness with pain. The arrest in England of the atomic scientist Klaus Fuchs had led back in the United States to one Harry Gold, whom Fuchs identified as the courier to whom he had given information to pass on to the Russians, and then to Morton Sobell and Julius and Ethel Rosenberg. The trial of the Rosenbergs and codefendant Sobell has been labeled by historian Stewart Easton as "one of the most bizarre in the United States history," and that "they surely would not have been executed if they had confessed or given useful information to the FBI—which waited hopefully for it until the end."

The Rosenbergs were found guilty and their execution was scheduled for June, 1953. As that time drew near, the *Worker* concerned itself more and more with that prospect. A despondent Ludlow wrote: "It is not a just age we live in. It is an age where guilt by association is fast becoming the accepted method of judging. . . . And our patriotic Catholics and our wretched publications do not see this as the leaders of the Church in France did not see it before the Revolution and as the leaders in Spain did not see it. And when they do see it (of course they never really do) then they will envision themselves as the innocent victims of devils." He concluded with a prayer. "May all Catholics, in union with the Supreme Pontiff who has already asked that clemency be granted the Rosenbergs, send one last plea that these lives be spared."

There was no clemency; the Rosenbergs protested their innocence to the last, and at eight o'clock on Friday, June 19, they began their walk to the death chamber. Dorothy Day was at the farm. "That June evening the air was fragrant with the smell of honey suckle. Out under the hedge . . . the black cat played with a grass snake, and the newly

cut grass was fragrant in the evening air. . . . I prayed for
fortitude for them both. 'Oh God let them be strong, take
away all fear from them, let them be spared this suffering,
at least, this suffering of fear and trembling.' "

She was glad that a rabbi had been with them, reading
the Psalms as he followed them to the execution chamber—
"those same psalms Cardinal Spellman reads every week as he
reads his breviary. . . . I have seen rabbis on all-night
coaches, praying thus in the morning. Who can hear the Word
of God without loving the Word? Who can work for what
they conceive of as justice, as brotherhood, without loving
God and brother?" If the Rosenbergs were spies, "they were
doing what we also do in other countries." Yes, she said, they
were serving a philosophy, a religion, but how mixed up religion could become. "What confusion we have gotten into
when Christian prelates sprinkle holy water on scrap metal,
to be used for obliteration bombing, and name bombers for
the Holy Innocents, for Our Lady of Mercy; who bless a man
about to press a button which releases death on fifty thousand
human beings, including little babies, children, the sick, the
aged, the innocent as well as the guilty. 'You know not of
what spirit you are,' Jesus said to his apostles when they
wished to call down fire from heaven on the inhospitable Sa-
maritans. . . ."

She was glad that Ethel Rosenberg's final gesture was to
turn to one of the two police matrons who accompanied her
and kiss her. "Her last gesture was a gesture of love. Let us
have no part with the vindictive state and let us pray for
Ethel and Julius Rosenberg. . . . May their souls, as well as
the souls of the faithful departed, rest in peace."

---

# 15

# CHRYSTIE STREET

In May, 1950, Dorothy Day alerted readers of *The Catholic Worker* that a crisis was at hand—the "most severe . . . in the seventeen years of our existence. . . . Today we begin our eighteenth year . . . and we are faced with the need to find ourselves a new home." The Mott Street house was to be sold by the lay religious group that owned it, and Workers were looking for twenty-five thousand dollars in donations to buy a new place. Throughout the summer Dorothy Day begged, writing an occasional letter whose tone was so trusting and so unrelated to the subject of money that checks came in and sometimes they were large. "You will find enclosed a check in the amount of three thousand dollars which I am loaning to the Catholic Worker in the name of our Lady of the Rosary," said one letter.

Then there was the problem of finding another suitable location and a rosary novena was resorted to. It—or something—worked, for when it appeared that they might be moved out onto the streets, they discovered a location at 221 Chrystie Street which they got for thirty thousand dollars. Dorothy Day thanked God and all of the readers. "Peter Maurin used to say that he liked things to come to a crisis and he certainly brought on a crisis for us this summer. . . . We have gotten far more than we ever dreamed of having"—a "big double house, red brick, high ceilinged, with its iron grilling over the porch and stairway, its iron

fence in front, its large yard, this is room indeed for our dining room, our breadline, and for those who come to stay
with us."

In September she climbed up to the fifth floor of the old
tenement for the last time. They had lived there for fourteen years and she wondered how they had stood for so
long all of the confusion, dirt, and noise that went with the
place. Yes, it had been bad: cold, damp, and drafty, surrounded with the noise of crying children, gossiping neighbors, jukeboxes, blocked traffic, and grinding trucks. But in
the midst of the filth and noise there had been the seed of a
swelling joy, the knowledge that the course was being followed aright.

She was sad at leaving the Italian neghborhood. "We love
our . . . neighbors. . . . We could never have lived so long
without trouble in any but an Italian neighborhood, while
our breadline was building up filling their halls on rainy
days, blocking the sidewalks."

In the September *Worker* there was news of yet another
acquisition. It was a small farm of twenty-two acres at 469
Bloomingdale Road, Pleasant Plains, Staten Island. It was
called the "Peter Maurin Farm," and Maurin was blamed
for its having been acquired. "I have often said that Peter
Maurin had so compelling a way with him, had so great a
moral force, that if he had asked me to get in the middle of
Madison Square Garden to speak, I would have obeyed,"
explained Dorothy Day. Thus, "this compulsion that was on
me to go on with the purchasing of the Staten Island farm
regardless of the fact that we had just finished purchasing
. . . headquarters on Chrystie Street, was due to Peter. He
has goaded us and bestirred us."

Talk of leaving the Newburgh farm had occcurred beginning in October, 1949. Dissatisfaction with it was occa-
sioned by its distance from the city, which made commuting
difficult, and by the presence of a nearby airport where military jets were continually landing and taking off. Since
Dorothy Day had gotten a thousand-dollar advance from
Harper's on her manuscript, *The Long Loneliness*, she and

the others decided then to buy the Staten Island farm. She
signed the purchase contract, but it was shortly voided
through legal complications. Who or what legally was the
Catholic Worker movement? Eventually this problem was
resolved by setting up a trusteeship, but for the moment
they had no purchase. Perhaps they should keep the Newburgh farm, she thought. "Peter had died there, then Charlie O'Rourke. . . . I felt most uncertain, not knowing what
to do."

Then one morning, "like the importunate widow, I asked
for a sign of the Lord. It was at Mass, and I kept saying to
myself, 'If I don't hear something by eleven o'clock this
morning I am going to drop the whole idea. . . . It was a
promise to the Lord." And sure enough, before eleven
o'clock a friend called and offered to lend the Workers several thousand dollars. Already the owners had come down
on the amount of down payment required, and they further
agreed to take the mortgage themselves. Dorothy Day had
all the signs she needed.

What she really had wanted, one might guess, was the
occasion to ride the Staten Island ferry again. She had gone
to the island to see their new purchase, and then as evening
came she was back on the ferry for the ride to the city. A
steady east wind blew and the swells rode heavy. "The taste
of the salt spray was on my lips, and the sense of being upheld on the water reminded me of 'the everlasting arms'
which sustain us. Gulls wheeled overhead, grey and blue
against the dark sea. On the Brooklyn shore the setting sun
shone red in the windows of the warehouses. . . ." It was, as
she wrote, a moment of peace and refreshment. Then she
said a prayer: "May the many who come to us on the island
feel this calm and strength and healing power of the sea,
and may it lift them to God as it has so often lifted me."

After the Workers made their move to the new house,
Tom Sullivan changed the name of his column to "Chrystie
Street" and brought to readers, as he had for Mott Street,
the little dramas of comic pathos that seemed always to be a
part of life at a Worker house. Sullivan described one that

occurred at Chrystie Street one Sunday afternoon in February, 1952. Some of the men of the house were sitting around the television, watching Bishop Sheen (who conveyed to Sullivan the feeling that he was getting his "final instructions just before The Last Judgment") give his Sunday afternoon talk. As Sheen sermonized, a guest of the house named Frank provided a running commentary:

> When the Bishop mentioned the woman at the well asking Christ for the Living Water, Frank snarled, "everybody is always asking for something." As the Bishop made the point that the worst sinners against impurity stood a better chance for salvation than those who had sinned against pride, Frank broke in at the pause and said, "I wish you would come down here and tell that to this gang who are running the Catholic Worker."

There was the night a young woman came in and ate with the group. She had never been there before, nor did they ever see her again. That night she ate her meal in silence, then got up from the table. Instead of walking toward the nearest door, she made her way toward the counter separating the dining room from the kitchen where she stopped and addressed the cook and the entire kitchen staff. "I am not thanking you bums for a bit of the meal I just ate," she said. "I am thanking the Man on the Cross," pointing to a crucifix hanging on the wall.

It was Sullivan who kept readers informed about what the critics were saying about Dorothy Day's new book, *The Long Loneliness*, that came out in January, 1952. As a sequel to *From Union Square to Rome*, it brought the Worker story up through Peter Maurin's death. Just about everyone, Sullivan said, had given the book good reviews.

It was, possibly, the publication of the book that led the writer Dwight Macdonald to believe that Dorothy Day would be a good subject for an article, for he shortly set about gathering material for one. Sullivan reported on Macdonald's research: "Now a man sporting a beret and a beard is rushing around interviewing people for a profile on

Dorothy Day to appear in *The New Yorker*." He was concerned about what *The New Yorker* could do to a person or institution. Witness, said Sullivan, who was a loyal Chicagoan, "that atrociously unfair series that they recently completed on our fair city of Chicago. After they finished tearing Chicago down I got the impression that there was less left than there was after the Chicago fire."

Dwight MacDonald's Profile appeared in two sections, the first on October 4, 1952, and the second a week later. Sullivan reported the reaction from Chrystie Street. All things considered, everybody thought the articles were "pretty fair pieces of writing." There were, however, some reservations. One person thought that it had been a terrible mistake to have become involved with a magazine that was "an outstanding source of nourishment for the *bourgeois* mind." Another person was annoyed with some of the complimentary statements that the articles had contained about the Worker house. He said that *he* had lived there a year and *he knew* what the truth was.

Running through the history of the New York houses were those occasions of visitations from one or another city department, insisting that, since the Worker ran something in the nature of a public house, it fulfill the requirements of city safety codes. There was always the feeling among Workers that, since they were only trying to exercise charity, they should not be subject to bureaucratic regulation, but such reasoning availed them nothing, and from time to time they were forced to undergo renovations to meet safety standards. One time, as Tom Sullivan related it, a man from the city came demanding that metal holders be installed flanking each window so that a window washer would be properly protected. Sullivan's response was that they had no plans to wash the windows then or at any time in the future.

Six months later Sullivan and the Workers had an occasion to be profoundly grateful to the city. One morning about 5:30 A.M., a fire alarm sounded at the house. Those routed on the lower floors saw smoke pouring out of the third, fourth, and fifth floors with men stretched far out over the window ledges gasping for air. Sullivan gladly recognized that these men's lives were saved by the fire department. "The ladders were shot up in a matter of seconds to the windows where the men clung. Valiant firemen raced to the top of the ladders and helped our men . . . down into the waiting ambulances. . . ."

No lives were lost in the fire, but one man, who had been chronically ill, died later from the effects of smoke inhalation and exertion. Part of the cost of reconstructing damaged areas was met by insurance, and readers of the *Worker* again contributed generously. "We had a serious letter from a former guest of ours," reported Sullivan, "who . . . seemed quite sure that one of us had started the fire 'to provoke more contributions to the Catholic Worker.'"

Over at Peter Maurin Farm a Worker life was commencing. Some of those who had been at Newburgh were moving down. For a while the Hennessys were at the farm, having been forced to leave West Virginia because of the rigors of trying to rear a large family on an undercapitalized family farm. Just before Christmas, 1951, they rented a house at Rossville, Staten Island. In January, David and Betty Dellinger came to the farm with their three children, while Mrs. Dellinger awaited the birth of their fourth. They had just returned from Europe, where Dellinger had been distributing pacifist literature behind the Iron Curtain.

In 1953, Peggy Conkling came to live at the farm. As Peggy Baird she had been Dorothy Day's friend and companion when the latter first came to New York as a student from the University of Illinois. They had been jailed together in 1917 when picketing the White House with suffragists. In the mid-twenties the two were together again when Peggy, as the wife of Malcolm Cowley, lived near Dorothy Day's beach cottage on Raritan Bay. As the twenties ended, the Cowleys were divorced, and Peggy briefly was engaged to the poet Hart Crane until his suicide on April 26, 1932, on a return voyage from Mexico. Then Peggy had married again and for almost twenty years she and Dorothy Day saw little of one another. Now she was at the farm, reading paperbacks and flower gardening. In the summers, when her flowers bloomed, she made beautiful floral arrangements for the dining-room table.

For Dorothy Day there was more traveling. In 1950 she was on the West Coast again and met Archbishop Francis McIntyre. He greeted her warmly and she thought he might have been homesick for New York. The people of California loved him, she said, and that was the way she had always felt about him, remembering her early days as a Catholic when he had gone out of his way to help her.

In June, 1952, she was invited to an unveiling of the statue of the "Madonna of the Hudson," but she did not go. She was just as glad, "since I would have to run into that unsavory character, Joseph P. Ryan, president of the International Longshoreman's Union, attending the function, no doubt, with guns and bodyguards." She suspected that the whole thing was a public-relations stunt and she thought appropriate to the situation a quotation from Evelyn Underhill that "'our modern humanitarianisms and sentimentalisms, our ceaseless attempt to harness the supernatural in the interest of our dark Satanic mills, looking very cheap and thin over against the solemn realities of religion, the awful priority of God. . . .'"

In September, though, she did get to upstate New York and had a visit with Julia Leacraft, who back in the twenties had taken French lessons from Peter Maurin. She told Dorothy Day that her children had made comments on how ragged and unkempt Maurin was. "We were sure . . . that he never bathed, and he seemed to sleep in his clothes. When I put my question to him, why did he not take better care of his appearance, his reply was simple. 'So as not to excite envy.'"

The following month Dorothy began a long journey of four months that took her to Vancouver, down the coast to San Diego, then to Phoenix, to Memphis, down to New Orleans, over to Tampa and West Palm Beach and up through Atlanta to New York. One of her main objectives on this trip

was to visit a new house of hospitality at Memphis run by
Helen Caldwell, a young Black woman, described by Dorothy Day as beautiful and tremendously talented. With a
marriage gone awry, Miss Caldwell had been in New York
training to become a nurse when she developed tuberculosis. It was during her convalescence that she became acquainted with the Workers, and, influenced by their example, she became a Catholic.

In 1951 she returned to her hometown of Memphis,
where shortly she and a few young people and several families were meeting periodically at a Josephite parish house
as a Catholic Worker cell. It was Miss Caldwell who initi-
ated the idea of beginning a house of hospitality, a decision
she made when three little children were burned to death in
her neighborhood after their mother had locked them in the
garage while she went out to work. Such occurrences were
not uncommon. And so, in an old store front at 299 South
Fourth Street, the Blessed Martin de Porres house of hospitality was begun.

Dorothy Day wrote of her first night there. All day she
had been traveling across Arkansas over narrow roads on a
bus that seemed to have a broken spring, if not one of the
wheels missing. When she got there, Miss Caldwell told her
that she would be breaking the law if she spent the night
at the Fourth Street house, but she was too tired to give
much thought to that eventuality. Weary though she was,
she could not get to sleep because the rats seemed to have
been in a festive mood that night, running back and forth
and squalling in chorus. Finally, the house cat took a position on the foot of the bed, and reassured by its presence,
she went to sleep.

At five-thirty the next morning, the mothers began to
come in, depositing their little ones as they went off to the
day's work. The first was Annie Green, bringing her three,
as she headed off to the Arkansas fields to pick cotton.
Later, after the children were all in and affairs organized,
Miss Caldwell and Dorothy Day began the day by going to
Mass down the street in old St. Patrick's Church where Car-

dinal Stritch had once been a pastor but which now was staffed by Paulist priests.

What Dorothy Day recalled most vividly about her visit to the Blessed Martin House was her spooning out cod-liver oil "to that long line of little ones, standing so trustfully and so open mouthed like little birds." And this instance, like others that had struck her, was made the occasion of a re-·flection. No normal person would make a bomb to kill one of them, she said, but in the large and organized affairs of the object world, few had qualms about making bombs that would kill thousands of such children. Thinking of that wretched, crowded slum there in Memphis, where life early became soiled, she thought of the innocence of those children and the problems of poverty. Theirs were "so vast . . . and we think how little we can do. But with a sense of the Mystical Body, the knowledge comes that we can lower or heighten the strength and love in the Body, we can work as Helen does, among the least of God's children. . . . 'Go to the poor.' Not only to serve them, but to be of them, the despised, the forgotten, the neglected and needy, taking from others, beggars too, giving up job and hope and independence and becoming as Christ told us, one of the 'little ones.' Of such is the kingdom of heaven."

The Blessed Martin House, as a child-care center, survived for three years, and that in part because of the help of a young Memphian, Robert Steed. Having been in the Trappists for two years, he returned to Memphis "and found that The Catholic Worker had opened a house . . . I don't think anything could have been more welcome as far as I was concerned. . . ." Steed scrubbed floors, changed diapers and washed clothes, and otherwise found time to picket a local Bell Telephone office during a telephone workers' strike in 1955.

Others, too, helped at the house. Mothers of the cared-for children helped when they could, and another "Helen," who was expecting a child, lived at the house and took her part of the work. The Memphis Christian Brothers, as Steed observed, "more than once . . . literally kept food on the shelf and table." But support and interest dwindled, and finally Helen Caldwell could keep the house open no longer and it was closed in 1955.

Otherwise, on her four-month trip Dorothy Day witnessed a development that disturbed her. All over the country, many churches and church schools were being built, and, while some of them were no doubt needed, she also felt that there was too much building on too grand a scale. Building there should be, but for the poor, for families. She was also convinced that the clergy had been "taken for a ride by the contractors." And in the end, as the clergy deserted their mission of spirit in their concern to erect more churches and schools, they contributed, she thought, to that inevitable reaction that resulted in priests being "crucified to their church doors, hung from telegraph poles, stuffed into holes of prisons and left to rot." In America "We . . . are like Dives sitting at the banquet table, and the rest of the world, Asia, India, Africa, are like Lazarus sitting at the gate. God help us. One half of the world pledged to fight the Church, and we go on piling field on field, building on building." She did not want to emphasize the subject unduly, but were she to remain quiet "the very stones of the street would cry out. . . ."

Perhaps she was thinking back to a visit she had made to Chicago when she and some Workers went to see a monsignor about renting a church-owned house for a family center. All he had had to say to them was that the family was the responsibility of the state, and that the neighborhood had deteriorated so that it was full of truck drivers instead of doctors and lawyers which it once had had. He concluded by saying that he had bought the property to protect the church and that he did not want any shantytowns around him.

On that same trip to Chicago she had stopped over at Harrisburg, Pennsylvania, and had heard Louis Budenz warn that "the communists would try to foment anti-clericalism and divide the people from the heirarchy." Her reaction was that there was really no need of their doing it. It was already an accomplished fact. It was her hope that the Catholic Worker movement could help in bridging the gap between the clergy and that great body of people who were not part of the system of the established and secure middle class.

In 1954 and 1955, as Americans talked with confidence about full employment and the end of poverty, she wrote more of the poor. "Where Are the Poor?" she asked in the January, 1955, *Worker*. The poor were still with us, she said —in the slums, in those rural areas of the South where Blacks suffered inhuman deprivation, and, as she wrote in one article, "They are in prisons, too."

She thought of the poor in those areas of the world whose only contact with Western "progress" had so frequently been in the form of colonial exploitation. In May, 1954, the lead headline in *The Catholic Worker* was "Theophane Venard and Ho Chi Minh," which she wrote as the McCarthy-Army hearings displaced the afternoon soap operas on television, and while, on the other side of the world, a different drama, that of Dien Bien Phu, was in progress. Theophane Venard was a priest-missionary who had gone to Vietnam and who had been executed by a local chieftain in 1860. Venard, she said, was a missionary who opposed all forms of colonialism, including the presence of arms that might have saved his life. This was his position up until the time he was executed, a matter that he took so lightheartedly he obligingly took off his clothes for the executioner so that he might retrieve them unstained by his blood.

The point about Venard, she said, was its contrast with Dien Bien Phu. The latter was an example of the ease with which one could fall into the heroics of colonialism. It was difficult at such times to see things clearly. If Americans thought that a defeat of Ho Chi Minh by the French at Dien Bien Phu would result in a protection of their own interests, they were mistaken. It was the poor of the world, the exploited, who would have the last voice. It was the dominated who would conquer.

From Dien Bien Phu to Chrystie Street—the concerns of

Dorothy Day encompassed much, and in the spring of 1954 she had to confront again a problem within the Worker household. Over the years it had become the habit of Father Paul Hanley Furfey occasionally to ask Dorothy Day how she managed "to lose so many wonderful people to the work." It was a remark, she said, that they often quoted to one another because there was some element of truth in it. There was also that other comment that came to be a kind of saying—"in the Catholic Worker the gold is expelled and the dross remains." Certainly, in 1954 and 1955, the Worker movement lost some wonderful people who might indeed have been accounted its gold.

First it was Robert Ludlow. In the Feburary, 1954, issue of the *Worker*, Dorothy Day noted that Ludlow was taking a leave of absence. He had been at the house a long time, but finally he had come to feel that he would have to make his existence on his own terms. He would write occasionally for the paper in the years to come, but when he left, it marked the end of the most intellectually vital decade in the history of *The Catholic Worker*.

The following year Tom Sullivan gave the news that another Worker had left. This time it was Tony Aratari, who in the postwar years had added his own thoughtful and literary dimension to the paper. Two months later Sullivan wrote of the death of Robert (Shorty) Smith. He had died in the city hospital after his "fourth or fifth" operation for cancer. He was fifty-five years old and had been with the Worker for eigheen years. Like some others who were down and out during the Depression years, all he had wanted was some work to do he could call his own. Smith had worked in the kitchen. He must have averaged twelve to fifteen hours a day, Sullivan said. He never sat down in the dining room, even eating his meals while standing. But he sat down plenty during his last three years, when he was too ill to work. He had tried repeatedly to help in the kitchen but finally had to crawl off to the sidelines and wait for death. Sullivan knew that it was going to take a very long time to get over the loss of Smith. He had made an almost total contribution of himself to the ongoing life of the Worker house. He belonged, said Sullivan, on the honor roll with the great people who had died in the Catholic Worker movement. Sullivan noted along with Smith's death that of another cancer victim at the house, Henry Sanborn. Sanborn, too, had had a lingering death but he suffered with a bravery that few had seen. Sanborn said that he was offering that suffering to God for every soul on the Bowery.

Right after Smith's death, Sullivan left the Worker. He was trying to reach some decision about what to do finally with his life, and in an attempt to view the problem more clearly, he had decided to go for a while to the Trappist monastery at Conyers, Georgia. He had wanted to go for a year, Dorothy Day said, but Smith's illness had kept him there. When Smith died, he left.

It was true: some good people had been lost to the work; some gold had gone, but there was more gold at hand. In February, 1955, Deane Mowrer, who had once been an English professor, contributed her literary talent to the *Worker* with an article on a retreat at the Newburgh farm. With a gradually failing vision, Miss Mowrer thereafter made the Worker her home, and eventually she contributed her regular column, "Farm With a View," delicately written accounts of life and the world of nature at the Catholic Worker farm.

After the Blessed Martin House in Memphis closed, Bob Steed went to Chrystie Street, and for a while took over the job of writing the news of the house that Sullivan had had in his "Chrystie Street" column. About this time, Charlie McCormick moved in as house manager and contributed his own view of life at the house. And, dominating *The Catholic Worker* for the next five years, as no one else except Dorothy Day had ever done, was Ammon Hennacy with his very personal and highly entertaining accounts of his one-man contest with powers and principalities over the issue of war and the bomb.

Dorothy Day took the changes with equanimity. The vicissitudes, suffering, and tragedy of the world were but for a

Dorothy Day in office, 1955. Vivian Cherry photo.

time, and she always found within her life those contemplative and prayerful moments that came from the simplest of
sources and which seem so incongruous to those many who
would flow with the world and its signs. In January, 1955,
she, the Christian who consorted with Marxists and called
them brothers, who lived and preached revolution, visited a
little church in the poor section of St. Paul, Minnesota. It
was a small frame building, painted a deep green. It was
light and warm inside and, she thought, had the feeling of a
much loved place. There was a shrine to Our Lady of Guadalupe there, which despite the garish decorations, moved
her by its beauty. "I love to visit her shrines, and make special requests there," she said, because these shrines were
many times found in the neighborhoods of the poor. "What
was my joy," she said, to find "that this was a place where a
miracle had taken place back in 1944 when a woman on her
way to Rochester clinic had been instantly healed . . . by
her prayers."

# 16

# TWENTY-FIVE YEARS

One day in March, 1956, Dorothy Day was handed a summons ordering her to appear before a city judge to answer charges of being a slum landlord and running a firetrap. Moving from the primitive conditions of Mott Street into a house where toilets flushed and sunlight occasionally filtered into rooms seemed to Workers to have been a move into luxury. The summons was, therefore, a heavy blow. And it was compounded at her court appearance when she was fined $250 and informed that a notice to vacate had already been issued which would take effect within a week. Her first thought was to go to jail, but she quickly realized that becoming immobilized behind bars would do nothing for the fifty or more people at the house who would be turned into the street.

At this point the story got into the newspapers. It was of the stuff that could make a journalist's day when all else failed—the dedicated and selfless group taking the poor into their home, giving them unlimited hospitality, and asking nothing of them, only to be fined and charged with being a slum landlord. *The New York Times* carried a statement of what had occurred, and it was this story that brought significant reaction. Several days later, as Dorothy Day was leaving the house on the way to a second appearance before the judge, she saw a group of men assembled for a clothing handout. As she approached, one stepped out toward her.

Her immediate thought was that it was one of the unemployed men, but when she got closer she recognized the poet W. H. Auden. "Here is two-fifty," he said, pressing a piece of paper into her hand. She thanked him and after some brief talk she hurried to catch the subway to go up to the court session at 151 Street. On the train she looked at her check and discovered that Auden's "two-fifty" meant $250! She was delighted, and then at the court her mood was given another boost. The judge suspended her fine, explaining that he did not realize that it was a charitable organization she served. He gave her time to raise the $28,000 that would be needed to make the house conform to the building codes.

Then came a Cinderella sequence that saw most of the $28,000 coming in almost within a month. The plight the Workers had fallen into could not have been more appealing. The press and the radio gave it full publicity. By Easter Sunday donations had come in to the amount of $23,876.40. Some of this money came in as a result of an appearance Auden made on the television program "Strike It Rich." (But he was not allowed to say on the program, as he had planned, "The great thing about Dorothy Day is that she cares for both the deserving and the undeserving poor.") Dorothy Day found it distressing. What had she done wrong? she asked. It was, she said, in a way a matter for rejoicing when suddenly a great deal of attention was given to the Catholic Worker movement, but at the same time there was something distressing about all of the publicity. It had all been too easy, and from the standpoint of the Gospel, she thought, they had not been blessed. Not that she was overly concerned about all the things that had been written about her in connection with the affair. "If some aspects of my past life are brought out (the reformed sinner) I should not object . . . as to whether what is said is true or not true. 'We never get a lick amiss,' my mother used to tell us when she had slapped the wrong child in some family fray. So if I am blamed for what I did not do, I have too often escaped blame for what I did do."

When it was over she realized that her difficulty with "Holy Mother City" had been a small thing; one, in fact, in which the city had ended up by being quite decent about the whole business. She thought of this as she thought of another community in the South that had for months been facing difficulties far more serious. Throughout 1956 the Koinonia community farm at Americus, Georgia, had stood off assaults against its life, and in April, 1957, with the Chrystie Street affair long since settled, she took a bus for Americus.

The farm was the idea of Clarence Jordan, a Baptist minister who had come to a radical view of what he should be doing with his vocation. Dissatisfied with the role traditionally held by the Southern minister, he and Martin England in 1942 bought four hundred acres of eroded land to found a community. It was a new kind of community they wanted, a community of spirit, free from the taint of conforming to regional traditions where the issue of race was concerned; and free, too, to oppose the nation-state in its role as either a maker of myths or of wars that separated men from one another and violated their humanity.

For over a decade they seemed to have labored at their task without undue notice from the community around them, but in 1956 serious trouble began. In March of that year one of the members of the community signed an application for two Blacks seeking entrance to a Georgia business college. When this was reported in an Americus newspaper, the community began to receive threatening anonymous telephone calls. Shortly, egg customers were refusing to buy eggs; merchants stopped the delivery of gasoline, fertilizer, and butane gas for heating and cooking; mechanics refused to service farm vehicles.

The first violence came in June when an incensed segregationist sped along the state road fronting the farm and fired his pistol into the community's roadside market. On July 23, a charge of dynamite wrecked the market, and on November 27, a fusillade of buckshot destroyed a refrigerated meat case, The day after Christmas, with the holiday time available for working up outraged feelings, and fueled, no doubt, by spirits of local manufacture, the upholders of established tradition made their boldest move. Heavy-caliber rifle fire destroyed the community's fuel pump, with the sign at the farm's entrance providing an especially inviting target. At 1:15 A.M. on January 29, 1957, a speeding car raked the residence nearest the highway with machine-gun fire, and in February the main cluster of residences was subjected to rifle fire. On February 24, after instances of cross burning, the Ku Klux Klan held a mass meeting in Americus, following which members proceeded in a motorcade to Koinonia where two crosses were lit.

At this point Dorothy Day left for the farm. It was snowing when the bus left the station in New York but in New Jersey the snow turned to rain. It was still raining that night when, somewhere in Virginia, she fell asleep. She awakened the next morning in Georgia. The sky had cleared and the air was warm. Passing through small towns where old homes sat back from the street, she could see yards filled with blooming forsythia and azaleas. Arriving in Americus that evening, Clarence Jordan and his little son, Lennie, were there to meet her. After supper she was so tired she went to bed immediately and fell into a sleep that was undisturbed throughout the night.

The next morning she and Florence Jordan, Clarence Jordan's wife, with Lennie between them, started down state road 309, looking for seed for spring planting that they had not been able to buy in Americus. Where 309 intersects state highway 19, the main route south to Albany, is the little town of Smithville. There, they hoped, they might get seed peanuts, but as they brought the farm truck to a halt, a man dressed in a business suit approached, screaming incoherently. Trailing Mrs. Jordan into the store, he cursed the two women, calling them "dirty communist whores," "nigger lovers," and other such phrases reserved for women who violated the racial taboos.

There were no seeds in Smithville either, so they headed down the highway for the next town, Leesburgh, their adversary following close behind, having picked up more of his kind to add strength to his crusade. There were no seeds in Leesburgh, so on they went to Albany where seed dealers found it more prudent to turn the women away rather than face the wrath of the sizable group that now was following. And thus they returned to Koinonia.

The seed incident was not the end of the excitement for Dorothy Day. On Easter Eve she spent the night hours doing sentry duty by sitting in a station wagon, positioned under a floodlight beneath a huge oak tree near the entrance gate. But an unarmed woman, visible in the light, was no deterrent to those whose mission transcended a recognition of the chivalric code. A car came speeding down state highway 49, slowed as it passed the station wagon, and directed a shotgun blast at it. The shot peppered the wagon but touched no one in the car.

With all of the shooting and burning, that no one at Koinonia was injured was regarded as providential by farm residents. But for some of the people in the area, this fact was cited in support of a legend that they had repeated among themselves—that there had been no violence, that it had all been staged to elicit public sympathy and Northern contributions. The Albany *Journal* quoted the solicitor general of the county in which the farm lay as saying to an Albany audience that " 'It was possible for the participants in the Farm's cooperative and racially mixed . . . program to have planted [bombs] as a means of gaining sympathy and public attention.' " In the same speech the solicitor general had gone on to suggest that with affairs such as they were at Koinonia, maybe " 'what we need now is for the right kind of a Klan to start up again and use a buggy whip on some of these race mixers. I believe that would stop them.' " It was, therefore, to be expected that when the county grand jury made its report on the trouble, based on facts assembled by the solicitor general, the conclusion was reached that "Koinonia is probably committing the acts of violence against itself in order to get publicity and money; Koinonia is a Communist front; Negro residents are in a status of 'brain-washed peonage.' "

Dorothy Day went back to New York after Easter, distressed by what the people of the farm were having to put up with. But she was filled with the pleasant sense that comes from having lived in the company of good people and believing that their work represented what Peter Maurin had talked about when he would repeat the old IWW slogan about "building the new within the shell of the old." For their part, the people at the farm had found her presence a support in their difficulties, for she had scarcely gotten home before one member wrote her to tell her that she was missed very much and that she had been an inspiration to all of them.

Back in New York, Dorothy Day's life took on its accustomed proportions. In that summer of 1957 there was again the brief respite of imprisonment for violating civil defense regulations. From prison she went to the farm where she found Father Faley had returned after a long hospital confinement. But she was shortly at Tamar's house, looking after things as Tamar had her eighth child. The Hennessy place was a mile from the farm, and at nights from the small attic room where she slept she could look north to the Jersey shore a mile away. Now it was factory after factory that took the place of the pear and apple orchards she remembered from the twenties. Sometimes the children overwhelmed her. They climbed the highest trees, ran after John Filliger on his tractor, and disappeared in the woods for hours. They were bitten by cats, stung by nettles and jellyfish, and they had festerings of thorns and pieces of cinder in their feet.

As soon as Tamar was back on her feet, Dorothy helped the family pack for another move. The Hennessys liked open space and the area around their house at Staten Island was becoming industrialized and sometimes smog enshrouded. After much searching they had found, near Perkinsville, Vermont, an old farmhouse with land, and on a fine day in early September the family set out for its new home. Tamar and her mother drove with the children, and Hennessy traveled separately in the truck that carried the household goods. The trip was exhilarating, with the first signs of fall in the air and the children eagerly looking forward to their new life. When Dorothy Day saw the roomy old house and the land around, she was satisfied that the move had been for the better.

In the Catholic Worker nothing was as predictable as crisis, and with the new year of 1958 another loomed. The Chrystie Street house was going to be razed. The New York Transit Authority had authorized a new subway connection, and the house lay directly on the line of advance. But the crisis was still a time off, and in January Dorothy Day joined a group going to Mexico to make a pilgrimage to the shrine of Our Lady of Guadalupe. She visited the shrine many times and always came away marveling at the devotion that the common people had for this particular representation of the Blessed Mother. Communists might refer to "the masses, which can be moved and swayed and used in the tactic of class war," she wrote, but "the *people* are another matter." With all of their poverty, the Mexican people had endured and kept their faith.

Back from her trip she went out to Peter Maurin Farm, and one night as the wind howled about the house and tossed the branches of the cherry tree grating along her window, she lay awake, wondering what they should do. Someone had suggested a barge or a houseboat for the Workers. Would that be practical? Or maybe even a Liberty ship so that when people got tired of them they could move somewhere else. After sleep these fancies passed. The fact was, she said, that as long as there were slums Workers would have to live in them. For her part, she hoped that they could find something in an Italian neighborhood. She remembered the Italians from Mott Street days. Not only had they been hospitable, she recalled, but they had taken care of their own. The old and the senile were not put away in institutions but were cared for by the younger generation.

In the midst of the house crisis, the Worker had its twenty-fifth anniversary. In May, 1957, as that twenty-fifth year began, Dorothy Day restated the Worker position as still that of putting into effect Peter Maurin's program for a Christian social order. To present anew some of his ideas in his manner of phrasing, a whole page of "Easy Essays" was included. Then she restated the position that she herself had done most to make a part of the Worker mind: "In all these years we have maintained our pacifist position."

A year later, with the quarter century completed, there were no pronouncements or declarations, but there was some reminiscing. John Cort, one of the first-generation Workers, wrote a nostalgic article, "Back in the Old Days," and Tom Sullivan's "Mott Street" of May, 1948, was reprinted. Otherwise, there was little pausing to look backward. In 1958, it was Kieran Dugan who took Sullivan's place at the house and wrote about Chrystie Street for the paper. Dugan, like Sullivan, wrote of the people at the house, of people like Arthur Lacey, "the irrepressible itinerant" who would, though, settle down firmly into Worker life and become something of a chamberlain in its household. Beth Rogers managed the Peter Maurin Farm and with Deane Mowrer wrote of affairs there. When they were away Stanley Vishnewski filled in for them. Anne Taillifer contributed news stories and book reviews, and in the September, 1963, issue she had a fine interpretative editorial on William Faulkner at the time of his death.

In this era, too, the *Worker* began to feature an occasional article by one or the other of the Berrigan brothers and by Thomas Merton. With Ammon Hennacy, the paper continued to maintain the characteristic vitality that its predecessors had set for it.

Where Dorothy Day was concerned, the completion of twenty-five years found her preoccupied with the house crisis, since the subway down the street was approaching closer and closer. She did, though, indulge in a brief reflection over the past years. When the movement began, she said, she had thought that she was embarking on a career in journalism, but like a true revolutionary movement they had attracted all the cranks, the reformers, the theorists, and "the fools for Christ, who wander like . . . monks of St. Benedict's day." Some who came were holy, she said, some had not even begun to learn to keep the commandments.

Had it meant anything? She recalled how Cardinal Newman had written how tragic it would be if one came to the end of his life to find that he had never even begun to do what God wanted him to do. She hoped that that would not be the case where the Workers were concerned. "I do sincerely think that we keep trying, that we keep beginning again, over and over, each day. . . . God be thanked for the work He has given us to do."

On August 27, the city, after condemnation proceedings, took title to the Chrystie Street property. For the weeks that remained, the Workers would pay the city rent for its use. And then what? They could rent a loft for their office and someplace to sit. They could rent a floor of a hotel for the men and find an apartment nearby for the women. They could still give out clothes; they could still feed the hungry.

They found their loft at 39 Spring Street—a huge one on the top floor of a three-story building. The rent was one hundred dollars a month, which was reasonable, but the last tenant had been a theatrical group and had left the place cluttered with junk. They spent November cleaning the huge room where three sides of it was uninterrupted window space, and in December, Bob Steed began the work of moving.

By the end of January, 1959, they were in and settled. The Friday night meetings had been resumed and the line that had been served at Chrystie Street rapidly re-formed at the new location. Observing how quickly the line had been able to accept the new location, Dorothy Day recalled that the same thing had happened when they had moved from Mott Street back in 1950—the breadline had come right after them, up the ten blocks or so along the Bowery, over east another block, and there they were the next day waiting for their meal. She noted that one good thing about the Spring Street loft was that now many of the men could wait

Bob Steed and Janet Burwash. Lent 1960.

inside for their meal. Workers had never intended, she said, to submit men to the indignity of standing in line. She was always consoled, she said, when she saw people standing in line at an expensive restaurant or at a movie on Broadway.

The Spring Street loft did not work out well in the long run. There were some people in the neighborhood who objected to the presence of the Worker and who were unpleasant about it. For Dorothy Day, though, the greatest suffering was the stairs that had to be climbed. There were two long flights up to the loft and six to the apartment where she lived.

In the spring of 1961 the Workers moved again, this time to 175 Chrystie Street. The old Chrystie Street house had been adequate, and by Worker standards an even refined habitation. But such was the squalor of the new headquarters that visitors were sometimes shocked when they saw it. The ground floor was cement and impossible to keep clean with hundreds of people tramping in and out each day. Twenty persons could be seated there; the overflow went up one short flight to the "sitting room" floor where the clothes room was. The offices were on the third floor, and there, with the ceiling sagging and floor slanting, the paper was put out. With a little money and a few skilled workers, the place could be put in fairly good repair, Dorothy Day thought, but then wondered what this would avail them. The clutter and filth would remain the same.

It was in the course of its domiciliary problems that Dorothy Day did something that struck many people as preposterous. In the September, 1960, issue of *The Catholic Worker* there was printed a copy of a letter she had recently written to the city of New York. She was returning to the city a check for $3,579.39 which represented the interest on the $68,000 that Workers were given as payment for the property at 221 Chrystie Street. She was returning the money because Workers did not believe in moneylending at interest. She explained: "As Catholics we are acquainted with the early teaching of the Church. . . . All the Councils forbade it. . . . In the Christian emphasis on the duty of

St. Joseph House, Chrystie Street, exterior, ca. 1962.
William Carter photo.

St. Joseph House, 175 Chrystie Street, ca. 1966.
Nicole d'Entremont, center. Ed Lettau photo.

Next page: St. Joseph House, Chrystie Street house, interior, ca.
1962. William Carter photo.

Chrystie St. house, ca. 1966. Ed Lettau photo (published in *U.S. Catholic*, April 1966).

charity, we are commanded to lend gratutiously, to give freely, even in the case of confiscation, as in our own case— not to resist but to accept cheerfully."

Naturally some otherwise loyal friends of the Workers were hard put to justify this action. One reader, whose days were filled "with the need and struggle for money" could not at all understand why she had refused to accept money returned by the city. "Your smug righteousness on this matter loses forever whatever little aid I or my friends might have scared up. Since when do you examine the source of all your funds? Do you inquire how each of your various donors acquired the money he . . . sent you?" And now, to top off the whole madness, here he was with an appeal in his hands from Dorothy Day being asked "for a sinful dollar or two from my interest bearing savings account now $25 strong ($5 of which is interest)."

The exasperation seemed justified. E. I. Watkins, the English Catholic philosopher and pacifist, had once informed the Workers that he thought they had every virtue except a sense of proportion. But it was not in the character of Dorothy Day and Catholic Workers to deal with the world with an even logic. They were persons who knew so little of worldly affairs that evenness was beyond their competence. By returning the money she was making a point—exactly what kind of a point she may not even have been sure. But it had something to do with asserting her independence of a system, and especially of an aspect of that system, that in her view over the long term had been a prominent feature of those bourgeois values of the object world that had dehumanized man. It was also an affirmation of her conviction that the Church in one of its basic traditions had stood against this dehumanization. So, she concluded, "primarily our sending back the money was a gesture."

Apart from the stress of the large problems and issues, the daily life of Dorothy Day and the Catholic Worker movement was filled with the ordinary events of the passage of time. There was the daily mail, and sometimes there was news that cheered and warmed. One May morning in 1959 she got a letter from a former guest of the house. He had just settled in his cell in the Hart Island Prison after getting a thirty-day sentence. "What a break!" he exclaimed. "I sure expected a lot more. . . . I'll just be out in time to help with the July and August issue of the paper." Another letter that came almost at the same time was from Jacques and Raïssa Maritain. They sent a check and asked for Dorothy Day's prayers because they were both ill.

Because she was well known and represented an unconventional viewpoint, there were those who wished to have her presence at elitist gatherings, where in the warming presence of well-ordered surroundings, food and drink, and stimulating minds, the conversation would glow and ideas proliferate. Could she, one man of taste and position wanted to know, "join with a small group" at his estate over the weekend to meet with an author-lecturer? "As you know," the letter of invitation said, this special guest had "much to say to our day and generation." Dorothy Day's presence would be absolutely necessary for the success of the weekend since "I will want some discussion of the philosophical basis for a religious faith." Attractive though this invitation was, she probably passed it up, feeling that it was more the action of the object world than of the spirit.

The affairs of the world seemed to be speeding beyond control anyway, she thought. "So many things are happening in the world. . . . We are brought so close to them by newsprint and radio and television (ours does not work) that one feels crushed, submerged by events." The Eichmann trial in 1961 brought alive again the horror of the gas chambers. It made her think of Cardinal Newman's observation that mankind was implicated in some terrible aboriginal calamity.

The decade of the sixties carried within it the seeds of strange and tragic occurrences, suggestions of a time when what little remained that held the universe together and life in some proportion would be questioned and then denied. The Catholic Worker seemed not to change. Good people left and more came; there was the routine of life, and there

was death. Kieran Dugan noted in the paper that Roger
O'Neil, one of the young Workers, was leaving, "a prime example of the personalist. . . . A wonderful example of kindness and patience and devotion to the poor." And, as Dorothy Day observed, Llewellyn Scott was still running his
Blessed Martin House in Washington, D.C., as he had been
doing for almost twenty years.

One event especially in this period brought Dorothy Day
satisfaction and pleasure. In March, 1959, just after the
Workers had settled in the Spring Street loft, she traveled to
the Trappist monastery at Conyers, Georgia, to be present
at Jack English's ordination and first Mass. He was the first
*Worker* editor to become a priest, she observed in the
paper. The Mass was said early one morning at the monastery, and to get there on time she and all of English's
Worker friends had to rise early. It was bitter cold, and the
red clay roads were frozen hard, but compared to New York
there was already something springlike about the air—the
clear bright sky and the sounds of many birds.

The occasion was also a reunion for those who had been
at the Worker houses just as the war began. Dorothy Day
thought about that time and the bitterness that had divided
them when there were great arguments about the war. English had missed out on most of it, she recalled. After he had
become a bomber crewman, he was on his way to England.
In London he had run into an old Communist friend of
hers, Charles Ashleigh, who had been arrested in Chicago
during the First World War and had served a term in Leavenworth in Kansas. Meeting one evening in a tavern, they
had sent her a postcard.

The beginning of the sixties, like that of the fifties, was
the occasion of death for some who had been close to the
movement. Cathy Odlivak, a member of the Chrystie Street
family, had died in October, 1957. A gentle and retiring person, burdened with a bad heart, she had lived quietly but
helpfully at the house. "May she rest in peace and pray for
us, this little Cathy Odlivak who was so unspotted by this
world," Dorothy Day wrote in the *Worker*. Then in Decem-

ber, 1959, Father John Faley had died. Excused from duties that normally would have been assigned to him by a bishop, he had for almost a decade performed as chaplain at Peter Maurin Farm.

Ed Willock, one of the founders of *Integrity* magazine, died on a Sunday, December 18, 1960, after nine years of torturing illness. His passing, like Larry Heaney's a decade before, had an especial pathos. Still a young man and the father of twelve children, he had in his active years prodigally spent his energy in the cause of Catholic renewal, carrying out projects to which he could contribute his gifts as a thinker and writer. After the onset of his illness in 1951, some of his friends in the Worker helped him as much as they could with their time and sometimes with money when they had it. Once when Dorothy Day sent him a small check, he wrote to tell her that, since her gift was so unplanned for in his tight economy, he was going to do something wild with it. The Willock washing machine, running three and four hours a day, had become so hopelessly infirm that it leaked its contents of wash water all over the floor, causing the odor of wet laundry to pervade the entire house. He was going to use her check as a down payment on a new washing machine.

Over the course of his long illness, he was able to live out what he had written concerning his confrontation with death. His statement was published by journalist-columnist Dale Francis after Willock's death, the account of which Francis called "The Story of a Love Affair."

> Those who are chronically ill or handicapped, exemplify in their affliction, a taste of death. . . . So, in a sense we are called to the vocation of demonstrating how to die. Even if our handicap is so extreme as to rule out all work, it is no little thing to have nothing to do but to die. If Our Lord took upon flesh primarily so as to die, it is not a little thing to be asked to do the same. If we are asked to do it in slow motion it is only so as to permit us to demonstrate the lesson more clearly. The more we can think of our suffering as matter of factly as one accepts a job, remembering that hu-

miliation, frustration, pain and loneliness are tools of our
trade, the more Christ will grant us the serenity and cheer-
fulness to bear our lot gracefully.

Another member of the Worker group also met death
gracefully. Elizabeth Burrows wrote to Dorothy Day on December 12, 1960, to tell her that she was hurrying to finish
some writing because the cancer within her had become too
widespread for treatment. If God wanted her to complete
the work, "He will give me time to do it. Otherwise, what
matter?"

Dorothy Day visited her several months later and wrote
of the visit in her column: "We visited Elizabeth Burrows,
known to John Cogley, Tom Sullivan and our Chicago
friends in the earliest days of the Catholic Worker there.
She breaks our hearts with her courage in the face of physical and mental suffering; physical because she has cancer;
mental because of the hostility of . . . people . . . towards
the Negro." It was at the time of the Little Rock school crisis and this, with her physical suffering, made it "as though
she were flayed alive in a long slow martyrdom." She died
in April, 1962.

In July, 1963, Father Joseph McSorley died. He was "our
dearest friend . . . with whose encouragement and advice
Peter Maurin and I launched the Catholic Worker back in
1933," Dorothy Day wrote. As she sat through the Requiem
Mass, she thought how gentle and saintly a man he had
been, one whose person was entirely directed to the priesthood. Father McSorley's passing, as much as any other
event, was the mark of the end of another era in the history
of the Catholic Worker movement. The sixties would bring
the new crisis, when the flight from spirit and the ashes of
an exploding time would settle as a pall over all and obscure the vision of those who sought a way. Yet before the
fifties finally closed, there was for Catholics, and the world,
too, one bright sign of hope.

In the *Worker* of November, 1958, Dorothy Day noted
the death of Pius XII and the election of Angelo Giuseppi

Roncalli as the new pope. "What kind of a man is he going to be, this new pope?" she asked. As if to answer her own question, she quoted one the new pope himself had just asked: "Why should the resources of human genius and the riches of the people turn more often to preparing armies—pernicious instruments of death and destruction—than to increasing the welfare of all classes of citizens and particularly the poor?" The obstacles to this end were many, the new pope had said, "but they must be overcome, even if by force. . . ."

What had he meant in using the phrase, "by force"? some readers had asked Dorothy Day. "I find no difficulty in understanding it," she answered. "Heaven must be taken by violence, and working for a better order here in this world means a terrible struggle." Her "violence" though was not that of the object world but of spirit. "Our means are prayer and fasting, and the non-payment of federal income tax which goes for war." And indeed it was again of war that the world in the sixties would be forced to think.

# 17

# AMMON HENNACY

During the decade of the fifties, Ammon Hennacy dominated the action at *The Catholic Worker*. He was the *Worker's* most energetic salesman, ranging up and down Manhattan Island, pressing *Workers* with good-natured fast talk into the hands of tycoons and revolutionaries alike. He was an activist such as the Worker movement had not known before, and, at a time when young Catholic radicals were thinking more in activist terms, he came to be their hero. Hennacy was a native American radical from the Midwest, a Thoreaurian character who was honest and pure, who did all that a brave heart could do to end violence and cruelty. When Hennacy was living at the New York Worker house and engaging in his Spartan feats of fasting, picketing, and selling *Workers*, Dorothy Day made a comparison of him with Peter Maurin. "Ammon is deep and narrow, but Peter was so broad that he took in all the life of man, body, soul and mind."

Ammon Hennacy once observed that he had known two great men: Alexander Berkman, the anarchist, and Peter Maurin. But it is obvious in reading Hennacy's autobiography, *The Book of Ammon*, that Berkman was his model and that the scope of Maurin's vision escaped him. Hennacy's vision was his own, and at its end was the paradise of the anarchist, where oppression, injustice, and violence were all resolved in a community of free men, where no state or church could divide men, organize them one against the other, oppress them and take their lives. He could not philosophize over the problem of evil, but accepted it, like Job, as humanly incomprehensible and, therefore, resolvable only by God in a state that went beyond time. He reflected little on the suffering that came from the vagaries of a quixotic fate, but he knew well what the state could do—send man to his death, as in the case of war, or put him to death in the practice of capital punishment. He pondered little the most poignant of all tragic phenomena, that of suffering innocence. For Hennacy, seemingly immune to pain or stress, believing in neither germs nor doctors, it was the reduction of the state that was the object of his crusade. His "one-man revolution," as he called it, was to live apart from any aspect of an institutional life that contributed to the power of that institution to do harm to man, irrespective of the circumstances.

That Hennacy's one-man crusade should have, for a time, merged with the design of the Catholic Worker movement was not because of any deep and ranging reflection on his part, but because he admired Dorothy Day and got what he called, a "crush" on her. In his autobiography, he wrote that she had "more integrity about what is worthwhile than any two radicals or Christians I have ever known." When someone questioned the propriety of the "one-man revolution" adoring so unabashedly the head of the Catholic Worker movement, his rejoinder was "What the hell . . . can't a fellow love Dorothy without being romantic or rheumatic about it?" It was because of her that he gave seven years of his life to the Catholic Worker and was baptized a Catholic. "If she had been a Quaker or a Mormon . . . I would have been attracted to those religions," he said.

He subtitled his self-published autobiography *The Autobiography of a Unique American Rebel.* Further announced on the cover as an added attraction was an introduction by Steve Allen. If ever there was an autobiography utterly faithful to its subject, it was this one. Hennacy leaps into his life with the first line, and then carries himself vigorously through it with few pauses for rest or reflection for nearly five hundred pages. The story is Hennacy all the way and, if in the text he were to have substituted "our hero" for the "I's" that abound, one would scarcely have been startled or thought it out of place. But it is not offensive, it is Hennacy. And more than that, it is written with such vigor and humor and with such sensitivity to feeling and mood that parts of it are masterful. Dorothy Day is quoted on the back cover of the book jacket as stating that "The Story of his prison days will rank with the great writings of the the world about prisons," and this is not an overstatement. Nor would it be an overstatement to say the same of his descriptions of farming in the arid West, of Hopi Indians, and of his travel experiences.

He was, as he said, hardly born, for he weighed only three and a half pounds at birth and was put in a cigar box. That was on July 24, 1893, on a farm at Negley, Ohio, near the West Virginia and Pennsylvania line. Despite the Irish name, the Hennacys were native stock of some duration and were well rooted in the middle-class Protestantism of the area. Perhaps the only thing that set the family off from the predominant Republicanism of the community was that the elder Hennacy had once been a Populist and that Ammon's mother had baked ginger cookies for Coxey's Army when it encamped in a meadow near the Hennacy farm.

His childhood days were full and happy. He recalled a long hill behind the house down which the young Hennacys would sled in wintertime. Near the top was a pine tree that had been planted the day Lincoln was shot, and the hill was called Lincoln Hill. In the parlor hung a picture of John Brown, and about the only time that young Ammon felt the pulse of the martial spirit was when he was five years old and a neighbor girl taught him to play the chorus of a Civil War song on the piano: "Mid camp fires gleaming; mid shot and shell; I will be dreaming of my own Bluebell." When he played the song he wept because he had not been born to go to war.

When he was ten he began to go each summer to his

grandmother's to help her with her garden, and on Wednesday nights at prayer meeting and on Sundays, he met his family at the local Baptist church. When he was twelve, "after cringing at the terrible threats of damnation from the pulpit during a six weeks' revival meeting . . . I was baptized in the creek . . . the only sucker caught in the theological net. This was the swimming hole which I knew but the preacher did not, so he stumbled on a rock and nearly choked me."

Perhaps the choking was symbolic, for the young convert was soon beset by doubts. He took his problems to the minister, who advised him to pray. This he did, but the questions kept coming up. As a last resort he was advised to go to Youngstown and hear Billy Sunday. He went one rainy night and the result was disastrous. He went back to the church where he had been baptized and got up and told the congregation that he did not believe in God or the Bible. Young Ammon's father had wanted no public announcement of his son's apostasy, but, said Hennacy, "I told him that I had splashed in and I was going to splash out."

When he was seventeen he was reading regularly the Socialist *The Appeal to Reason.* He also read Upton Sinclair's *The Jungle* and became a vegetarian. The next year he went to live with his grandfather who had broken his leg and needed help. That winter he milked eight cows and studied at night behind a huge wood stove. When the Socialist Mother Bloor came to East Palestine, Ohio, to organize miners, Hennacy drove her to his hometown so she could organize there. "She was a wonderful woman and an inspiration," Hennacy recalled.

In the summer of 1913 he went with a crew from his hometown to Cleveland to sell cornflakes, house to house. He had never seen a streetcar before and got lost his first day, but when it came to selling, few could match him, and he made the fabulous amount of eight dollars his first day out. It was cornflakes that paved his way into college that fall and for the two years thereafter. His first year was at Hiram College in Hiram, Ohio. But the next summer, selling cornflakes in Portage, Wisconsin, he made a sale to a beautiful young lady "who seemed very nearly to glide down the bannister to answer the door." It was Zona Gale, the author of *Miss Lulu Bett*, who, as the young salesman noted, was holding a copy of Jack London's *Iron Heel* in her hand as he expostulated on the merits of his product. Since he, too, was reading London's book, the conversation moved to a wider subject range and in a short time Miss Gale, clutching her cornflakes, had persuaded Hennacy to go to the University of Wisconsin that fall.

At Madison he took journalism in a class with Bob La Follette, Jr., and wrote some articles for the New York *Call* about Socialists in the Wisconsin state legislature. He washed dishes in a fraternity house for his meals and delivered newspapers for living expenses. When he got fifty cents extra he would take "dark, cold, and beautiful" Miriam Gaylord, daughter of the Socialist state senator, to a movie. Randolph Bourne lectured on the campus that year, and Hennacy and his roommate gave up their bed to Bourne, who was traveling on a limited budget. Emma Goldman, who combined with her anarchism the interesting subject of free love, came to lecture and Hennacy introduced her. Along with his academic subjects he took military drill because he wanted to know how to shoot when the revolution came.

In the summer of 1915, the war raged in Europe and Hennacy sold aluminum ware in Milwaukee. It was still the city of *Gemütlichkeit* and sentimental song, where Fritzi Scheff sang Victor Herbert melodies at the Pabst Theater, and over on the other side of Wisconsin Avenue violinists, playing gypsy airs, strolled among the guests at The Schlitz Palm Garden. But the time left for such graciousness was short; the old world was dying.

For his third year in college Hennacy decided on Ohio State. There may have been a pretty girl there but, more likely, the move was made in the interest of economy. The day before he was to leave Milwaukee he was invited to a lawn party of young Socialists. There, among the young ladies drinking lemonade that August afternoon, he saw one who impressed him immediately. She was Selma Nelms, the daughter of the Socialist sheriff of Milwaukee. She had a glowing freshness about her and her youthful redicalism convinced Hennacy that she was the one woman for him. He lingered in Milwaukee two weeks more, nightly pressing his suit with such ardor that when he left they were engaged.

He left for Ohio State confident and happy, and the year turned out to be one of the most pleasant of his life. He was president of the Socialist Club, he started a cooperative secondhand bookstore on the campus, and in his classes he expanded on his radicalism. Professor Arthur Schlesinger, Sr., became his "very good friend" at the university.

The next year he did not return to college because he had to help out at home. Naturally, he went into selling; this time it was bakery products. He drove a wagon and built up a profitable route by featuring each day a special on some product that he was sure to have fresh. Shortly, his little baby sister was calling him "Ammon-cookie" because he brought his ten-percent allowable breakage home to the family.

He also devoted time to matters of the spirit, studying Yoga, Spiritualism, and Theosophy. Rosicrucian friends cast his horoscope: Leo with Saturn in ascendancy, which meant "that I would always be in trouble, but never defeated." Trouble was soon at hand. Selma wrote to tell him that their engagement was off. Later, when things had been patched up, he found out that two Socialists "had told her long tales about me which had but a faint basis in fact." What the two Socialists had charged him with he does not say, but perhaps they had told Selma of those nights at the movies with the dark and beautiful Miriam Gaylord and had neglected to emphasize that she was also "cold"!

When the war came, Hennacy began actively to fight conscription. Carrying a bundle of leaflets, he would go into a town and look up someone whom he had previously known as a radical. But often, Hennacy found out, his "comrade" had turned prowar and he would have to leave town in a hurry. Driven from Cleveland, he went into Pennsylvania and then to Huntington, West Virginia. From there it was back to Columbus, Ohio. In Columbus he spent a day two jumps ahead of the police, crisscrossing the town as he distributed anticonscription leaflets and pasted placards on storefronts. Finally, in the middle of the afternoon, he was caught and put in solitary confinement. He had made it easy for the police to spot him, for during all of his anticonscription pamphleteering, he had worn a huge button marked "Peace."

He was six weeks awaiting trial for refusing to register for the draft, during which time he was held in solitary confinement on the grounds that patriotic prisoners would have killed him. On July 3, 1917, the district attorney summed up the case against him. Hennacy, either from memory or from a trial transcript, included a portion of the summation in his autobiography. The prosecutor harkened back to the days when Americans had freed themselves from the tyranny of George III. Now it was "the Beast of Berlin," and if it had been 1776 Hennacy would have been a Tory. "He calls . . . himself . . . by the resounding name of 'conscientious objector.' I tell you this man does not have a conscience." And there was more.

He was sentenced to two years in the Atlanta federal penitentiary. The morning after his first night in jail, he was handed a note by another prisoner—"A note from Alexander Berkman, the great Anarchist!"—the man who had shot and stabbed Henry Clay Frick during the Homestead strike. Berkman suggested they meet and talk, otherwise advising Hennacy that he was in a cell with the most aggressive homosexual in the prison and offering suggestions on how to deal with him. That afternoon Ammon met Berkman in the prison yard. He told Hennacy how to get out letters and explained how he could train himself to talk in his throat without moving his lips. Then he gave four rules for survival: "Don't tell a lie . . . Don't tell on another prisoner . . . Draw your line to what you will do and will not do and don't budge . . . Don't curse the guards."

Hennacy stayed out of trouble for nearly a year, but just short of the anniversary of his first year in prison he was sent to "the dark hole," charged with plotting to blow up the prison with dynamite. What he had been doing over a period of nearly a month was organizing the inmates in a strike against the rotten fish served on Fridays. When nine hundred stayed in their cells during a Friday-night meal instead of going to the dining area, the warden felt that Hennacy's capacity for making trouble had to be curbed.

He stayed in the hole for ten days, getting one slice of cornbread and a cup of water each day. Then he was transferred to the "light hole," a cell large enough to walk up and down in—"exactly 8½ steps from corner to corner." A bunk was attached to the wall to the right; a plain chair and a small table with a spoon, plate, and cup on it was on the opposite wall, along with a toilet and a washbasin. A small twenty-watt light, turned on and off from the outside, was his illumination. Three times a day a Black lifer brought him his meals, ladled out of a bucket.

He had been in solitary for nearly three months when the warden came in one day and asked him to sign a paper. It was a registration form for the second war draft. "I told him I had not changed my mind about the war," said Hennacy. "He said I wouldn't get anything around here acting that way. I told him that I wasn't asking for anything around here: I was just doing time. He said I would get another year back in the hole for this second refusal to register. I told him that was O.K."

Shortly the warden was back. Hennacy would be released the next day, he said, but he had a question. Had Hennacy been sneaking any letters out of prison. Yes, he had. Who had taken them out? A friend. What was his name? "That is for you and your guards and stool pigeons to find out. I won't tell you," Hennacy replied, "good naturedly." The warden left, raging, promising Hennacy another year in solitary.

That night Hennacy had a crisis. "I paced my eight and a half steps back and forth for hours and finally flung myself on the bunk. It must have been in the middle of the night when I awoke. I had not had a note from anyone for a month. Were my friends forgetting me? I felt weak, lonesome and alone in the world. . . . I wondered if anyone really cared." He thought of cutting his wrists with his spoon. He finally fell into a restless sleep, hearing the long wailing whistle of a freight train as it passed somewhere outside the prison walls.

The next day he was told that, if he did not get out of solitary, he would probably die of the flu, that thirty in the prison had died the past week. Then the warden asked Hennacy if it was a prisoner or a guard who had sent out the letters. "I walked up to him closely," said Hennacy, "and in a confidential tone said, 'It was a prisoner or a guard.' "

That afternoon he was taken across the hall for a bath. Crossing over, he could see a prisoner called "Popoff" in the next cell, hanging by his hands, a torture to which he had been subjected for eight hours a day over a period of several months. Just then the guard came down the hall, opened Popoff's door, and, dipping his tin cup in the toilet, he threw the dirty water in Popoff's face.

Hennacy wondered how long he could stand it. When it was dark, he sharpened his spoon. If he cut his wrists at midnight he could be dead by morning. But he would wait another night; he had to wait for daytime to write a note to Selma and his mother. That night his dreams were a mixture of Victor Hugo's stories of men hiding in the sewers of Paris, IWW songs, blood flowing from the pigs that had been butchered on the Hennacy farm, and the groans of Popoff.

The next morning, for the first time in weeks, the sun shone in his cell and, crouching by the door, he could see Berkman's bald head in the prison yard. Berkman had suffered far more than he; could he not resist more? He decided he would try and began to sing the verses of the IWW prison song. He would try to live and make the world better. If he gave up, how would the world know about such things as Popoff's torture?

He began to take long exercises in his cell every day and

he studied the Bible. Reading the Bible, he decided to try to work out a philosophy of life. For a time he thought in terms of assassination, violence, and revolution. Then he read again of Jesus, of overcoming evil with good, of hatred with love. Which was the better way? He recalled that when he was a child he had been frightened by the threat of hellfire into proclaiming a changed life. Now he had a lot of time to think, and he spent several months weighing the worth of violence as against the way of Jesus. Gradually, Hennacy wrote, "I came to gain a glimpse of what Jesus meant when He said, 'The kingdom of God is Within You.'"

At this point Hennacy was becoming what Peter Maurin called a personalist. If the Kingdom of God was within himself, he reasoned, then it had to be in everyone—"in the deputy, the warden, in the rat and the pervert." He read and reread the Sermon on the Mount and the fifth, sixth, and seventh chapters of Matthew. It was the opposite of the Sermon on the Mount that the world had been practicing— "hate piled on hate had brought hate and revenge." So, he concluded, "it was plain that this system did not work."

This was Hennacy's conversion. He was a man wound with a spring of steel that could not be locked. He ran with an energy along his narrow track that could not be diffused, and when that energy brought him to a roadblock, it was either a matter of killing himself or of pausing to choose a better course that offered not frustration and bitterness but fulfillment. With desolation upon him he rejected the sharpened spoon and turned to life—he turned to God. Being Hennacy, he hastened to add that it was not the orthodox bourgeois God that he had turned to but one which he spelled "with a little 'g' and two 'o's."

In February, 1919, after seven and a half months in solitary, the superintendent of federal prisons visited Hennacy in his cell and he, too, tried to plumb the secret of how contraband mail got to the outside world. Failing, he began to swing his arms about and berate Hennacy as a fool and a coward. But the warden, standing by, interjected: "If he's a

fool or a coward he must be a God's fool or a God's coward," for "no one ever stood more than three months in solitary without giving in." Thus "God's Coward" became the
title for Hennacy's account of his time in solitary which was
published in *The Catholic Worker* in the issue of November,
1941.

The federal prison superintendent, however, suggested
that Hennacy have his "good time" restored, which meant
that his release would be on March 20, 1919. The night before, the prison deputy came in and tried again to find out
who was getting out the contraband mail. When Hennacy
refused to tell, the deputy said that he would then have to
serve out his full sentence with another year for refusing to
register. "After he left I wept," said Hennacy, "but I was at
the stage where I felt strong enough to take it." But the next
morning he was released.

After prison came the happiest time in Hennacy's life. On
Christmas Eve, 1919, he and Selma "kissed each other and
made the mutual pledge that 'we would live together as
long as we loved each other—for the Revolution.'"
Throughout the year 1920 they were activists in radical
causes, going to meetings, distributing leaflets, and crusading for Margaret Sanger's birth control program.

In the spring of 1921 they began a leisurely vagabond's
tour of the country. They started by hiking over Staten Island, worked their way to Norfolk, and from there rode for
three weeks on a leaky coal barge to Boston. "We climbed
Mt. Washington one night; and found the New England
people the kindest folks of the whole country." Crossing
over into the Midwest, they revisited Milwaukee and then
went down to Chicago and placed a rose on the graves of
the Haymarket anarchists. With winter coming on, they
headed south to Georgia and in Atlanta, Hennacy took
Selma on a tour of the penitentiary. As they went through
the kitchen, the Black lifer who had given Hennacy his food
in solitary recognized him and winked at him.

They left Atlanta in the spring, climbed Mount Mitchell

in North Carolina, went across to Texas and then up to Milwaukee again in time for the state Socialist picnic in August. Going south once more into Alabama, Hennacy was persuaded to remain at the single tax settlement of Fairhope and to teach at the School of Organic Education. When a local minister, who "was head of the Boy Scouts and of the KKK," declared from his pulpit that Hennacy should be tarred and feathered and then drowned in Mobile Bay, Hennacy invited him to the school to give a talk on the Ku Klux Klan. The minister said he would come but he did not, and shortly afterward he was "called" to preach in another town.

When the school year was over, they went westward across Texas and climbed Pikes Peak on the night of July 4, 1924. They stopped off at Leavenworth to visit some Wobblies in prison there, and Hennacy ran into his old warden from Atlanta. That winter Hennacy settled in Berkeley, California, and sold Fuller brushes. Because of his outstanding sales record, the company gave him a turkey which he and Selma ate for Thanksgiving with Mother Bloor and a radical Berkeley campus news vendor as guests.

They had planned to go to South America when summer came, but said Hennacy: "One evening in May I came home from a meeting and said to Selma: 'Suppose we don't go to South America. Suppose we go to some place in the country near Milwaukee; start farming on a small scale; rest up . . . and have some children." Selma said she had been thinking the same thing.

Arriving in Wisconsin with $105, they put $100 down on a wooded tract near Waukesha. Hennacy got a job in a dairy, and shortly he was building a house for them at the top of a hill. He dug a basement and carried rocks of all colors to a stone mason who laid the fireplace. Then came the two daughters they had wanted: Carmen was born in 1927 and Sharon, in 1929. For Hennacy, life was at its richest. "Here by the blazing wood, on the Navajo rug near Fritz, our police dog, and mother and child, with the wind whistling outside and June, the Jersey cow, securely nestled in the small barn, was a feeling hardly to be improved upon."

The idyll ended in 1931 when Hennacy was discharged by the dairy for organizing a strike. Unable to make the payments on their land, their home was lost. From Waukesha they moved into Milwaukee where Hennacy got a job as a social worker and where he encountered "the second great influence of my life: that of the Catholic Worker movement." It was, most appropriately, the friend of the Catholic Worker movement and able editor of *The Catholic Herald Citizen*, Monsignor Franklyn Kennedy, who gave Hennacy his first copy of *The Catholic Worker*. "I at once subscribed," said Hennacy.

In 1937 he began working with Nina Polcyn, Larry Doyle, and others at the Milwaukee Holy Family House, and it was probably through his influence that a strong infusion of anarchist-Communist viewpoints were represented in the forums that took place at the house. When Dorthy Day came the next year to speak at the Social Action Congress called by Archbishop Stritch, Hennacy went to hear her at another session at Marquette University. He met her after the meeting and was pleased to hear her speak well of the Wobblies and Communists. When she spoke again the next day, Hennacy was there, too, sitting in the front row.

He heard Peter Maurin speak at the Holy Family House one night. Hennacy relates that a Communist friend came to the meeting, and when the time came for questions, the Communist got up, made a point, and to back it up began quoting Marx. After he had finished, Maurin said that Marx had not been quoted correctly and gave the correct version. When Hennacy interjected with, "Peter, you talk like an anarchist," Maurin answered, "Sure, I am an anarchist; all thinking people are anarchists. But I prefer the name personalist."

Soon Hennacy was putting his gift for selling to work as a newsboy. With a bundle of *Workers* under his arm, he made the rounds of the Catholic churches in Milwaukee, catching the crowds as they left Mass. His favorite spot was in front of Gesu, the big church of the Jesuits, where in wintertime the wind swept down Wisconsin Avenue to swirl against the church's massive exterior and numb passersby.

After Pearl Harbor, Hennacy noted that some of the "religious folks" at the Holy Family house were reluctant to distribute the paper, but so far as he was concerned World War II was no different from World War I. In the May, 1942, issue of the *Worker*, Hennacy's letter to the local United States District Attorney appeared. In it he declared again that he would not register for the draft and would without protest accept the sentence of the court. He knew that soldiers and sailors were sacrificing for what they thought was right, and he was willing to do the same. He had refused to serve in World War I because as a Socialist he would have nothing to do with a capitalist war. In World War II he was a Christian anarchist and would not serve the government.

But times had changed and the authorities were not anxious to make an example out of Hennacy again. Besides, he was forty-eight years old. His continuing radicalism, however, brought a personal problem. As the Hennacy girls began to grow, Selma's enthusiasm for radical causes began to wane. She wanted some security and acceptance for her daughters. With the passing years there was no mellowing in Hennacy, no altering of his conception of the "one-man revolution" as anything but Ammon Hennacy against all forms of the objectivized world—always leading a charge against these forms, the first to go over the top, to give an example to lesser man who struggled with clay feet, and whose policy of no retreat, together with a pyrotechnical display of polemical brilliance, invariably brought him victory over the hapless adversary who, in the end, was either converted or went away shaking his head as if he had seen a great light.

When the war clouds began to gather, Selma took their daughters and left. She knew that another crisis was at hand and that there would probably be another test of strength between her husband and the state. Already, she could see, he was laying down the lines of battle. In time, she and the girls ended up in Los Angeles where, as Hennacy described it, she joined "one of the esoteric cults that spring up in the unhealthy atmosphere of Los Angeles."

Selma was the one woman he ever really loved, Hennacy told Dorothy Day once; but on another occasion he also said that he never remembered the time when he was not in love with some woman. This may have been true, but it *is* true that the woman he loved the longest was Selma Nelms, for it was she who was the full focus of the ardent and pure passion of his youth, who represented the dimension of his hope during the time that he suffered in the Atlanta penitentiary, and who bore him his two daughters. Their leaving hurt him greatly, and sometimes at night his loneliness brought him to tears. He did not forget them, and until his daughters were through college, he sent them practically everything he made, little though it was.

In 1943 he went west, working as a farm laborer and living at times among the Hopi Indians, for whom he came to have a great admiration. He continued this way for seven years, and it was during this time that he wrote his pieces, "Life at Hard Labor," for *The Catholic Worker*. He had not seen Dorothy Day since September, 1941, when she had visited Milwaukee, but for the next nine years he wrote her often and occasionally she would answer. On December 29, 1948, he met her at the Phoenix bus station. They visited the Jesuit Father George Dunne, who had been an uncompromising spokesman for racial justice at a time when the issue customarily was swept under the rug.

Later, they went with another priest to an Indian mission in the desert southeast of Tempe where the Indians, who were very poor, had built a church "without . . . bingo parties." Then they visited several anarchists one evening who tried to convince them that a belief in God was incompatible with anarchism. The talk, and the clarity and depth of Dorothy's radicalism, stirred Hennacy. When she left, he said, he felt a new reason for continuing his one-man revolution. Dorothy had brought him to a rededication; she gave him a sense of warmth and of sharing with her a glorious struggle for the Holy Grail. His love was indeed of the spirit, for as he said, "With my Life at Hard Labor, vegetarian diet, and mind on the One Man Revolution, I did not have to have physical contact with any woman: I had work to do."

On Easter, following Dorothy Day's visit, Hennacy visited Mott Street to see what it was all about, although he was by far "not yet sold on the advisability of majoring in 'feeding bums.' " He remained at the house for two months, and during that time he began writing his autobiography in the library at Peter Maurin Farm and became acquainted with the staff. He found in Tom Sullivan a fellow Irishman whom he loved, and he generally found something good to say about most of the people who staffed the house. And then he was off again for two years, propagandizing, meeting people, giving lectures, sermons, and talks wherever he was invited, but touching back from time to time at Mott Street.

As his life became more and more Worker oriented, speculation arose as to when he would become a Catholic. Father George Dunne answered someone that it would happen, he supposed, when the Church had all gone underground. Presumably he did not think that Hennacy, with his temperament, could bridge the gap between the objectivized Church of the world and that of the Mystical Body that lived in the spirit of Christ. For Hennacy, the bridge over that gap was Dorothy Day. She had never spoken to him on the subject, although once in a group she had said to him that he should never think of becoming a Catholic because of her and the Catholic Worker, but only because he loved the Church.

It was in the presence of Dorothy Day and in that special and rare atmosphere of the Catholic Worker movement that he came to have a sense of the Church as spirit and found fading those attributes of its worldly life that he had found so objectionable. Two things, he relates, led him to take the final step of becoming a Catholic. In August, 1952, he attended a retreat given at the Newburgh farm by Father Marion Casey, a priest of the Minnesota diocese. Afterward, he felt that there was a substance to the Church that he had not known and which he felt that he should have. From then on, he went to Mass daily "because I was at the Catholic Worker and loved them all."

The second immediate influence came when he had heard Dorothy Day describe an experience she had had when going to Mass at a large church during the war. Immediately after Communion, the organist had launched into an all-stops-open rendition of "The Star-Spangled Banner." Then Hennacy told the story: "This was a most holy moment after partaking of the body of Christ and it was broken up by this war-mongering. Everyone stood up in honor of this God of Battles. Dorothy did that thing which only St. Francis or Gandhi would have had the spiritual insight to do: *she knelt and prayed.*" And Hennacy emphasized her reaction, so much did it impress him.

When she told the story, Hennacy said, he got the biggest jolt in his life since his experience in solitary in Atlanta. It swept aside for the moment the armor of his pose. He suddenly realized that he was just "a stubborn smart-alec—perhaps with more knowledge than many others I met, but still moving along with a handicap of a lack of spirituality. . . . How was I going to get it and where? I did not dare admit to myself . . . that I was slipping, but I did say then with tears in my eyes to Dorothy, 'You have shown me a great light; you have made me ashamed of myself.' "

He was baptized on November 17, 1952, at Hutchinson, Minnesota, by Father Casey, with Dorothy Day as his godmother and Robert Ludlow his godfather. "It was all very sacred and solemn," Hennacy said. "I saw the water, salt, oil —necessary parts of nature—were linked with my entry into the Church, and as Dorthy had told me once, sensing my objection to holy water, 'All water is holy; it makes the corn grow for the Hopi.' "

# 18

# HENNACY AT THE CATHOLIC WORKER

Hennacy brought to the Worker movement the breezy self-confidence of a fighter who knows that he is invincible. He gave complex social and theological problems simple, direct answers and backed them up with such self-discipline and bravery that sometimes young Workers were awed into looking upon him as an oracle. But others, who felt that over the years they had become a part of the Worker's formation, regarded him with some apprehension, wondering perhaps if the movement was not moving toward a new "truth." Specifically, he led the movement into a new level of pacifist activism, the most widely publicized form of which was the annual resistance of some of the Workers to New York City's air-raid drill, which, according to the Civil Defense Act, required that all take shelter for at least ten minutes during a sham air raid.

"It was Ammon Hennacy's idea," Dorothy Day said. He had always emphasized the duty of civil disobedience as a means of calling attention to the terrible threat of atomic warfare that hung over the world. And, she continued, it was a small matter when compared to the terrible choice the Germans had had to make when called upon to obey Hitler. The Workers could make their witness, and the jail sentences would be light.

Their first violation occurred on June 15, 1955. As was their custom, they informed the police beforehand of their

intention to violate the law. There were seven Catholic
Workers and twenty-three others, variously from the War
Resisters League and the Fellowship of Reconciliation, who
sat unmoving on benches in City Hall Park when the alarm
went off at 2:05 P.M. As they continued to sit, a number of
blue-clad auxiliary police, sporting a full display of ribbons
and brass, marched up and told the group to take shelter.
When they refused, they were declared to be under arrest,
loaded in a police van, and driven away to the station. The
only unscheduled part of the operation occurred when a
shoeshine boy named Rocco Parilli walked into the park to
get a drink of water when the sirens sounded and was
hauled off with the protesters. After nine hours of uncomfortable detention, they were released on fifteen hundred
dollars' bail.

When their case came up on December 22 before Judge
Hyman Bushel in the Criminal Courts Building on Centre
Street, they made the statement customary in such cases.
They had practiced civil disobedience because they did not
wish to participate in an action whose purpose was to create
a wary psychology, which was the only meaning of the drill,
since the idea of taking cover from an atomic attack was ri-
diculous. They wanted to think of their action as a small act
of penance for the dropping of the atom bomb on Japan.
Judge Bushel listened, found them guilty, and suspended
their sentence.

The affair produced a small flurry of reaction. *Commonweal* was the only Catholic publication that explained and
defended their action. *The New York Times* wrote it up and
explained it as a penitential act for the use of the bomb.
Fulton Lewis, Jr., the well-known radio commentator, found
it reprehensible that a group that appealed to the public to
help it support the poor would use that money to hire lawyers. But, as Dorothy Day pointed out, they had actually refused to have a defense. Their only appeals were made for
the poor, she said, "with whom we live and share." A priest
wrote in to ask that his name be taken off the subscription
list. Having *The Catholic Worker* around embarrassed him,

he said, since the Workers had embarrassed the Church by their ill-advised fuss over the air-raid drills.

The following year they repeated the performance. Dorothy Day heralded their gesture of disobedience with an editorial in the June, 1956, *Worker* on the current testing of the hydrogen bomb. It seemed to her as if it was a contest between man and God. It was as though man was trying to shut off earth from heaven, from God himself. The hydrogen bomb was a symbol of "utter atheism"—the saddest thing of all—for it was the final result of equating God with country and with ideology, the ultimate step in making God serve the objectivized impulses of man.

After their demonstration this time, they were sentenced to five days in jail. "God knows, it is suffering," Dorothy Day said. She did not think that anyone enjoyed the demonstrations, not even Hennacy. It was so much easier to sit somewhere and talk about the issues. She hated the public spectacle, the tension—"police worried about bombs (certainly the government has set . . . the example in violence, in bomb-making and throwing)," she added.

The 1957 drill was scheduled for Friday, July 12, and as usual the Workers announced beforehand (in a phrase that was Hennacy's) that again they did not plan "to play war." They were sentenced to thirty days. Dorothy Day made it clear that she was putting herself in no hero's role as a sufferer of the villainy of the state. "We love our country and are only saddened to see its great virtues matched by equally great faults. We are a part of it, we are responsible too." From jail she wrote a letter back to the Chrystie Street group giving instructions for putting out the paper, and then added she wanted to make it clear "that we do not want to harass people who are only doing their duty . . . we bend over backward to show our respect for the desire for the common good which most laws are for." She had no complaints in jail; the food was as good as that at Chrystie Street. "Certainly Holy Mother City tries to do right by everyone here." It was obvious that Judge James Comerford, the city magistrate who sentenced them, bore them no

ill will, for when St. Patrick's Day came around he sent
them tickets for seats in the stands at the parade. "Hope you
and friends will enjoy it," he wrote.

So it went, every year until 1960, by which time Hennacy
and Dorothy Day had been imprisoned four times and
Deane Mowrer three. That year over a thousand turned out
to defy the alarm, and when the arrests were made, the
Workers were passed over, prompting Hennacy to inquire
of one of the arresting officers if he were not shirking his
duty. After 1960, the city gave up its annual little war game.
Small thing though it was, the Workers by their resistance
had helped to make a point.

Dorothy Day valued the days she spent in jail as an instruction in the life of the spirit. The Catholic Worker had
for years performed all the works of mercy except visiting
the prisoner, she said. Now they had visited the prisoners by
becoming prisoners themselves. For her and Deane Mowrer,
however, the going in among the women prisoners evoked
no grateful murmuring from them. The ribald, obscene chorus stunned them. Later Dorothy Day thought about her
own defensive reaction. Hating the sin and loving the sinner
had proved in this instance to be a difficult thing to practice. She recalled a story by J. D. Salinger she had read in
*The New Yorker* about a girl who compulsively prayed as
an escape from mankind. Especially she remembered Father
Zosima's discourse on love in *The Brothers Karamazov*. Her
love, she was afraid, had not been equal to the reception
they had received from those tormented women.

She did come to know some of her fellow prisoners, one
especially. During her imprisonment in 1958 she once was
talking with some of them when the subject of heaven came
up, and she quoted to them as she remembered it St. Augustine's description of the beatific vision, where "that voice
sounds which no tongue can take from me, I breathe that
fragrance which no wind scatters," where "I eat the food
which is not lessened by eating, and I lie in the embrace
which satiety never comes to sunder." Did she really believe
that? asked one who listened to her. When the woman who

asked the question was released a short time later, she put on her finest clothes and visited the Worker house.

Living in the presence of persons so wretched and desperate, brief though her sojourns in prison were, caused her to ponder those lives that might have been made more gracious had the burden of indifference and cruelty in the world not touched them so heavily. Who was responsible for this cruelty? She remembered stark episodes of it— seeing some boys stoning a cat that had been hung up by its tail—some women laughing at a man trying to eat whose arms were so palsied that he could not get the food to his mouth—a Puerto Rican woman taken off to Bellevue for psychiatric observation; when a social worker went to the tenement where she lived, he found the stinking bodies of the woman's children. All who professed the good, and then chose first to solace their own lives with ease before helping others, were guilty. "If we do not correspond to the grace God gives us He will withdraw it," she said.

There was a certain surface compensation to going to prison. It was good for a week or so to live completely under someone else's direction and not have to plan and meet emergencies. Things happened anyway. During the excitement of picketing and arrests in 1955, Dorothy's seventh grandchild was born. The cadre that had remained at the Newburgh farm after the acquisition of Peter Maurin Farm had left 'Newburgh. Now all would be together at Peter Maurin Farm. The men were all housed in outbuildings and only women were in the house—except for Stanley Vishnewski, who had a small cubbyhole room for his press.

Prison for Hennacy was an interlude in his activist life with the Worker. It was natural that with his salesman's personality he would become an aggressive street vendor of *The Catholic Worker*. In the manner of successful salesmen, he had his success formula, which was understanding "the value of being at the same place the same time with the same article for sale, and not to jump around." On Monday nights he was at Cooper Union to sell to those who went to the lectures; on Tuesday noon he sold in the Wall Street district; then in the evening at the New School on Twelfth Street. He spent Wednesday afternoon at a spot at Fordham University, which, with the elevated there and students running like mad to make the train, he considered to be the noisiest place in the world. He was at Fourteenth and Broadway on Thursday, and Forty-third and Broadway on Friday, where he became "really a part of the pillar by the Peerless store." On Sunday there was no better spot than in front of St. Patrick's Cathedral. This was his routine for several years.

There were adventures and confrontations. One night he was in front of the New School selling when a cabdriver, waiting for a fare, hailed Hennacy and told him, " 'There's a guy in there talking against you folks, name of Blanshard.' " Soon, related Hennacy, "a man whom I knew by his moustache was Paul Blanshard . . . came out." Stepping up to him, Hennacy thrust a *Worker* into Blanshard's hand, then to be met by the question, " 'How much?' " " 'Nothing, you need it bad,' was my reply. He gave me a nickel." Perhaps Blanshard felt the better course was not to be beholden to the opposition, but, on the other hand, not to overdo it.

Sometimes when he was selling in front of a church, a cop would ask him to move on, acting on the request of the pastor who was concerned about the radical message of the *Worker*. But Hennacy held no antagonism toward the police. His experience had been that they were like everybody else; they would respond at once to kind and generous attitudes. Priests and nuns, he noted, were usually friendly, but pastors resisted having the *Worker* in their churches. At the rectory of the St. Francis Church near Penn Station, he was received cordially, but was told that there was no room for the paper on the church's reading rack.

Hennacy was also one of the *Worker*'s editors and columnists. The title of his column, "In the Marketplace," had been suggested by Tom Sullivan, and, in its wit, liveliness, and spontaneity, the column was reminiscent of Sullivan's. The difference was that Sullivan had written about the house and the people who lived in it, while Hennacy wrote about the world and Ammon Hennacy—the quick-witted, indefatigable salesman of *The Catholic Worker* in some personal and epic battle against the dark forces of established society. But his concern with self missed the deadliness of megalomania. He told his tales with lively humor, and those who might have been made into the supervillains in the camp of the establishment turned out to be simple and good men with whom he frequently established some tie of comradeship. Writing was so much of a gift with him that his words did not intrude themselves irritatingly into the thought or action, but were ready conveyers of that always youthful zest and poetry that were part of his nature. It was this zest and this disposition to do battle in epic proportions that made him real and not the braggart that some people thought of him as being.

The column was a great storehouse of anecdotal material about the radical movement in America at the time of the First World War and the decade following. He liked to reminisce about some of the lesser known whom he considered to be the real heroes of the movement, like 'old man Marquardt of Grasston, Minn.," who "did time in both wars for refusing to register for the draft" and who had "made a brave fight all along the line." He invoked the memory of friends, not infrequently identifying them by the prison number by which he had known them from his days in the Atlanta penitentiary.

One could travel with Hennacy in other special circles. He had just made a telephone call to his "old friend" Professor Arthur M. Schlesinger, Sr., he chattily told his readers. He had also spent a recent Sunday noon "with Prof. Schultz at Dartmouth at whose class I . . . spoke on my last trip." He had taken the occasion to talk with the professor's five daughters and was then "goin' on my way" to see "radical vegetarian friends." Amidst this flurry of consorting with academicians, he had worked in a short visit with Aldio Feliciani, secretary of the old Sacco-Vanzetti defense fund.

As a Catholic, Hennacy's piety showed itself in unusual forms. "I believe in God the Father, in Jesus Christ, His only

Son, in the Holy Spirit, in the Holy Catholic Church and the Communion of the Saints," he wrote, adding immediately that he also believed in the economic interpretation of history and the Marxian theory of surplus value. But, he added, he was little interested in either Marxian or theological hairsplitting. Marxians, he thought, were too right wing. They were as timid as Victor Berger used to be, and he ought to know about Victor Berger because he had lived in Milwaukee eighteen years.

Nor did he think that social change was going to come about by just saying prayers or going to church without following what Jesus had said. He went to Mass daily, but would still quote a phrase he had heard someone say: "2000 years of Mass and all we've got is poison gas." What was needed was "the true spirit of men like Debs." Hennacy said that he prayed, but for whatever and whomever else he prayed, he also prayed for the souls of Sacco and Vanzetti and the Rosenbergs.

His comment on some of the practices associated with American Catholic life delighted his loyal readers. One reader of "In the Marketplace" was "very happy" to learn that "the Legion of Decency is a right wing organization." Like Hennacy, he, too, "would not arise and take their pledge for their social conscience is blurred by their puritan attitude." The writer revealed himself as not only an anarchist and pacifist but also a nudist, believing in the possibility "of returning to the pristine life of the Garden of Eden before the Fall, where there were no tyrannies, no wars, and no clothes."

Hennacy could go beyond the Catholic experience in criticizing the very proper institutions of American life, and in this he caused further glee. There were, he said, real pacifists and sentimental pacifists, and the difference was that a real pacifist "will have nothing to do with the Girl Scouts and Boy Scouts. . . . The Boy Scouts are errand boys for the military. . . . If any of our readers doubt this let them ask the leaders of the Girl Scouts or the Boy Scouts to invite a pacifist to speak to their groups and see what re-

sponse they get. It is not difficult to speak about militarism
in South Africa or Russia but to oppose it in your own block
is something else."

To be sure, many objected to him. Some thought he was
insufferably self-centered and some thought his talk was
wild. "Can you hear him on Judgment day telling the Lord
about himself?" one friend of the Worker asked. Two students from a Catholic college wrote to tell him that they
read his column as a source of amusement. If he were a real
anarchist, they said, he would insist on destroying all the
bridges and roads in the country.

Hennacy said that he had heard all these criticisms before
and had answered them before. He admitted that he was
"perhaps 10% inconsistent," but that did not require him to
take correction from those who supported the system ninety
percent. His basic point, he said, was that one person could
secede from the system, refuse to pay taxes for the support
of the system, and take the alternative of a life of hard
labor. He was not, he said, going to complicate his message
by substituting highly detailed blueprints for a complete anarchist system which would not work anyway unless the
heart was changed.

As for the two young men who had written him, he
brushed them off with a good-humored return shot that was
characteristic of the kind of answer his critics got when they
undertook to joust with him. He would not drop by to talk
with them as they had suggested, "for the duties of a Catholic revolutionist are very arduous in these days of devil worship." He had a final word: "Keep on with your studies,
boys, and may your minds be enlightened, but not too
quickly, for perhaps you could not stand the change."

Every year on August 6, the day the bomb was dropped
on Hiroshima, he and his friends would be found picketing
a federal building in protest of bomb stockpiling and testing. At four o'clock on Hiroshima Day they would move to
the Empire State Building where, as in 1956, Dorothy Day,
A. J. Muste from the Fellowship of Reconciliation, and Bayard Rustin of the War Resisters League would take a letter

up to the office of the Japanese embassy which expressed sorrow over the destruction of Hiroshima and Nagasaki.

The unusual feature of Hennacy's Hiroshima memorial picketing was its rigorous penitential character. With his picketing he fasted, and his fasting would continue for as many days as the number of years that had elapsed since the dropping of the bomb. Thus, in 1955 his picketing and fasting went on for ten days. That year Bob Steed had just come up from Memphis, and he immediately offered to accompany Hennacy to give out papers and to assist in case Hennacy fainted. That year Hennacy's sign read, "The Individual Conscience Versus the Atom-bomb? Yes, There is no Other Way." A young actress named Judith Malina Beck who had joined the Workers in the air-raid demonstrations carried another sign that said, "Love and Life, not Death and Taxes."

It went on for the next five years: Hennacy, Dorothy Day, and friends of the Worker picketing the federal tax office. Yearly, Bob Steed stood with Hennacy; and in 1960 there was also Hugh Madden, an ex-farmer and ex-Trappist novice who wore a scratchy rope around his neck and made a strange appearance with his long whiskers and strange getup. Madden, too, fasted, and as they patrolled slowly up and down the street, he would occasionally fall to his knees and pray.

The picketing did not go unchallenged, and frequently the challengers were Catholic. One demanded that the picketers recite the Rosary as proof of their authenticity. Why did they not picket the Russian embassy, too? they were asked. Hennacy's response was that the Russians were not asking him to pay taxes for their bomb. Once a group of teen-agers pushed Hennacy and Dorothy Day up against a car, calling them Communists. A woman called the Chancery Office, asking that the picketers be disavowed, but someone there said that the office was not for them nor against them. On another occasion, when they were being menaced by a crowd, an important-looking man came up and told the crowd that he was not going to let any harm come to the picketers. He thereupon pulled out his Knights of Columbus membership card and in a few minutes the sidewalk was clear.

With Hennacy everything was in the open. He built no romantic conspiratorial air around himself; he was the "one-man revolution" mounting the parapet, if need be alone, and in the full light of day. "I always notify the FBI, the tax men, the police, etc. of my picketing," he wrote in his autobiography. Tax authorities also were fully notified that they need expect nothing from him when the time came to file a return. In 1953 he considerately restated his position to the director of his local tax office since the man was new on the job. He told the director that he had been a C.O. in both wars and he did not now plan to assist in the financing of the H-bomb and napalm warfare. "I am not helping out in this plain murder."

The tax men could find no place where Hennacy had earned money so they gave up on him. In 1956, however, another new man came in the tax office, and when Hennacy began to picket outside, he received a summons to the tax office on the seventh floor where he was asked about his "hidden assets." Not having had to confront a case like Hennacy's before, the official said he would pass the matter up to his superiors. After a few years the tax men got used to the picketing and would come out of the office and greet Hennacy, take a *Catholic Worker*, and then pretend to argue among themselves how Hennacy got away with it.

In 1957, with the Atomic Energy Commission planning a series of nuclear tests at Las Vegas, Hennacy decided to shift his activities there. Accordingly, he wrote the authorities in Las Vegas, the Catholic bishop in Reno, and priests in Las Vegas that from June 17 through June 28 he would fast and picket the Atomic Energy Commission. In Las Vegas, with temperatures running well over a hundred degrees, he picketed daily, carrying signs that quoted Pope Pius XII in his denunciation of war and atomic testing.

The kindness that the tax men had shown him in New York was exceeded by the military at Las Vegas. One offi-

cer, a Colonel Hunter, greeted Hennacy and said he would
do what he could to help Hennacy except call off bomb test
drops. The colonel even had a guard bring out a chair each
morning so that Hennacy could rest for a while in the
shade. Hennacy noted that everyone there was most cordial
to him except two Irish Catholics. He said two Spanish
Catholics outdid themselves in their effort to be friendly.

The bishop of the diocese, Hennacy felt, had not been so
friendly. In his autobiography, Hennacy quotes a news article from the *Las Vegas Review Journal* that gave the bishop's reaction to the picketing. First, it was the bishop's opinion that a recent appeal of Pius XII to the nations of the
world that they cease testing atomic weapons was a general
statement and not limited to the Nevada proving grounds.
And then, when asked about the status of *The Catholic
Worker* as representing the mind of the Church, the bishop
responded that it had no official status. Nonetheless, he
said, he subscribed to the principles of free speech and free
press, although he thought that certain forms of extreme liberalism could be very dangerous.

In April of the next year, Hennacy was off to Florida to
picket another government installation. The plan was that
on Sunday, April 13, Hennacy and some of his friends
would each choose a church and there distribute leaflets
protesting the missiles at Cape Canaveral. They spent Saturday night at the home of a reader of *The Catholic Worker,*
making signs to carry the next day. The church Hennacy
was to picket was in Rockledge, a suburb of Cocoa, and, following his custom, he telephoned twice to announce this intention of distributing leaflets there the next morning after
Mass. But the housekeeper failed to relay the message to
the pastor, and the next morning he unexpectedly confronted Hennacy picketing in front of the church. As Hennacy reported it, the following exchange took place:

> "Take the word Catholic off that sign and leaflet. You
> don't have permission from the Bishop or from me to use
> it. You give Catholics a bad name," said Father. . . .
> "We are laymen and we do not need permission from the

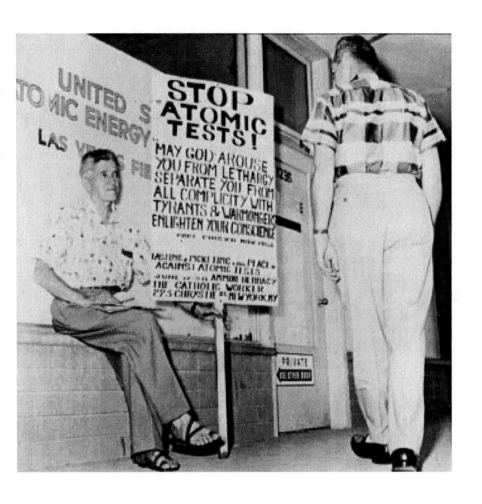

Ammon Hennacy picketing against atomic testing.
Las Vegas, 18 June 1957.
UPI photo.

Bishop or from you to oppose missiles for murder," I answered, and continued, "The Church has had a bad name long enough supporting wars. I like the name Catholic and I am trying to make it mean something like the early Christians meant it to be when Christians couldn't go to court or kill in war. I venture that in the years to come the Church will be proud that we Catholic Workers opposed missiles and war and that we gave the Church a good name."

As Hennacy talked to the pastor, the ushers tore up his sign and broke into pieces the stick to which it was attached. As Hennacy wondered what his next move would be, he was picked up by the chief of police. The chief, convinced that he had an authentic Communist in his hands, advised Hennacy to vacate the town immediately and, were it not for the fact that he had his uniform on, he would beat the hell out of Hennacy himself. But Hennacy had a stack of leaflets left, so he headed back to the church to catch the people coming out of the next Mass. As he returned, the chief of police eased up behind him in his car and gave him a parting word of advice: "Better get your ass out of town or these guys will get you . . . I'm warning you."

Reflecting disconsolately on what possible fate awaited him—drowning, lynching, tarring and feathering—he sat on the church steps and listened to the sermon. As the church emptied, the ushers again strove to take care of what they regarded as undoubtedly the advance agent of the Communist menace. One heavy, red-faced usher seized him by the arm and rushed him across the street to the opposite sidewalk as his comrades closed ranks behind him. If he handed out any more leaflets, they said, he would be taken "over the hill."

At this juncture the chief again appeared and motioned Hennacy into his car. This time he took Hennacy to the mayor's house. Leaving Hennacy in the car guarded by another policeman, the chief engaged in a long and earnest discourse with the mayor. Returning, he said that Hennacy could be arrested for loitering and for disturbing religious services. Hennacy responded that he had disturbed only the

"Catholic Vigilantes," and the policemen could arrest him under whatever law they chose; he would not sue them for false arrest because he did not believe in the courts. This observation caused the chief to become thoughtful. Hennacy's declaration that he would not sue them sounded like a Communist trick, he said. So he took Hennacy back to the police station. There the officer in charge repeated several times that, were it not for the fact that he was in uniform, he also would beat hell out of Hennacy. This time Hennacy was no longer just a Communist; he was a New York Communist! Finally, they took his leaflets and ordered him to leave. Since Mass was over anyway, Hennacy gave up the confrontation and returned to his friends.

Immediately after the Florida excursion, Hennacy's protest took a more rigorous form than any that he had before undertaken. As the 1958 anniversary of Hiroshima drew near, he planned a fast and picketing of the Atomic Energy Commission's headquarters at the nation's capital. He would fast and picket for forty days. The leaflet he had printed for distribution read: "I am fasting not to coerce or embarrass the A.E.C. but as a penance for our sinfulness in bombing Hiroshima and Nagasaki and for our continued testing of hydrogen and atomic weapons in our mad race for a supremacy that means only death. I am fasting to awaken the consciences of those who are a part of the war machine, those who are half-hearted pacifists and those Christians who see no contradiction in following Christ and Caesar."

The Atomic Energy Commission office was at 1717 H Street. Taking a room nearby, he would rise early, go to Mass, then buy a *New York Times* which he read until nine o'clock, at which time he began his picketing. The employees of the commission treated him respectfully and one, who declared that he knew well the effects of radiation, told him that he was completely right and wished him good luck. Daily, as commission chairman Admiral Lewis Strauss entered the commission office, he would see Hennacy and the two would exchange mock salutes. Once he came up to Hennacy and told him that he looked fine. Each day of the fast Hennacy wrote Dorothy Day. He gave her a recital of what had occurred that day and how much weight he had lost. When the fast was over he had lost thirty-one pounds. The first thing he ate was some strawberries mixed in buttermilk with a juicer. He drank this as Mrs. Stewart Udall, the wife of the Arizona congressman, drove him to an appearance he was to make at a Mormon church.

One of the last episodes in the confrontations that Hennacy had with the federal government in his role as a member of the Catholic Worker group was going "over the fence," as he called it, at the Omaha missile base. It was an act of civil disobedience that had cost other pacifists six months in jail, one of whom had been a Catholic Worker from Chicago, Karl Meyer. Meyer, a dark-haired, intense young man, was the son of a former Vermont congressman. A graduate of the University of Chicago, he became a messenger in Dean Acheson's law firm. But a life of "service" that operated from behind the security of an established existence, graced by the amenities and controlled by the proprieties, did not appeal to him. Not yet a Catholic, he rented a store in Washington and started a house of hospitality there. In 1959, as a Catholic, he began running the St. Stephen House in Chicago. It was then that the construction of missile sites and the continued testing of atom bombs struck him as a hideous madness that required the most desperate resistance.

When Hennacy learned of the tactic that Meyer and his associates had employed, he decided that he would put on a repeat performance. So the day after his New York tax picketing vigil was over, he began a leisurely trip to the missile base at Omaha, Nebraska. With the news of his coming announced for several days in a row over a local radio station, base personnel were not surprised when he arrived. "You're the pacifist," a guard greeted him, and then added helpfully that Hennacy's picketing place was two miles down the road. But Hennacy did not want to picket; he wanted to effect an illegal entry, and this he managed by taking a back route into the base. Heading toward the main building, he handed out *Catholic Workers* as he proceeded. Eventually he was accosted by a clerical worker who ceremoniously escorted him to some top officers waiting for him at the front gate. There a United States marshal handed him an order: "You are being removed as a trespasser from the Offutt Missile Annex B . . . and ordered not to re-enter the confines of this installation without the permission of the Commander."

It worked simply. He was escorted out of the gate; he immediately climbed the fence back onto the base and was arrested. For his action he was given six months in the Sandstone, Minnesota, federal penitentiary. His days at Sandstone could be accounted as an almost restful interlude compared to his Atlanta experience. The inmates lived in dormitories, the food was good, and his duties were light. He worked in the library, but he never got to read much because, as he explained it, "I was busy shuffling Zane Grey and other rubbish."

There was, of course, one confrontation with his keepers. When he was ordered to take his shots, he refused, ascribing them to a part of that body of superstition with which he believed modern medicine had surrounded itself. But the chief medical officer was obdurate and threatened to have Hennacy strapped down unless he cooperated. As he wrote his daughter, Carmen, there was just "no way out of it."

He liked the Catholic chaplain at the prison who requested that the men not think of themselves as prisoners but as members of his parish. He went to church with a Lutheran friend and twice sang "Faith of our fathers! living still." His stay at Sandstone brought some reflections on the prison system. Jesus, he said, had not been speaking sentimentally or idealistically when he had said of the sinful woman that only he who was without sin should be the first to cast a stone at her. This statement illustrated full well, he believed, that the Christian could not cooperate with the prison system.

When he left Sandstone in January, 1960, he told the warden that his time in prison had not been wasted. He had tried to give his fellow prisoners the idea that there was a

different way of looking at life, and that as a radical he had
work to do in the prison as well as out of it. As he walked
out of the gate, he posed with Dorothy Day for a snapshot.
She was making one of her Midwest tours and had come up
to Sandstone to see him.

In June that year, he, Hugh Madden, and Charlie Butterworth of the New York Worker house joined a group of pacifists walking from New York to New London, Connecticut,
to picket the Electric Boat Company plant that had built
the atomic-missile-carrying submarine, Polaris. It was a
small group that made the walk: some students who said
they were atheists, two Quakers, and a young priest. The
devout Madden, feeling uncomfortable in the company of
atheists, walked either ahead or behind the group. In New
London others joined them, and then, en masse, they
marched over a long bridge bound for Groton and the boat
works.

Hennacy stayed with the picketing and leaflet distributing for a while, but he wanted to get back to New York
where he was scheduled to make one of the speeches at a
Communist rally at Union Square on June 30. When the affair was held, it was cast in the spirit of a Fourth of July cel-
ebration, but Hennacy's brief remarks were not in keeping
with the patriotic theme. "When I was asked to speak here,"
he said, "I did not know for sure who was running the meeting, but when it opened with 'The Star-Spangled Banner' I
knew it was Communist. Now you can't sing the song, and
you don't believe it, and you are not fooling anybody. I
hope the next time you invite me we can all sing the Red
Flag as we did in the old days."

That fall he picketed for the last time as a member of the
New York Catholic Worker group. From October until January, 1961, he and his friends kept a daily vigil from noon
until 2 P.M. in front of the civil defense office at Forty-sixth
Street and Lexington Avenue. The leaflets and signs asked
that the public cease cooperating with any more civil defense drills. On January 2, he left New York, heading north
and west. The northward leg of his journey carried him to

Canada where he spent a week visiting Helen Demoskoff, a member of the Russian Doukhobor sect whose curious religious practices had from time to time been visited with coercive restraint from the Canadian government. Hennacy had known Mrs. Demoskoff for some time, and had admired her for her courage and independent spirit. After the visit he headed for Salt Lake City, and from then until his death it would be his home. There he would establish his own house of hospitality, the Joe Hill House, and there, too, he would continue to picket and fast to protest what he regarded as the colossal inhumanity of the state.

"He had been planning for a long time to go," Dorothy Day wrote in her chapter on Hennacy in *Loaves and Fishes*. She felt that in the agitated life of the city he missed the desert and sky that had become a part of his being in the years immediately after World War II. He had missed the "Life at Hard Labor" that he had written about in *The Catholic Worker* and which truly served as food for his spirit.

And then, as Dorothy Day wrote, Mary Lathrop had come into his life. When he returned to New York from Sandstone, she was there at the Worker house, "a lively young woman . . . slim, beautifully built, with the strong legs of the dancer." She had worked in a burlesque show, an occupation she regarded simply as a job. But whatever release it had provided for her restlessness, it was not finally sufficient, and she had gone, seeking anew, to the Worker house. After Hennacy's return, she began to join him in many of his activities in his life at the Worker. He would begin his day by going to a seven o'clock Mass at the old St. Patrick's Church on Mott Street, and if she were not up to join him, he would go to the door of the apartment she shared with Dorothy Day and wait until she appeared. They went for mail together, and then throughout the morning he supervised her typing of the replies. When all the mail had been answered, they went out onto the streets to sell *Workers*. In the afternoon they picketed and in the evening they went to meetings.

After a while Hennacy began to say that Mary wanted to marry him and would go with him to Salt Lake City. Overhearing, she would say that what she really wanted to do was to go into a convent. Marriage did indeed shortly enter into their plans, and so it might have been except that, as the Church viewed it, Hennacy was already married. Unwilling to separate, she followed Hennacy to Salt Lake City where they lived together as friends. But as Dorothy Day wrote, their "Gandhi-and-Mira" situation was not generally understood, and finally, on the advice of a priest at the church where she went to Mass daily, she left.

Her departure was without a good-bye, and Hennacy was shocked and hurt. He blamed the priest and he blamed Dorothy Day as well, for Mary Lathrop had regarded her as a mother. But he did not desert his work and he continued, as usual, to write his column for *The Catholic Worker*, calling it "Joe Hill House," the name of his own house of hospitality. The name honored the IWW songwriter who was executed by the state of Utah in 1915 and whom old Wobblies regarded as their special martyr to the vengeance of the state.

Later, when Dorothy Day wrote asking him if he planned to live on the Pacific coast, he replied that he would remain in Salt Lake City for the rest of his days. "He loves its beauty, he loves all that is good about the Mormans," she explained.

pear to worry *The Catholic Worker*. In a series of articles in
the *Worker* written by William Worthy of the Baltimore
*Afro-American*, peace activist David Dellinger, and Ed
Turner of *The Catholic Worker*, the revolution was accounted as not only justified but highly desirable.

There was, again, the response of outrage. *The Wanderer*,
conservative Catholic paper of St. Paul, Minnesota, said of
Worthy's article that it "might well have been featured in
the Communist *Worker*" and that unfortunately "*The Catholic Worker* has become only too notorious over the years
for its maudlin proclivities where anarchic beatnikism and
outright Communist interests are involved. . . ." A *Worker*
reader called Dellinger's article the product of "another
fuzzy thinker who writes quite well and sounds convincing.
. . . If he isn't a communist he should be paid by them for
this propaganda effort. . . ." There were more letters expressing such sentiments.

These were the outcries of those who believed they were
balancing the equation on the side of Providence in the progress of the object world. But others, friendly to the Worker
movement, were also concerned, feeling that the movement's stand on nonviolence was compromised by an uncritical attitude toward Castro in the face of his daily use of
firing squads in Cuba immediately after the revolution. A
couple wrote in: "Because we love you, we are sick at heart
over the CW's undiscriminating cheers for anything Cuba
does. Traumatic on the subject of Capitalist aggression, the
United States remains the villain of the piece even when enduring the most hate-filled speeches in silence. . . . This is a
very strange one-sided Pacifism." Robert Ludlow, one of the
most controversial of past *Worker* editors, wrote in to say
that he was "puzzled" by the attitude of the *Worker* on Castro. Had not the *Worker* during World War II maintained
that the use of force against the Nazis could not be justified?
But now, he said, *The Catholic Worker* apparently justified
the use of force by Castro. Why? he wanted to know.

Ludlow's letter appeared in the July–August, 1961, issue
of the paper. In the same edition, Dorothy Day wrote an

Ammon Hennacy, Salt Lake City, Summer 1966.

# 19

# ON PILGRIMAGE

In the decade that Ammon Hennacy was with the Catholic Worker movement, he gave focus to a conern that was, after World War II, increasingly central to the movement—opposition to war. Some of the Worker's old friends were complaining, Dorothy Day wrote in the June, 1957, *Worker*, that the paper was not what it used to be. "Too much stuff about war . . . and the duty of building up resistance." It was clear why this should be, she said. In Peter Maurin's day the problem was unemployment. There had been an emphasis on economic conditions because they had seemed closest to those fundamental human problems of sin, sickness, and death. Now it was the buildup of armaments and the threat of war that concerned them.

When she was asked—as she was repeatedly—why she did not object to the Russians, who also were testing atomic weapons and making missiles, she did object, she said, but the personalist way was not in name calling. There was no point in contributing to the sum total of hatred already in the world. She noted that the day on which she was writing her thoughts was the feast of Sts. Cyril and Methodius and that the Gospel for that feast had given the directive of Jesus Christ: "Go, behold, I send you as lambs among wolves. Carry neither purse nor script, nor shoes, and salute no man by the way. Into whatsoever house you enter, first say, Peace be to this house." It was in this spirit, she said, that these two brother saints had gone into the land of the Slavs and had converted them. The Workers' troubles had come from the Christians at home. She knew, of course, that the Communists believed in arms and in the use of force, with the threat of liquidation to all who do not conform. But it was that very use of force that was the heart of the problem.

Dorothy Day's pacifism and that of the Catholic Workers was now much clearer than it had been in the days before World War II, when the "lessons" of history had been invoked to justify Worker pacifism. The "lessons" of history were those equations built in the time and space of the object world, whose application would, presumably, enable time to progress more harmoniously. With Dorothy Day and the Catholic Worker, history had already ended. All was the present and what mattered was bringing the spirit into the world. A cleric sought to dissuade her from tampering with the world. "This world is an imperfect one, Dorothy, and even you know only a fraction of the ills which need correction. Had you stuck to the one work of assisting the needy you would have pleased God more." A seminarian wondered if she could not "let pacifism ride for a while. . . . We Catholics are already a minority and not over loved in America, without cutting ourselves off further and stopping the growth of Christ's Mystical Body, by having us branded as 'unAmerican.' God knows, this has been thrown at us enough already. . . ." And a *Worker* reader, outraged at the paper's seeming obliviousness to the necessity of keeping the equation balanced, declared that "Anyone who is apparently so sincere in the effort to uplift the masses ought to detect as hypocrisy the claims of the communists. . . . You are defeating the very purpose for which you have supposedly dedicated your life."

On January 1, 1959, the question of Communism took on a pointed reference for her and the American people. That was the date of the successful revolution of Fidel Castro in Cuba, and the concern of the American government and people was soon aroused over the rapid movement to the left that the revolution took. It was a movement that did not ap-

editorial: "About Cuba." She said she would do her best to try to clarify her position. The Communists, she pointed out, had stood with the poor; thus it was hard to say that the place of The Catholic Worker movement was with the poor without sometimes finding itself on the side of those who persecuted the Church. Further, the persecution of the Church was both deserved and undeserved. As she many times did when making a point, she went about it in a roundabout way, and now she spent some time explaining why the persecution of the Church, as possibly in Cuba, could be provoked by its insensitivity to the poverty around it. Only recently she had gone to a church in the heart of a slum where Puerto Ricans were crowded together and where some of the worst gangs of the city hung out. She observed that at night the streets there were filled with children who could not go to bed because their rooms were too crowded. Yet in this particular slum there was a Catholic boys' academy, and as she went to the eight-thirty Mass, she could see crowds of well-dressed, well-fed students crossing the street to go to their nine o'clock classes. The contrast of their lives with those of the Puerto Rican inhabitants of the area was painful, she said.

She knew of a convent built in the slums for twelve nuns that cost eighty-five thousand dollars, but she knew, too, of a family of twelve Puerto Ricans living in a two-room tenement. Such things should not be, she said. "Billions of dollars in buildings, plants, as they have come to be called, including Church, school, convent and rectory," but in so many instances there was little thought for the poor. "Even worse, it was the family that paid for all of this, the workingman who wants his children to have a 'Catholic education,' who is afraid of delinquents, who thinks of the sisters and priests as a police force to keep his own children protected, and the Sacraments as an insurance policy against suffering in the life to come." What a corrupted view of the Church, she thought. "Yet it is to the Church we must go or starve for the bread of life."

What had this to do with Castro and Cuba? "Fidel Castro

says he is not persecuting Christ, but Churchmen who have betrayed him . . . (After all, Castro is a Catholic). . . ." American Catholics had not persecuted churchmen, but were they not guilty of ignoring Christ? Castro's revolution had been *for* the poor, and if one *had* to choose between the violence done to the poor by the acquisitive bourgeois spirit of many Americans (among whom were churchmen) and the violence of Castro which was aimed at helping the poor, then she would take the latter. "We do believe," she wrote, "that it is better to revolt, to fight, as Castro did with his handful of men . . . than do nothing."

Ludlow was thus answered. Did this mean that Dorothy Day had at last been forced to admit that there was some ultimate point where circumstances became so desperate that only violence could resolve the problem? It sounded like it, but she said not. "We reaffirm our belief in the ultimate victory of good over evil, of love over hatred and we believe that the trials which beset us in the world today are for the perfecting of our faith. . . ."

Even so, it was still true that the tone of *The Catholic Worker* during the revolutionary period of Castro's coming to power remained studiously uncritical of Castro and criticism of it continued. A woman, a Cuban refugee, wrote to Dorothy Day to tell her that she was "pretty confused (and confusing)." The woman had, she said, "collaborated enthusiastically with the Castro regime during the early period, when we believed his statements that he was with the poor," but she had become "disillusioned" as every aspect of Cuban life had been taken over by the militia.

The Cuba editorial brought one of the editors of *The Register,* a national Catholic newspaper, to a boiling point of outraged feelings. He had just read Dorothy Day's "piece of Uriah Heepism. . . . What is your game. . . ? If you could be honest with yourself, Miss Day, you would acknowledge that you are rotten with pride. . . . In plain words, Miss Day, you and your movement are phony. . . . I think I know your game." Another rejoined with sarcasm. "After all Castro is a Catholic. Well, well, how do you like that? And what has happened in Cuba is all in the name of the poor and the socialism of Castro is not the Marxist brand and it is all very religious, really. . . ."

In a manner reminiscent of the high feelings of the beginning days of World War II, the Cuban debate continued. From Havana came a letter from a Cuban intellectual, Mario Gonzalez, printed in the June, 1962, *Worker*. Wondering if Dorothy Day had the courage to print his letter, he offered the opinion that Worker *readers* "should face the fact that most of the Cuban priesthood was slavishly committed to the Cuban oligarchy. They commerced with suffering and poverty in a very profitable way." The Church had "no right to be sumptuous while people starve to death in some blind alley." This was a "truth which all catholic workers should accept. It is obvious that before they can expect to change society they must try to change their own prostituted establishment." Gonzalez wondered what Dorothy Day would do if she were in Cuba. "Some plutocratic servants feel that she would be in jail but I think she might be working in some cooperative or helping the bearded rebels teach the socialist morality of generosity and sacrifice."

Dorothy Day responded in the same issue that Gonzalez' letter was printed. "I must assure Mario Gonzalez that I would not be teaching 'socialist morality of generosity and sacrifice' but would certainly try to speak always in terms of the generosity and sacrifice of Jesus Christ, our brother and our God." For one professing Christ the issue was not rebellion, but "to grow in love, to rejoice, to be happy and thankful even, that we are living in such parlous times and not just benefiting unwittingly by the toil and suffering of others—rejoicing even that there is every sign that we are going to be given a chance to expiate here and now for our sins . . . and so to help the revolution and convert the revolutionaries. This is a dream worth dreaming, and the only kind of vision powerful enough to stand side-by-side with Marxist-Leninism. . . ."

Gonzalez responded, impressed. He thought the Catholic Worker movement was "one of the few real solutions to save your Church from an inevitable collapse under the pressure of Marxist-Leninism or in the Ash Wednesday of a nuclear disaster. The Catholics cannot fight poverty with bullets but with the renunciation of privileges which they are bound to lose by force sooner or later anyway. If the Catholics and other Christians do not want to accept your secular monasticism they will face the day of judgment unprepared. . . . And then they will find out that a camel cannot pass at all through the eye of a needle. . . ."

More letters: "I wonder if you are being played for a dupe by this Mario Gonzalez. Are you, perchance, blindly opening your columns to a purveyor of Cuban government propaganda?" And, "I can only hope and pray that the views he expressed are his alone, and not those of 'The Catholic Worker.' . . . priests, too, are only human."

And now, said Dorothy Day in the September *Worker*, "I am going to take our readers with me to Cuba." She knew she would be accused of seeing only what *they* wanted her to see, or of seeing only what *she* wanted to see. Of course she knew the island was an armed camp. "But it is too late now to talk of non violence, with one invasion behind them and threats of others ahead of them. . . . No one expects that Fidel will become another Martin of Tours or Ignatius and lay down his arms. But we pray the grace of God will grow in him. . . ." She got her permission to visit the island from the Czechoslovakian embassay, and with an eighty-dollar ticket she left Jersey City on September 5, on a Spanish line vessel.

Despite the passion that had developed around the subject of Castro and Cuba over the two years that the *Worker* had been discussing it, Dorothy Day's brief visit to the island turned out to be a solitary pilgrimage of seeking "concordances" with the Cuban people rather than making it an occasion to arm herself with dramatic new weapons of "fact" and personal encounter to add fuel to the controversy. She did go to a rally where Castro spoke and her reaction was that he was a "great speaker," but she commented no further. She tried to live in a spirit of communion with the

lives of the ordinary people, where she found deprivation
but also rich resourcefulness. It was a narrative of her personal experiences among these people that she gave.

Her Cuban reports brought praise. One person, explaining that "I am not a Catholic," thought the articles so fine
that she was "overcome with emotion, and said aloud, tho' I
was alone, 'Thank God for people like Dorothy Day!' And I
am a person who practically never uses the word 'God.'"
Jack English, now Father Charles in the Trappists, thought
that she had never done such a good job of reporting unless
it had been back in the thirties when she was writing about
the efforts of the CIO to organize the steel mills. Another
wrote simply, "Thank you for your courage on Cuba."

Returning home through Mexico, she was back at Peter
Maurin Farm by Christmas Day, celebrating the occasion in
the company of those enduring members of the Worker
household, Hans Tunnesen, Joe Cotter, and John Filliger.
Jean Walsh, the house manager, was there and so was
Deane Mowrer, down from Boston where, since the onset of
her blindness, she had been undergoing training at the St.
Paul's Rehabilitation Center.

But she was soon away again, and on January 6, 1963, she
was writing her column from Detroit, hoping fervently that
the snow would hold until she could get back to New York.
If she were to be snowed in, she wrote, she would like to be
at the little beach cottage she once had had on Staten Island. She thought back to that time, some four decades past,
when she had walked the beach with her friends and had
gathered driftwood and dug for clams. "It was the observation of those beauties along the sea shore that brought me to
a stunned recognition of God as creator of infinite beauty
and variety," she recalled. How good it had been "to go the
few miles on the five cent ferry over to the island, and down
to the beach where there is the rich life of the shore."

Dorothy Day was now in her mid-sixties, seemingly at the
full tide of her energy and force. It was a time when people
began to recognize that the world was beginning to move
with a new momentum and the word "explosion" became a

commonplace in the vocabulary of learning. It was the time, too, when the Catholic Church began a reevaluation of its position in time. In Rome, on October 20, 1962, Pope John XXIII issued a "Message to Humanity," thereby opening the Second Vatican Council. "We wish to inquire," the message began, "how we ought to renew ourselves, so that we may be found increasingly faithful to the gospel of Christ." For Catholics, it was a heady time and many believed that marvelous consequences were at hand. For Dorothy Day, the rising spirit of Catholic expectancy caught her in a new sweep of conferences and appearances, for it was recognized by many that the call for renewal had long since been made by Peter Maurin and that for thirty years Catholic Workers had been trying to live in the spirit of that call and give life to it.

In April, 1963, with her fare paid by friends, she joined a group of fifty women on a pilgrimage to Rome—"to the representative of Christ on Earth to present ourselves as though a first fruits of his great encyclical Pacem in Terris, to thank him, to pledge ourselves to work for peace, and to ask too, a more radical condemnation of the instruments of modern warfare." She left Rome more convinced than ever that "the particular vocation of The Catholic Worker is to reach the man in the street, to write about the glorious truths of Christianity, the great adventure of the spirit, which can effect so great a transformation in the lives of men if they would consent to the promptings of the Spirit."

While she was in Rome, the Catholic Worker movement had its thirtieth anniversary. On May 15, the fourteenth anniversary of the death of Peter Maurin, she went to a memorial Mass for him in the crypt close to the tomb of St. Peter, under the altar in the Great Basilica of St. Peter.

That fall she crossed the ocean again, having been asked to be one of the main speakers at a British Catholic peace conference. She went over on the *Queen Elizabeth* and had a relaxing trip, the details of which she related in a letter to her sister Della (Mrs. Franklin Spier). "Gray white capped seas and stormy skies, the seamen on deck battening down

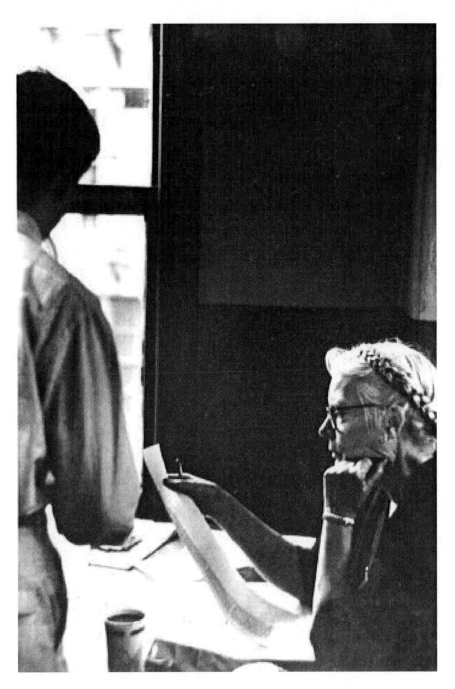

Dorothy Day reading galleys, ca. 1962.
Mottke Weissman photo.

the hatches. Very low clouds and wind whistling thru the rigging." Then she wondered whether phrases like "battening down the hatches" and "wind whistling thru the rigging"—"all that sea language"—could be applied to the *Queen Elizabeth.* Anyway, she was comfortable. "I'll spend the morning writing a few notes . . . read a little, and watch the whitecaps and think of dolphins, which symbolize the resurrection (since they leap out of their natural element, water, I suppose)."

The English were quite taken with her. The English *Catholic Herald* called her a "Joan of Arc holding a glittering and angry pen," who had "encamped within the forecourt of the Catholic Church of America, conservative, pious, uncomprehending, entrenched." Her talk, given at Spode House, Staffordshire, also impressed. "She says what needs to be said, and nothing more. She practices voluntary poverty in words, as well as in goods. . . . Something of early Christianity, you feel, is still with us, and like early Christianity, one of its strengths is its indifference to the organs of power in society, its non-participation in war and politics and civil defense. 'What can you expect,' she says, 'except suffering?' "

She gave her talk on October 18, and that evening she wrote her sister about the events following the talk. There was a reception and then she went with two young English Catholic Workers to Highgate Cemetery to visit Karl Marx's grave, standing out from the others because of the huge bronze bust of Marx over it. She noted that fresh flowers had been placed there. Then they said a prayer. "I remembered his wife Jenny especially," she wrote.

She was back in the country in November, in time for the publication of her book *Loaves and Fishes.* On the afternoon of November 22, she was in Chicago, having just gotten off the bus from South Bend, when she heard of the assassination of John Kennedy. She met her friend Nina Polcyn and together they went to Mass. She spent Christmas back at Peter Maurin Farm, where "we had just enough visitors to make things festive." There had been some snow, but now, several weeks later, it was springlike and "people were grumbling about pneumonia weather. . . . So I shall overcome the doldrums by getting under covers early at night and reading Jane Austen." Marty Corbin, recently graduated from college and interested in communitarian ventures, was there, visiting the farm to discuss a new move. With Peter Maurin Farm now sold, the plan was to move to a place they had bought on the Hudson, at Tivoli. Dave Mason, who had kept the Mott Street house together during the World War II days, was back for a visit. At Chrystie Street all was peaceful. Ed Forand, another young man who put his lot in with the Workers in this period, had a great deal to do with that, Dorothy said. He was energetic and cheerful.

From Salt Lake City Ammon Hennacy reported a fine Christmas at Joe Hill house. Mary Lathrop, who had come back for four days, had sung Christmas carols, gypsy songs, "and even the one Carl Sandburg sings about Sam Hall." She still held to her "exalted ideas about the Church," Hennacy said, which were in contrast to Bob Steed's "ironic" attitude and "my realistic frame of mind."

The news from Chicago was not good. Karl Meyer, two years married, had developed an active case of tuberculosis, and his Christmas was spent in a sanitarium. Meyer had become the most passionately committed of antiwar activists. After he was arrested and imprisoned in 1959 for having gone "over the fence" at the Omaha missile base, he had written to Dorothy Day of his pacifist conviction:

> If war comes, if we do not win for man a reprieve from the immensity of sin that weighs upon us all and threatens our destruction, nothing that we have done, however right or courageous, can be any consolation for the loss of our brothers. We must follow Peguy's words in *The Mystery of the Charity of Joan of Arc*, that we can not do what is right ourselves and leave the nations to their fate. . . . It is not enough to have always taken our stand and made our witness. It is only enough to have succeeded. Therefore I appeal . . . to everyone who agrees intellectually with what

we have done and supports us, to welcome an upheaval in their own lives, to refuse to go to war, to refuse to pay for war, and to dedicate themselves completely to the work of peace and leave any job that is not in very truth a necessary service of love to God and man. In the critical year ahead twenty-five new radicals must spring up for each of the four of us who have been cut off and imprisoned here.

By 1961, he had thought of a new project, a peace pilgrimage to Moscow, walking wherever circumstances permitted. He had written to Dorothy Day: "I have great hopes for the walk, and a deep desire to carry the spirit of the Little Brothers and Sisters of Jesus into Russia. . . . It is an absolute act of peace that I am seeking for as an opening of reconciliation."

The walk had started from Chicago on Easter Monday, April 3. Others walked with him; sometimes there were as many as thirty-five. When it was cold and rainy he was miserable, and then, as he wrote in the *Worker*, he thought of those in prison camps and on battle fields. In Pennsylvania the weather warmed, and they walked through a country of Quaker farmers who were wonderfully hospitable and who put them up at night in their meetinghouses.

They flew to London on May 31 and from there they boarded a boat to France. But the French would not permit them to disembark. So fourteen of the group jumped over the side and began to swim in different directions toward the shore. Meyer had not been eager to face the ice-cold water and then the French police, but he thought, "if the salt lose its savor what is it good for but to be cast out and to be trodden on by men? . . ." Thus, philosophically consoled, he leaped into the water and swam laboriously toward the police-lined shore. By the time he reached land he had, presumably, gotten his fill of salt, for his energy was expended. The police reached down to seize his leaflets and then to grasp him. Meyer gasped out his protest and stated his cause. Later, a somewhat bemused and apologetic French policeman put him back on the ship.

All of this had been recorded in the July–August, 1961,

issue of the *Worker*. The September issue carried his account of the journey through Belgium, and finally in October came the account of his arrival in Moscow. There in Red Square he had been permitted "for fifteen minutes" to distribute his leaflets and talk to students.

During the days that Meyer was recovering from his tuberculosis, it must have seemed to him that his hope for twenty-five pacifists to arise for every one he had known in 1959 was coming true. Whatever the causes for this development, the phenomenon of young Catholics becoming pacifists was especially obvious. It was also obvious that there was no likelier place for them to converge upon than the Catholic Worker movement.

By the early sixties Worker pacifism seemed to be resting on a new foundation of respectability. It was no longer a matter of Dorothy Day, Ammon Hennacy, and their devoted young friends seeming to defy alone the traditional conventions of church and state where war was concerned. The utterances and person of Pope John bespoke peace so pervasively that whatever had been said in the past about "conditions of a just war" now seemed only a tired formalism in the new light of hope and warmth for all men, generated by his person. Then, as Vatican II gave voice to its deliberations, there was frequently found enjoined on the Catholic world the necessity of taking a more urgent approach to the task of ending war. To the young zealots of Catholic pacifism, it appeared that the peace emphasis of Vatican II culminated on October 4, 1965, in Pope Paul's address to the General Assembly of the United Nations where he asked the world, "in God's name," to cease its fighting, "war, never again."

The peace theme was even more emphasized in *The Catholic Worker*. In the fifties Hennacy had kept the issue before the *Worker* readers as after him Karl Meyer had contributed accounts of his activities. Then it was Tom Cornell, a graduate of Fairfield University, who had as an undergraduate read something written by Dorothy Day. He was immediately impressed, for it seemed to him that what she said was the true focus "of what we were all studying . . . Christianity, Catholicism and doctrine," whereas his Catholic education had been "very heavy on apologetics and personal piety and novenas and that kind of thing." After his graduation Cornell became a peace activist, picketing in 1960 with Hennacy the Polaris submarine project at New London, Connecticut.

Since Dorothy Day was traveling afar more and more often, Cornell, with Marty Corbin's help, became the editor of *The Catholic Worker* in the fall of 1962. He contributed his own material to the paper and included articles by a growing list of others concerned with peace. There were the Berrigan brothers, writing of their concern with injustice the world around and seeing the attainment of peace as the central and sacred action of human and social purification.

By 1965, Dan Berrigan had become the prophet of the young in the peace movement. He moved into this position when his probing of the issue of poverty produced in him a new level of feeling and of eloquence, especially after a year's journey to Africa and Europe that had begun in the fall of 1963.

On his journey Berrigan wrote a letter to Dorothy Day. It was April 24, 1964. He was in Cairo. He had just spent two weeks in South Africa at the invitation of Archbishop Patrick Hurley of Durban. It was a country "lost in the worst repressions of Hitler's Germany—indeed Gordon Zahn's book [*German Catholics and Hitler's Wars*] could be read there and the implications for the Catholic community could be played there without changing a major note." In the course of the discussion that followed a Berrigan interview with the priests of Durban, the archbishop had remarked "that what was needed in D. was fewer Masses on Sunday and a few priests in jail."

Thomas Merton also contributed peace articles in this period. "What are we to do?" he asked in the October, 1961, *Worker*. "The duty of the Christian in this crisis is to strive with all his power and intelligence, with his faith, hope in Christ, and love for God and man to do the one task which

God has imposed on us in the world today. That task is to work for the total abolition of war." A month later he was writing a criticism of "The Shelter Ethic" that justified compulsory air-raid drills, and in February, 1962, he discussed the peace demonstrations that were beginning to occur. "Of course the tragedy is that the vast majority of people do not understand. . . . In their . . . blind craving for undisturbed security, they feel that agitation for peace is somehow threatening to them. They do not feel at all threatened by the bomb . . . but they feel terribly threatened by some little girl student carrying a placard."

Over its thirty-year history there had been a time in the Catholic Worker movement when the special concerns of persons who thought of themselves in some sense as Catholic Workers prompted them to form a separate organization to deal with a specific complex of problems. In the thirties it had been the Campions, seeking a more active approach to social problems, and in the years of the war there had been the organization for Catholic conscientious objectors. As the problem of war in the mid-sixties again became more direct, a new group of young men, drawn to the Worker because of its pacifism, organized the Catholic Peace Fellowship. Jim Forest, a Navy veteran, who upon his discharge in 1961 went directly to the Worker house, was one of the principals forming the new organization in February, 1965. Marty Corbin and Tom Cornell were also involved, the latter serving as the new organization's publications director. The Peace Fellowship saw as its first job the initiation of educational programs that would acquaint Catholics with a Church history that emphasized the hitherto neglected areas of its peace traditions. It was also concerned with counseling young men who as a matter of conscience would resist the draft. By the end of its first year the Fellowship had eight hundred members, Forest said.

And now there was Vietnam, that hard fact of despoliation and slaughter that weighed heavy on the nation's conscience—a conscience that frequently was lulled and blurred by promises of victories soon to be won, for America had always won. But the young men of the Worker, of the nation, who burned their draft cards, who burned draft records, saw the war as a bankruptcy of the value life of the nation. As they saw it, it was the spectacle of the American government interjecting itself into a process, in which previously it had taken no large and notably charitable concern, and insisting that the process go according to America's own formula as to what it conceived as its vital interests; insisting that the people of Vietnam continue to function within corrupt and moribund institutional arrangements, divinely sanctioned, it would seem, with an importance that transcended all decency and life because, somewhere in the plethora of verbiage used to justify death and inhumanity, could be found that battered word symbol, "freedom."

But what a curious freedom! It was of the order of the Grand Inquisitor's freedom. It was a freedom uncomprehending of the spirit and with but only a passing reference to it. Even the Grand Inquisitor had spoken of freedom in terms of work, song, and "innocent dances," but the "freedom" looked to by the American government was one that found its life in the exercise of that dubious process of ballot casting and which sought to uphold this exercise at whatever the price in violence. In the name of this freedom the men of the Pentagon, of the State Department, of the White House, wrote their memoranda, cloaked their thoughts with an eye to the stylistic effect of their verbiage, planned the "scenario" of war, and played tennis to relax from the tension of work. They spoke as men of high faith, knowing all the while that they possessed the power to destroy finally and fully. Thus they fashioned the diplomacy of "the carrot and the stick," and when the carrot failed to beguile, their conscience and that of Americans was consoled, even with the killing and debauchery that followed.

They, the men who played tennis, who played with words, and who played with power, were, after all, Americans, upheld by the American people, and like the American people trapped by words which had themselves been caught racing with the object world and which had lost touch with spirit, yet professed to be of spirit. Thus the "fire" of freedom came not from that spirit once carried into Vietnam by a Theophane Venard, but from napalm, bombs, defoliation, and disease; from the debauchery of a people where watches and motorbikes came to be the only consolation of life, and no price of body or soul was too high to pay for them.

In the minds of the young—those who had been taught the reality of spirit and who, through the Worker movement or whatever source, had grasped pacifism as its sharpest weapon—the war was a monstrosity. Thomas Merton had spoken for them when in the May, 1962, *Worker* he had written, "We Have to Make Ourselves Heard." It was a cry that by 1965 reechoed more insistently in the thoughts of those young whose sensitivity to what they considered the injustice of the war had reached desperate proportions.

In September of that year, 1965, Dorothy Day went again to Rome with her friend and longtime peace advocate Eileen Egan, to observe the proceedings of the Vatican Council. For Dorothy Day and the party with whom she traveled, it was to be the occasion of a ten-day fast. She described her experiences in the *Worker* of November, 1965. The night before the fast began, there had been a feast with a bishop from India, an affair she felt somewhat guilty about, since she was offering her fast for the victims of famine over the world.

Fasting was a difficult penitential exercise for her, and the pains of conscience soon gave way to those of the sense. "They were certainly of a kind I have never had before, and they seemed to pierce to the very marrow of my bones when I lay down at night. . . ." It was a small offering, she concluded—she an American, from a nation where there was so much of everything, giving up her food for ten days. "God help us, living as we do," she concluded.

Back in New York some of the young Workers were thinking of what they might do in some striking way to focus the attention of the nation on the injustice of the war.

On August 4, there was passed a law that made it illegal to burn or mutilate a draft card, and on August 30, President Lyndon Johnson signed the bill. Some immediate gesture of noncooperation would have to be offered.

Tom Cornell had already set what seemed a worthy precedent. As early as 1960, he had decided that he did not want to have anything to do with the "system" because, in the matter of the draft, neither nonreligious people nor nonpacifists were protected by the law. So he did not want protection either, he concluded, and at the Polaris submarine demonstration at New London he burned his draft card.

As a dramatic act it was an immediate success, and thereafter Cornell was in much demand for performances, so much so that his draft board must have been hard pressed to keep him supplied with cards. After New London, he burned a number of cards during the 1962 "strike for peace." He burned one for a national television audience. Actually, "I burned two cards, because the cameras didn't get the first burning," he said. Fortunately, he had another one with him. In 1963, he burned his remaining cards at a demonstration at Union Square. Altogether, at that demonstration, twelve cards were collected and burned with three FBI men looking on. Cornell explained that the FBI men were recognized "because of their sun glasses and drip dry suits." The drip dry suits are "what gives them away," he said.

Now, wrote Cornell, with the new law making the destruction of the draft card a crime, "the card was made something for which there had never been a place in the American tradition, an internal passport, a license to breathe for every male between the ages of 18 and 36. The draft card became the symbol . . . of involuntary servitude for the works of death, and the symbol of moral and intellectual suffocation. It deserves to be burned."

The most appropriate gesture of defiance to the new law was, of course, to burn a draft card. Already this had been done by another young man with a Worker orientation. Producing something of a sensation, David Miller had burned his card on October 15, at a protest demonstration. Perhaps to add momentum to Miller's action, Cornell and his group planned a demonstration at Union Square for November 6.

Two thousand gathered at the square that day, among whom was Dorothy Day just returned from Rome. So also was the only other man in the United States who could rival Ammon Hennacy for length of service on the active front of the peace movement. This was A. J. Muste, Presbyterian minister, labor leader, revolutionary, uncompromising pacifist, now old, but still battling. It was an especially solemn gathering, for four days previous, Roger Morrison, a thirty-two-year-old Quaker, had immolated himself at the Pentagon. The meeting began with a moment of prayer for him, and then Muste and Dorothy Day gave talks. "They spoke from age and experience, with such depth of conviction and commitment that we were deeply moved," Cornell wrote in the *Worker*.

Dorothy Day's talk was brief:

When Jesus walked this earth, True God and true Man, and addressed the multitudes, a woman in the crowd cried out: Blessed is the womb that bore you, and the breasts that gave you sustenance. Jesus answered her: Rather, blessed are those that hear the word of God and keep it.

And the word of God is clear, in the New Testament and the Old. "Thou shalt not kill; love your enemies; overcome evil with good." To love others as He loves us, to lay down our lives for our brothers throughout the world, not to take the lives of men, women and children, young and old, by bombs and napalm and all the other instruments of war.

Instead He spoke of the instruments of peace, to be practiced by all nations; feeding the hungry, clothing the naked, not destroying their crops, not spending billions of dollars on defense, which means instruments of destruction. He commanded us to feed the hungry, shelter the homeless, to save lives, not to destroy them, these precious lives for whom He willingly sacrificed His own.

I speak today as one who is old, and who must endorse the courage of the young who themselves are willing to give up their freedom. I speak as one who is old, and whose whole lifetime has seen the cruelty and hysteria of war in the last half century, but who has also seen, praise God, the emerging nations of Africa and Asia and Latin America, achieving their own freedom, in some instances with nonviolence. Our own country has, through tens of thousands of the Negro people, shown an example to the world of what a nonviolent struggle can achieve. This very struggle was begun by courage, even in martyrdom, which has been shared by little children, in the struggle for full freedom and human dignity. . . .

I wish to place myself beside A. J. Muste to show my solidarity of purpose with these young men, and to point out that we too are breaking the law, committing civil disobedience, in advocating and trying to encourage all those who are conscripted, to inform their consciences, to heed the still, small voice, and to refuse to participate in the immorality of war.

As she spoke, a counterdemonstration broke out on the other side of Seventeenth Street. The cry went up: "Moscow Mary" and "Give us joy, Bomb Hanoi." Then Cornell and four others on a raised platform held up their draft cards and ignited a cigarette lighter. As they held their cards over the flame, they were suddenly doused with water. But Cornell persisted. The cards were torn and resubmitted to the flame and were burned.

Across the street, the counterdemonstrators became frenzied. "Burn yourselves, not your cards," they shouted. Watching the proceedings was a young man who had been with the Worker about two weeks, Roger LaPorte. Three days later, November 9, at 5:20 in the morning, LaPorte sat in the middle of First Avenue before the United Nations Building, poured over himself gasoline from a two-gallon can, and then struck a flame. He died thirty hours later at Bellevue Hospital.

For much of the time before his death, he was conscious and lucid, nor was he in pain. He spoke to the ambulance attendants who took him to the hospital: "I am a Catholic Worker. I am antiwar, all wars. I did this as a religious ac-

tion . . . all the hatred of the world. . . . I picked this
hour so no one could stop me." At the hospital a priest
heard his Confession and anointed him. To some of the
Catholic Workers gathered in the hall outside his room, he
sent out word that he wanted to live.

His immolation shocked and perplexed Workers. Many
had not known him, for he had moved into the Worker
Kenmare Street apartment only a week before his death.
They began to put together information they had about
him. He had attended a Catholic prep school at Tupper
Lake, New York, and had spent two years in a Trappist
seminary. Recently he had been working at a library on the
Columbia University campus and was taking a course in
"philosophical ideas in imaginative literature" at Hunter
College in the Bronx. The instructor in that course, Walter
Arnold, recalls him as a serious student who sat in the rear
and spoke little, but when he did, thoughtfully. (Ironically,
Mr. Arnold recalls, one of the works read in that course was
Aeschylus' *Antigone*.) Most people at the Worker house
considered him reserved and quiet.

But there were some at the Chrystie Street house who
had come to know him well and who were aware of the
depth and warmth of his person. One was Nicole
d'Entremont, the house manager. She remembered that he
had come every evening around five o'clock to wait on tables. "He appeared at the door, and, pursing his lips and
smiling at the same time, would look around for someone to
kid with. He had a special affection for Julia, a modern Tug-
boat Annie. . . . Roger would grab Julia's arm and tease her
by pulling the funny yellow knit cap she wears down over
one eye."

Julia had a mammoth shopping bag, and one night before
Roger left, he scribbled something on it. "The next morning
while I was washing my face," Miss d'Entremont related,
"and Julia was sitting on the couch in the kitchen, she said
to me chuckling, 'Hey, Nicola, look what my honey wrote
on my bag.' In his angular script, Roger had written a simple 'I love you.' He was a man who understood how people

spoke from their needs and he answered them as spontaneously and completely as possible."

Miss d'Entremont remembered most vividly the evening of the day of LaPorte's burning. Most of his friends had gathered at the Chrystie Street house for the evening meal, seeking the comfort of each other's presence. They had begun serving the food when the lights began to flicker and then went out. Twenty-five million people in the northeastern United States and southeastern Canada were thrown into darkness. Someone noticed that the lights had gone out at 5.20 and that at 5.20 that morning LaPorte had been in flames. Candles were brought down from the third floor, and then someone brought in his bicycle with a light on it and the men took turns pumping the pedals to make it burn. As they ate, a bedspring, hung from the ceiling with candles stuffed into its coils, turned slowly, making light and shadow pass over the faces of people. Someone broke into a chorus of "This Little Light of Mine."

After the house had closed, a group decided to walk over to Tom and Monica Cornell's apartment. It was a strange kind of New York they found on the streets. Miss d'Entremont thought how suddenly people in the great, impersonal city found a need to talk to one another. A Puerto Rican joined them, speaking Spanish, and although none could respond, he continued on with the group for a block. "I thought," she wrote, "of how Roger would have smiled if he had heard that civil-defense teams were out directing traffic and escorting people across the streets, military vehicles were used to transport the elderly and sick to hospitals, armories were opened up as Houses of Hospitality. All over New York were candles. . . . It was if the technological world had revolted so that the stars and candles could forever witness that this day was a prayer."

Those Workers who knew LaPorte could not think of his action as coming from madness or despair. Anne Taillefer wrote of their feelings in her *Worker* article, "Requiem for a Flame":

✿   ✿   ✿

The indignation of the young is a terrible thing. The call
and the witness of Antigone, to protest overbearing power,
have been taken up all through the ages. But here is no
stark Greek doom. Even if we must view it as a unique action, never again to be imitated by a Christian for fear of
destroying its purity and making of it a monstrous parody
through pride or fanaticism, it stands out as an impulse of
extraordinary innocence. . . . Faced by extraordinary, overwhelming evil, he had no good choice and cried out "murder," "murder" in the best way he could to the entire
world; . . .

Julia Porcelli Moran added a passionate affirmation of
Miss Taillefer's view. Some of her acquaintances had tried
to tell her that there was some relationship between La-
Porte's action and the philosophy and style of life of the
Catholic Worker movement. "Yes, but I kept saying, some
of the zeal of St. Francis of Assisi, ripping off his clothes in
front of his parents, was in this boy. It was an excess of zeal
and love."

Some others, outside the Worker, took a different view.
LaPorte had been one of "these Catholic Communists" one
columnist had said. John Leo in the *National Catholic Reporter* thought that the Catholic Worker movement had
been "terribly important for the American Church" but that
it had "a sort of built-in rejection of complexity that I hope
was not operative in LaPorte's death." The movement, he
continued, "has practically never been well-grounded intellectually and is traditionally intolerant of distinctions which
are not its own."

Many of the people who wrote to Dorothy Day thought
they understood and tried to comfort her. A nun said she realized "you must be feeling very sad. . . . I, for one . . . am
convinced his sacrifice will not be in vain." A priest wrote
saying that he hoped "the unkind and bitter words" that
had been said about LaPorte would not discourage her in
her work. No one could judge LaPorte, "it was God alone
who was able to read his heart . . . and God alone who
knew his sincerity."

The people up at the Tivoli farm had not known LaPorte, but Deane Mowrer was troubled and depressed by his death. It should not be taken as an example for others, she said. The Worker had had too many deaths of late. Little Jimmy Hughes, Marge Hughes' son, had recently suddenly died. He, with his mother and the other Hughes children, had lived at the Staten Island Peter Maurin Farm. Then, German George had died. He would be remembered as one of the most faithful workers at the old Chrystie Street house, Miss Mowrer wrote. At Tivoli he had gotten cancer and the operation had taken most of his tongue and part of his jaw. But he did not give up his work, and in the summer of 1965, he was back setting tables—laying out plates as he clutched a towel under his dripping chin. This had been his job for years and no one now was going to suggest that he do something else, least of all Jean Walsh, who managed the Tivoli house and who had so tirelessly nursed him in the critical moments of his illness.

Miss Mowrer reviewed the deaths and then thanked God for those still alive. Hans Tunnesen, Joe Cotter, and John Filliger were the ties with the past—also Hugh Madden, Mike Sullivan, and Arthur Sullivan. The Corbins were there, Marty spending the late night hours editing the paper and his wife, Rita, doing artwork. Arthur Lacey, the wanderer, seemed finally to have settled into regular ways. Every morning he walked the two miles to the village to get the mail and at mealtime he led the devotions. Sometimes in the late summer afternoon, when the children of Tivoli had vacated the swimming pool, he would mount the diving board, poise his eighty-five-pound frame for a moment, and then dive in for the brief wetting that he accounted as much a bath as relaxation.

In the summer of 1965, Jean Walsh was helped by Alice Lawrence, who had the job of housekeeper. Both of these capable women had much to do, for there were many guests, especially young people. Among them were two Japanese students who had come for a while to work in the gardens that John Filliger had planted. After dinner, washed and freshly dressed, they would come out on the broad lawn in front of the house and teach judo to the delighted young people. Down below, at the foot of the cliff, the Hudson flowed. Over on the other bank the Catskill Mountains rose. One night that summer as the children raced about and the grown-ups sat talking, a ship passed and its muffled pulsing was scarcely heard. Only its lights, distinct against the dark background of mountains, seemed to move steadily on.

# 20

# THE LAMB AND THE BEAST

After 1965, when she was not traveling, Dorothy Day made the Tivoli place her headquarters, going down to the city to the Chrystie Street house when the occasion required it. It was at Tivoli that her friends had gathered, and much of the support she got at this time in her life, when more and more the discordancies of a new phase of speeding time was sending its reverberations into the heart of the Worker idea, came from members of this group.

There was Stanley Vishnewski, now nearly fifty years old. Over the years he developed some areas of disagreement with Dorothy Day—her pacifism, for example—but he was not one to magnify differences and brood over them. To the contrary, his witticisms about the foibles and vagaries of Catholic Worker life became a part of its legend. And after thirty years he would still say, as he did on the morning of December 27, 1965, in the dining room of the house at Tivoli, that he believed in the personalist message of the Catholic Worker. He had been close to Dorothy Day for all those years, and if she was not real—if what she stood for was not true—then "there is no hope for any of us."

Marge Hughes was there. In the days before the war at Mott Street she had been the closest thing to a secretary that Dorothy Day had ever had. Her course had been hard, but she had endured the blows and held to the movement. At Tivoli she did what she had done at Mott Street. She helped with the management of the house and kept Dorothy Day's affairs in order when the latter was traveling.

Helene Iswolsky came to Tivoli late in the sixties. She had known Dorothy Day since the years of the Second World War and had from time to time visited the Worker house and farm. She began her Worker life at the retirement age, but she did not come seeking care and security, or the felicity of an atmosphere of comforting piety. She came believing that the personalist idea was right, and she hoped that with her talents as a writer and lecturer she might contribute whatever she could to the vitality of that idea.

Miss Iswolsky was a remarkable woman who did have something more to contribute—an unusual intellectual background. She was born in Russia in the years just before the turn of the century, the daugher of Russian diplomat Alexander Iswolsky. When World War I began, she was in Russia, but left immediately on her father's orders for Paris, where he was the Russian ambassador. When the Russian Revolution came, the Iswolskys remained in Paris and became members of the colony of Russian refugees from the revolution. When Alexander Iswolsky died in 1919, his family remained in Paris.

There, Miss Iswolsky and her mother received into their apartment one day a fellow Russian émigré. It was Nikolai Berdyaev, Christian philosopher and fellow exile of the revolution. He dropped in almost casually, Miss Iswolsky later related, to suggest that she participate in the work and discussions of an ecumenical group of thinkers of which he had become a member. Thus she came into contact with the personalist thinkers who lived in Paris in the decade of the twenties—Mounier, Maritain, and, of course, Berdyaev. Though she became a Catholic and Berdyaev throughout his life remained in the Orthodox Church, she was a devoted friend, and he influenced her considerably. She took on the social dimensions of his personalist position, one that made her quite revolutionary in the eyes of her countrymen who lived in Paris.

In World War II the Iswolskys left Paris for southern France two days before the Germans came and from there they made their way to the United States. In New York Miss Iswolsky met Dorothy Day, and for the next twenty years, as she made a livelihood by interpreting, teaching, and lecturing, she established her association with the Catholic Worker movement. It was, therefore, appropriate that this intelligent and resilient woman, who also deeply appreciated Dostoevsky, should become a part of the Catholic Worker household.

Deane Mowrer, now fully blind, nonetheless continued to write in her column of the sights and sounds of life about her at Tivoli. She, better than most, understood the depths of the Worker phenomenon and set herself to document a part of its past by making taped interviews with persons who had been a vital part of its history. She was a woman of taste and culture, of reason and order, who found painful the harsh, atonal discordancies that came with rushing time.

It was this group that sustained a spirit of community at Tivoli, for after 1965, time, the despoiler of community, took an increasing toll of those who through the years had been a vital part of the movement. In October, 1966, Dorothy Day received a letter telling her that Jane Marra, who, in 1934, had organized the Tremont Street Boston Worker house, was dying. "She remembers you with a smile," the letter concluded. Miss Marra died on November 15, and Dorothy Day went up to Boston for the funeral. Most of the people associated with the early days of the Boston house were there: Arthur Sheehan, Ignatius O'Conner, Catherine Ahearn, John Kelly, and Charles Dastoli. In the December 10 issue of *Ave Maria*, the magazine published by the Holy Cross Fathers at Notre Dame, Dorothy Day wrote a memorial to Miss Marra. Jane Marra had spent a long and useful life in the service of others, she said. It had been a celibate life and also, one might add, one of poverty and obedience. She had been a part of the past, of the early days of the movement, which were now gone.

In February, 1967, the Workers lost a friend. Eighty-two-year-old A. J. Muste died. He had just returned from a journey to Hanoi, seeking "concordances," as Dorothy Day might have said. In his last days Muste had an office in the same building with the Catholic Peace Fellowship. Tom Cornell, who worked on the Fellowship *Bulletin*, wrote in it that "A. J. was a lot more to us than the odd looking, quivering old gentleman down the hall."

Mike Gold, columnist for *The Daily Worker* and companion of Dorothy Day's early years in New York, died on May 14. His passing brought that time again to mind. She had last seen him in 1965, in Oakland, California, where he lived with his wife, Elizabeth. Dorothy Day knew Elizabeth Gold. Some ten years before the two had gathered shells together on the beaches of Staten Island "just as Mike and I had explored the beaches forty years before, picnicking with artists Maurice Becker and Hugo Gellert. . . ." It had been the year *The Masses* was suppressed, and while they knew that they could do nothing about the war, they found hope in the Russian Revolution.

> We all went to meetings, to picnics, to dances at Webster Hall, stayed up all night and walked the streets, and sat on the piers and sang. Great things were happening in the world, along with the senseless capitalistic war, which to us represented the suffering and death that came before the victorious resurrection. I thought in those terms then. . . . The suffering and death that accompanied war and revolution seemed to make the keenness of our joy the more poignant. The revolution was world-shaking, it liberated the people, and opened up to them a new life. We longed ourselves to be able to take part in that suffering.
>
> We were young, we had found ourselves . . . we had a cause. . . . I walked the streets of the East Side, which I had come to love. . . . I knew the Jews and their life there, I bathed with the women in those little bath houses. . . . I visited Mike's home on Chrystie Street, down the street from the present location of the Catholic Worker, and his mother, a stern and beautiful woman who wore the wig and observed the dietary laws, offered me food, even though I was a shiksa, but she did not speak to me.

Then, eight years later, when she bought her beach cottage on Staten Island, she saw more of him. Two of his brothers had had a cottage near hers, and they all swam, dug clams, and fished together. When she decided to become a Catholic, Gold never tried to argue her out of it. "He seemed to understand my misery and to sense that there had to be a price to pay, sometimes a heartbreaking price, in following one's vocation. Neither revolutions nor faith are won without keen suffering. For me Christ was not to be bought for thirty pieces of silver but with my heart's blood." On June 16, a memorial meeting was held for Gold in New York. It was organized by some of his friends who had been part of those stirring days when they were young. Matthew Josephson, Louis Untermeyer, and Dorothy Day were among the members of the memorial committee.

There was also a death in the Worker family that year. The world knew little of Hugh Madden, but at the Catholic Worker house he for several years had been among its most colorful residents. He was one of the first hippies, the original wearer of a floppy hat which he covered with religious medals and badges, the external marks of his inward piety. Madden was given to long-distance bicycle riding, and one day in September, as he made his way southward, he was struck by a car on a North Carolina highway and killed.

On October 11, Dorothy Day was in Rome again, this time as a member of the Third World Congress for the Lay Apostolate. For her, at least, the congress did not seem to produce a sense of the Church's moving into the world with a hopeful certainty of its mission. There was colorful pageantry and there were addresses by delegates, ranging over those subjects considered vital at the moment. She reported the character of some of these speeches in her column and then added an account of what she described as the high honor paid to her and the Catholic Worker by the congress.

What deep emotion, what new enlightenment of spirit had she received on that occasion? a journalist asked her. Mainly, she said, she had been concentrating so much on the proper procedure of walking up the carpeted stairs, and

of turning away and walking back along the priceless carpets past the red upholstered chairs where the cardinals sat
that she thought of nothing and felt nothing. She had
prayed fervently for Pope Paul, she said, and then had
prayed for the dead, including Che Guevara, whose death
had been reported just the week before.

The trip to Rome was noteworthy on another account. On
her return home, she traveled from Italy to England by air,
a form of transportation which hitherto she had not used,
partly because of fear but also because of considerations of
economy. Apparently this trip converted her into an air
traveler. Some trepidation about flying would remain, but
she recognized that the factor of economy, especially on
long trips, operated in favor of the airplane.

The Vatican Congress for the Lay Apostolate, coming
soon after the work of the council, suggested to the minds of
many Catholics an expectation of some Church-inspired
movement into the world that would represent a departure
from the traditional past. But nothing like this occurred,
though many of the delegates spoke of dissatisfaction with
established Church procedures. Perhaps Dorothy Day had
hoped for some new sign, but her inner feelings about the
character of the situation may have been revealed in her
sense of the disturbing presence of priceless carpets and upholstered chairs as she had gone to Communion.

Nonetheless whatever Vatican II had inspired or had not
inspired, there were well-publicized and highly controversial cases of American Catholics moving aggressively—
indeed radically—to confront social problems, especially
those that had enjoyed the benevolent toleration of
ecclesiastics—racism and war. In Milwaukee, Wisconsin, a
priest assigned to a Black inner-city parish came to the conclusion that his neighbors and parishoners suffered terrible
injustices. Soon he was organizing demonstrations of Blacks
against those injustices. Father James Groppi was not a man
of great learning but he could see a situation for what it
was. Further, he seemed not at all awed by the time-held
traditions of some of his fellow churchmen or of established

society concerning exploitation of Blacks. As Groppi-led demonstrations became more frequent, reactions became more bitter and insistent.

The protest of Father Groppi and his Black associates was spontaneous, but many who joined the marches had a Worker orientation, for Milwaukee had been well seeded with Worker ideas from the days when a Worker house had been there. Also, Karl Meyer came up from Chicago to give his help, and one of the most tireless in a day-after-day regimen of marching was a rosy-cheeked elderly man from Boston. Ignatius O'Conner, from the early days at the Boston house, had come to Milwaukee to join a march, but he was so taken with the rightness of the cause and the spirit of the marchers that he remained. "I wish I could tell you more about this most worthy movement—non-violent—the most dedicated group I have ever met," he wrote Dorothy Day.

Also marching regularly was the founder of a new Worker group in Milwaukee, Mike Cullen, with his wife, Nettie. Cullen was a young enthusiast from Ireland where he had been in a seminary. Deciding that the priesthood was not his vocation, he left Ireland for America. After his marriage he began to make for himself a place in the secure and "proper" ranks of mid-America. But he still felt a strong call to make some special and sacrificial effort with his life, and in 1966, when he heard about the Catholic Worker movement, he decided to give up his job and open a Worker house. This new course was almost immediately beset by serious difficulties, but he and his wife persisted.

Shortly, he was involved in the antiwar protest. With the beginning of Lent in 1968, he began a fast for the duration of that season. Daily, at the noon hour, he stood outside the federal building on Wisconsin Avenue, holding a sign that stated he was fasting and the reasons for it. Occasionally, others from the Casa Maria House that he and Nettie had begun came to stand with him, and once in a while a few students from Marquette University would share his vigil. But as the Lenten season wore on, the number who joined him fell off. Finally, it was usually Cullen alone who stood there, his thinning figure postured with an uncertain-appearing strength against the winds that swept down the avenue.

That fall he registered his protest in the dramatic manner that had become established by the Berrigans. On October 4, 1967, Philip Berrigan and three others had entered the office of a Selective Service Board in Baltimore and had poured blood on the board's files. Then on May 24, 1968, Philip and Dan Berrigan, with seven others, napalmed the draft files of the Catonsville, Maryland, board. With these examples before him, Cullen and thirteen others entered Milwaukee's Brumber Building, seized draft board records, and burned them in the street outside.

One of those with Cullen in the draft file burning was Jim Forest. In the October issue of the *Worker,* Forest wrote of their experience in jail during the several weeks of bail raising. Every night there had been a vigil outside the jail. One night Dick Gregory and Father Groppi led two thousand people to the jail from Marquette University. It was all exciting, brave, and solemn, and during that period in jail there was an outpouring of verse and prose from the inmates calculated to register more intensely the depth of their antiwar feeling. For a person like Cullen, family oriented, and well aware of the first call of his family upon him, this new experience and the prospects of future imprisonment must have been sobering.

That year found other Workers going to jail for their antiwar beliefs. In June, Tom Cornell began a six-month sentence for draft card burning; David Miller, another draft card burner, faced sentencing, and Bob Gilliam, a recent college graduate was already at Sandstone in Minnesota for refusing induction. Before imprisonment, Gilliam had lived at the Worker house, and in a letter from Sandstone, he told those who remained of his homesickness. What were they all doing? Who had been sentenced; who was up for parole? Had the "Feds" made a move toward anyone else? He observed that there were "about a dozen J.W.'s [Jehovah's Witnesses] here for the draft. They are very straight and keep to themselves. There are also a couple of Muslims. There are five of *us.* . . ."

From a jail in Little Rock came another letter. "I have just finished devouring the February issue of *The Catholic Worker* while awaiting trial," wrote another young man who was influenced by the Worker. Mike Vegler had been arrested for refusing to accept alternative work as a C.O. His parents, he said, were distressed, but they did not complain, accepting, rather, "this burden with joy and patience."

Certainly, in 1968 Dorothy Day must have felt, with more and more young people going to prison, that something of the spirit of the Catholic Worker was beginning to take hold and that these young were the vanguard of a new day for the Catholic Church. They were the ones who were building the new earth of peace and justice. Yet with these signs of the new creation there were also signs of faltering. There were the disaffections of the young, of those with religious vocations, even of those who were so closely and creatively a part of the active, forming mind of the Church that their loss seemed to atrophy a vital segment of its being.

Now it was that some of those young who came to the Worker house, to Tivoli, eager to demonstrate against the war, to sacrifice their freedom by years in prison, if need be, could no longer affirm the Church. "Catholic" was a label to be discarded. It was an idea that was dead, a weight they had been forced to carry which now, in the spirit of honesty and sincerity, they rejected. Their feeling for the Church ranged from a disposition to relegate it politely to the limbo of an interesting mythology to a bitterness at having been forced so long to live by codes that precluded the free pursuit of the golden path of dream and sense.

The time-wounded now sought refuge at the Catholic Worker. They could use the old word symbols but these meant something different from what they once had. They spoke of "community," using the word so frequently as to imply that the idea was novel. But it was not the community of spirit that they meant. Increasingly, they felt the

lure of community in terms of polarizations of sentiment derived from the action of the object world. Christ and the
Church (when the Church was considered) became catalysts
in the thrust for change. Christ was the spirit that bound
men and women in community as they cut cane together in
Cuba, that stood with the people as they demonstrated for
peace, that was indeed in every good work, conspiratorial
and romantic, that looked to the removal of all institutional
roadblocks to the free flow of change.

In *The Catholic Worker* there appeared at times a disposition to treat with weary indifference whatever meaning
the past might have for what was now. Tradition was forgotten, or perhaps the time-wounded never knew it. In the
April–May, 1967, issue of the paper there appeared an account of a penitential fast at the Shrine of the Immaculate
Conception at Washington by several young men of the
house who were deeply concerned over Vietnam. The account of the fast in the *Worker* seemed to emphasize more
the penance that came from having to sit in the shrine than
in the fasting. The writer, an especially talented person,
wrote of it as "grotesque," . . . "Truly a Vision of Error"
which made it "increasingly clear to us that the Shrine was
at once the epitome and symbol of American Catholicism. . . ."

Some might agree that architecturally the shrine was mis-
begotten and that it stridently symbolized the bourgeoisity
of American Catholicism, yet it was, nonetheless, the place
where on December 8, 1932, Dorothy Day had gone to pray
that she might have some special mission to perform in her
new life in the Church. Her prayer, she said many times,
had been answered immediately. Was there not in this a
sort of striking personalist symbolism—that at the very center of this contract-let splendor of the American Catholic
Church, her prayer for a revolution of the gospel of Christ
should be heard?

Dorothy Day recognized the sense of frustration out of
which the article had been written. It did, she said, give a
picture of American Catholicism as it appeared in the eyes

of the world—"the picture of comfortable, materialistic Catholicism, of which we are all very much a part. We have come from this bourgeois background ourselves, we have partaken of its comforts. But our eyes have been opened to see more clearly the words of the Gospel, and the words of the Pope today. We must pray that those same visitors [to the Shrine] may make the prayer, 'Lord, what wilt thou have me to do?' God takes us at our word, and will answer each one, will call each one to his vocation. . . ."

Always in the past Worker houses had harbored the poor and distressed, but now the problem of drugs and immorality began to insinuate itself into its daily life. On one occasion Dorothy Day was compelled to take action against a group of young transients who behaved in a fashion that contrasted shockingly with accustomed standards. As she wrote of them, they had moved into a Worker apartment where they had "reversed all standards, turning night into day, clinging together. . . ." It was a case of " 'The corruption of the best is the worst,' " for these people had come from good families, had good educations, and had been given every advantage. She understood why Lenin had had to write to Rosa Luxemburg of the bourgeois morality of the young. "This whole crowd goes to extremes in sex and drugs. . . ." It was "a complete rebellion against authority, natural and supernatural, even against the body and its needs, its natural functions of child bearing. It can only be a hatred of sex that leads them to talk as they do and be so explicit about the sex functions and the sex organs, as instruments of pleasure." This, she said, was "not reverence for life, this certainly is not natural love for family, for husband and wife, for child. It is a great denial, and is more resembling Nihilism than the revolution which they think they are furthering."

In the end there was a difference of opinion among some at the Chrystie Street house as to the course they should follow toward the group. Charles Butterworth and Ed Forand shared Dorothy Day's abhorrence of its conduct and had spoken to some of its members about their behavior. But they responded with indignation, saying that their freedom was being trespassed upon. Even so, Dorothy Day turned them out. Certainly, she said, "people do not support the Catholic Worker to support a group of young ones who live from hand to mouth. . . ."

These new ways were tragic to witness because, as she had said, of their contempt for life. This was the generation that had been freed from want. The concerns and trials of the Depression years no longer plagued middle-class America. It was as Berdyaev had said, the curing of social problems could make life appear outwardly less tragic, "but inwardly its eternally tragic nature is deepened and intensified." The deification of sense that was one of the marks of the new age was perhaps the sign of a movement into a deeper tragedy.

The drifting and rootlessness of the young was the bitter fruit of the collapse of the bourgeois world, and at this point in time when tradition had faded and perspective lost, the teachers in the Catholic Church seemed incapable of issuing in accord a convincing call to spirit and peace. The call that was made sounded like discord, its abrasive penetration heightened over the issue of Vietnam. "In Peace Is My Bitterness Most Bitter," Dorothy Day wrote in a *Worker* editorial in 1967. Her concern was Cardinal Spellman's Christmas visit to Vietnam and his call for victory in the war. "I can sit in the presence of the Blessed Sacrament and wrestle for that peace in the bitterness of my soul, a bitterness which many Catholics throughout the world feel, and I can find many things in Scripture to console me. . . . 'Our worst enemies are those of our own household,' Jesus said. . . ." She said that she had often thought it was a brave thing for the cardinal to visit American troops around the world, but "oh God what are all these Americans, so-called Christians, doing all over the world so far from our own shores?" And "what words are those he spoke—going against even the Pope, calling for victory, total victory? Words are as strong and powerful as bombs, as napalm. How much the government counts on those words, pays for those words to exalt our own way of life, to build up fear of the enemy. Deliver me, Lord, from the fear of the enemy. . . ."

There was another sign of ambiguity within the Church that could not but magnify a sense of the Church's inability to lead positively. Many priests and nuns who found it a continual frustration having to make their vocational life conform to the dry rigidities and stereotypes of bourgeois conventions, decided to leave the relgious life, and once in a while one would write to Dorothy Day seeking counsel. "I am a parish priest," began one letter, "striving to choose one of three alternatives: (1) to go along with the institutionalized, respectable Catholicism, saying yes to the bishop, celebrating Mass in a swank church, administering the sacraments in thermo-controlled conditions and accepting the terrible ordeal of filling out the . . . marriage forms from the chancery offices of the land, or (2) to revolt . . . or (3) to stick with the institution and at the same time go plodding along, intensely conscious of Christ's real work and, in an undramatic way, try to instill in the comfortable, respectable Catholic what it means to be a true Christian." The writer concluded by saying that he would stick with the institution, although this course, he felt, would be the most difficult. For her part, Dorothy Day would have agreed with this decision.

Certainly, then, she understood the dismay and even the cynicism of the young, of young Catholics and young Catholic Workers, of all who behind the flow of their cynical words hoped in their hearts that the Church would bring men to a new level of community. But there was no turning from the Church. "Where else shall we go," she asked, "except to the Bride of Christ, one flesh with Christ? Though she is a harlot at times, she is our Mother. . . . 'Love is indeed a harsh and dreadful thing' to ask of us, of each one of us, but it is the only answer."

To those engulfed in bitterness, forever pointing their finger at the Church for its weaknesses, for its inability to lead, she gave the personalist answer by quoting Newman: " 'Let us but raise the level of religion in our hearts, and it will rise in the world.'" She recalled that the Worker movement had been started and carried through its almost forty years of history without asking permission of anyone. "This business of 'asking Father' what to do about something has never occurred to us." She wondered if those who were bitter had their vision in perspective. She had recently read a life of Lenin by his widow, and she thought how quickly he had taken over so much of the modern world. Thinking of this, she reflected on how strange it was that "our youth dares to be discouraged, with Christ as its leader, with the Church at its back—its wealth in writings, the very deeds and virtues of the saints to draw upon—and wishes for numbers, for demonstrations, for something to do!"

There was, finally, this problem: existence could be cast into the flow, or it could be set toward eternity. However much Dorothy Day may have suffered personally at the compromises with time that the Church had made, the Church remained, more than the chemistry of her body, the coordinating element of her life. Only a complete madness could change her, but even then it would be the appearance of change. Her most fundamental being, beyond blood, flesh, and bone, had been formed and set in the Catholic Worker movement—in the "clarification" that Peter Maurin had talked about. The Church was the point where time was synthesized into eternity, where man and nature would be redeemed, and where community was completed. Nor would it be the Church if it abandoned eternity to cast itself into time's flow to become time's catalyst, its handservant, giving moral sanction to the new and exciting dimensions of action of the sensate world glowing ever more luminously and beckoning more insistently. And as long as there were those who stood with eternity, who indeed were the Church, then there was always a point to which those who had taken flight might return.

The object Church of the world was a symbol of its inner spirit, yet as many despaired and turned away from that object Church, there were signs that its spirit was alive. In the

September, 1969, issue of *The Catholic Worker* there appeared an article on Dom Hélder Câmara, the archbishop of Recife, Brazil. Here was a religious leader whose example and counsel might well direct the spirits of the young. His vision was that of the personalist and he spoke as Peter Maurin had spoken. Especially, the *Worker* quoted his advice to the youth of the world's rich nations: "Instead of thinking about going to the Third World to try to promote violence, stay home and help make your own wealthy countries realize that they also need a cultural revolution that can bring about a new value structure, a new world view, a global strategy of development, a revolution of man." Hélder Câmara's vision was based on the hope for the rise of a radical, personalist, communitarian spirit within the Church as against its character as an objectivized, institutional form trapped in the fiber of bourgeoisity.

There were others. Two bishops of the Church, Joseph Durrick of Nashville and Carroll Dozier of Memphis, like Hélder Câmara, brought to their pastoral duty a mood and spirit that was reminiscent of the first band of Workers that had gone into Union Square in May, 1933. There was news to be proclaimed, and the time was now. In Nashville, Durrick set about to erase the stain of racism in the administration of his diocese. His actions were not gestures, carefully measured so as not to upset the smooth running of administrative forms. He saw the Black man as one who had been greatly sinned against and to whom reparation was due. No concern for diocesan administrative tranquillity was large enough to stand in the path of his efforts, and the efforts of some of the priests and nuns of the diocese, to atone for past transgressions.

In the diocese of Memphis, Dozier sent his first pastoral letter to Catholics during the Christmas season of 1971. The letter surveyed the long history of the Church's attitude toward war, then concluded by saying that war under any circumstances was no longer tolerable for a Christian. It specifically named the war in Vietnam as morally reprehensible and declared that the diocese of Memphis would actively support anyone who for reasons of conscience sought a draft status of conscientious objector.

Readers of *The Catholic Worker* would find Bishop Dozier's letter making the same points the *Worker* had been making for many years. How had this come to be? It was a new air that the men of the Church breathed in 1971, but, certainly, insofar as their Catholic mind and conscience were concerned, Peter Maurin's idea and four decades of the Catholic Worker movement had done much to make it different. It was also different because of all those who for the sake of conscience had refused to be drafted and had gone to prison, beginning with the Heaneys and Ludlows of World War II, right up to a Karl Meyer who shrank from no personal sacrifice to affirm a community of spirit against that of violence.

This was a time when Dorothy Day must have thought much of these people. She thought of the Berrigans, imprisoned and surrounded by controversy. To what extent these priest brothers had become symbols, perhaps unwilling symbols, for those who sought community in an active struggle of the object world, no one could know. But in the December, 1970, issue of the *Worker* she wrote that she wanted to tell "the Fathers Berrigan, and all those who are suffering imprisonment now, that not a day goes by that we do not think of them, and hold them in our prayers together with all prisoners, who are the poor, at Compline and Rosary at the Tivoli Farm, and at . . . St. Joseph's House of Hospitality. Our love goes out to them, and love, like wisdom, is the most active of all active things, according to the Book of Wisdom. You have chosen suffering for your lot, dear friends, suffering and depression and hopelessness, which must in many ways be compared to that which is suffered in Vietnam and in all those parts of our struggling world. . . ."

She also knew that there were many others who acted and then quietly paid the price, continuing as they could to live in those ways hidden to the world where the force of spirit burned brightest. And who could know or measure the extent of those quiet and spreading currents, moved by an active love, that sought no response from the world— only that time be ended? No one could answer that question because the force and life of love were endless, making finally the great confrontations and conflicts of the time world seem only as barriers to eternity.

This was as Dorothy Day saw it and it was what she and her friends had tried to work out in the years since she had caught Peter Maurin's radical vision. As the Worker movement approached four decades of life, it could point to one kind of evidence that it had remained, as a movement, true to Maurin's personalist precepts. It still could cite no satisfying statistics of "progress" having been made, of a growth of organizational efficiency, of having established an economically "sound" basis for its structure, and of having had large and victorious confrontations with the forces of evil in the object world.

Indeed, things had changed little. *The Catholic Worker* still sold for a penny a copy, with an outward appearance that was much as it always had been. There was also a familiar content. Dorothy Day's "On Pilgrimage" column was there, and Deane Mowrer wrote of life at Tivoli. There was the familiar column on the New York house, written by various members of the group who lived there. Peter Maurin's "Easy Essays" appeared frequently, and once in a while Father Hugo, as he had in the forties, contributed some of his thoughts on the current interests in theology. And well into 1969, there were Ammon Hennacy's accounts of his work in Utah. If anything had changed, it was a loss of the excitement and Church-focused concern of former times. The young people who wrote for the paper were of a different age. For them the old words did not come easily.

In the summer of 1968, St. Joseph's House of Hospitality was moved again, this time to 36 East First Street. It was a large house and it conformed to all of the city's codes. The marks of the Catholic Worker were still about it. The poor were there; the street was filled with people—now Puerto

Ricans—and there was the same old problem of getting in enough money to pay the mortgage and feed those who were hungry. Once it had been the Zarellas, Sullivans, and Dugans who had struggled with these problems. Now it was Walter Kerrell, Ed Forand and Charles Butterworth who continued to work in the tradition of those who preceded them.

The passing of people who had been closely associated with the Worker movement occurred with increasing frequency. It was on a Wednesday, December 11, 1968, that Dorothy Day received a telegram from the abbot of the Trappist monastery at Gethsemani, Kentucky, telling her of the accidental death of Thomas Merton. "He was about to leave the monastery," someone at the Worker house had said. In the article she wrote on his death, she included a part of a recent letter Merton had written to her: "I know that I cannot really expect them [activist friends] to take the slightest interest in the peculiar problem I have, trying to live an authentic life of solitude (which I certainly think will do more for the peace movement than anything I write)." Merton then mentioned a particular friend who had argued in a long letter "that my whole monastic life was a pure evasion, that I ought to be back in the world leading a life of authentic involvement like himself. . . ." But Dorothy should not worry, he said. He knew where his true involvement lay. "I am more determined than ever on my present course."

In March, 1968, she wrote in her column that Ammon Hennacy had just brought out a new edition of his autobiography in which he had included an additional chapter explaining why he no longer considered himself a Catholic. This was all that she said about the matter, and Hennacy's pieces continued in the paper. In the March–April *Worker* of 1969, he expressed concern over developments in the antiwar movement, what "with many of the recent opponents of the war in Vietnam taking the violent instead of the non-violent stand." It was time "that these matters were thought through again. That is, if people can think when they are excited." Then he retold the story of his days in solitary in the Atlanta penitentiary during the First World War and how he had become a Christian and a pacifist.

Hennacy died January 14, 1970. Picketing and fasting, his heart collapsed. He was anointed in the hospital, but there was no deathbed reaffirmation of the Church. "Whether I left the Church or the Church left me depends upon how you look at the question," he had written in the last edition of his autobiography. It really was not a point of much importance, for, as Dorothy Day once wrote about Hennacy, his life itself spoke much louder than his words.

Dorothy Day wrote of Peggy Baird's death in the October–November, 1970, issue of the *Worker*. Peggy had been her companion in the years of the First World War, and later it had been she who had helped her find her little cottage on Raritan Bay. She could never forget, she said, that spring day in 1925, when she and Peggy had looked at the cottage and then had walked along the beach collecting shells and clams.

Once Peggy had thanked her for not having tried to convert her, but one day when some of the people at the house were talking to Jack English, long since Father Charles, English asked her if she would not like to join the rest of her friends when they went to Communion at Mass. She said that she would, and one May Sunday her former husband, Malcolm Cowley, came to Tivoli to visit her, and there he found her, as Dorothy Day related, " 'clothed in her right mind' as my mother used to say, surrounded by her kittens and flowers and books studying the Baltimore catechism, of all things!"

These were old friends of Dorothy Day's; in one way or another they had been her companions in arms. She did not, however, take their passing as an indication that she should be slowing her own pace. In the summer of 1970, she and Eileen Egan visited Australia, India, and Africa. In Australia she went to a farm commune begun by a priest who had been at the Easton farm in 1940. It was Father John Heffey, and he reminded her of Father Roy, the priest who had been so vital to the life of the Workers at Easton. Like Father Roy, she wrote, Father Heffey "leads in all the manual labor and teaches others." He reminded her too of Peter Maurin in the way he made schedules for himself.

In the spring of 1971, she told *Worker* readers of her plans for a journey that she hitherto had not made. She would go to Russia in the company of some old-time radicals whose passage, like her own, was being paid for by Corliss Lamont. Lamont was a man of considerable wealth. He was also a dedicated humanist who in the thirties and forties had written philosophical and literary works against the use of religion as a basis for humanism. The fact that he was extending his beneficence to Dorothy Day was a matter of wonderment for some *Worker* readers, but for him it was perhaps no more than his recognizing in her, religion or not, a time-tested upholder of positions and attitudes that he thought worthy.

The trip that summer was a stimulating one for her and in a certain sense it was a homecoming. She walked along the Kremlin Wall and was moved when she saw the graves of Bill Haywood of the IWW and Jack Reed with whom she had worked on *The Masses*. She thought of Rayna Simon, her roommate at the University of Illinois, who had died in Moscow in 1927. She, too, like the other Americans, should have had a flower-covered grave, she felt, but Rayna had been cremated, and the niche where her ashes were placed could not be found.

It was homecoming because she was in the land of Tolstoy, of Solzhenitsyn, and of Dostoevsky. She had wanted to visit Zagorsk, the monastery outside of Moscow, but she had been prohibited from doing so by travel regulations. Was not Father Zossima, the monk in *The Brothers Karamazov*, from Zagorsk? she asked. At a meeting of Soviet authors she was able to express her appreciation of a Russian literary tradition that had produced those writers who had meant so much to her. Her inclusion of Solzhenitsyn, however, provoked annoyance, since the official disfavor in which he was

held was also reflected in the attitude toward him of some
of the writers in the group to which she spoke.

The felicity of such traveling and the joyous knowledge
that the Church seemed to have begun to move toward the
message that Maurin had taught in Union Square could not
wall out from Dorothy Day and the Catholic Workers the
impact of the world in a new phase of crisis. Time was im-
posing a new and pervasive tyranny over man; the object
world with its institutions, manners, and values was coming
undone. New ways and new ideas came rocketing into what
was assumed to be a clear, new focus, but burned and then
blurred as others crowded more urgently in their wake.

From the position on which the Catholic Worker stood,
this new offensive of time, parading itself before the world
in a brilliant and bedazzling coloration of rapturous sense
experience, meant a dimming of the time-ending force of
spirit. And this was the new and severest testing of the
Worker position. Through all the years of Worker history,
Dorothy Day had declared that its mission was ending time.
How eagerly she had accepted Maurin's vision of a new creation outside of struggle and conflict and the conventional
definitions of "progress." How many times she had quoted
St. Catherine of Siena: "All the way to Heaven is Heaven";
how many times she had emphasized "now" in the building
of the new earth, and how unconcerned she had always
been about the time-made judgments of success or failure
where the Catholic Worker movement was concerned. It
was the mission of the Worker to free man from his enslave-
ment to history and process. It heard, as Nikolai Berdyaev
had written, "a call to transfigure this evil and stricken
world. It is a witness to the end of this world of ours with
its enslaving objectifications, religious, moral, social and
philosophical alike."

Most of the personalist thinkers, Peter Maurin included,
had had a vision of the triumph of objectification, when,
after World War II, Berdyaev wrote his "Final Philosophical Outlook." He saw "a terrible judgment" over history and

civilization. The new tryanny of time and sense was, in the apocalyptic image, "'the beast rising out of the sea,'" the "last demonic attempts of the kingdom of Caesar to dominate and to enslave man and the world." And so it seemed to be occurring. Caesar's kingdom, the object world, came hurtling into full phase. But Berdyaev was a Christian and the victory of time was not final. The Lamb was eternal and in the end "The Beast will . . . be cast once more into the abyss of hell and shackled, not to eternity, but to time; for hell is that which remains in time; that which, obsessed by its evil nightmares, does not pass into eternity."

The crisis of the times fell upon the Catholic Worker movement. There was no longer the sense of community that had marked the early days when Workers had trooped behind Peter Maurin to Union Square and had thronged into the crowded room and backyard court at Fifteenth Street to hear a lecture where the mind was sent racing over the path of an idea, converging, finally, one knew, at an answer. Now at Tivoli some lived, almost, in private isolation. From the woods behind the house came the notes of a delicate air played on a recorder; at some other spot there was a dabbling in paints; and somewhere else another labored over a manuscript.

But what could these young know of the harsh and dreadful way of spirit and life when at every hand a dazzling sense world called? Dorothy Day thought of that hypnotic quality of racing time that lured the spirits of the young into oblivion. Who was to blame? she asked, and then she gave the personalist answer. "We are all responsible. . . . And there is so little we can do, so little we have done, to bear one another's burdens." When "we are able to bear some small share of the sufferings of the world, whether in pain of mind, body or soul, let us thank God for that too. Maybe we are helping some prisoner, some black or Puerto Rican youth in the Tombs, some soldier in Vietnam. . . . We can indeed hold each other up in prayer. Excuse this preaching. I am preaching to myself too."

It was February, 1971. The war in Vietnam went on, exfoliating a madness that was excused in the name of "honor." In the face of the suffering over all the world, it was hard to endure. What should one do? she asked. Read the book of Job "and then go on reading the psalms." Also, "remember the importunate widow, the importunate friend. Both are stories Jesus told. Then pray without ceasing as Paul urged. And just as there was the interpolation in Job— that triumphant cry—'I know that my Redeemer liveth,' so we too can know that help will come, that even from evil, God can bring great good, that indeed the good will triumph. Bitter that it is today with ice and sleet, the sap will soon be rising in those bare trees down the street from us."

Dorothy Day, 1972.
Harriet B. Norris photo.

# SOURCES

The principal sources used in the preparation of this book were the Catholic Worker papers, located at Marquette University; the files of *The Catholic Worker;* Dorothy Day's books about her life in the Worker movement; the oral history of the Catholic Worker movement; and my own personal interviewing and association with persons involved in the Catholic Worker idea.

Historians will continue to be interested in the Worker phenomenon, and a further word about the last two of the above sources may be helpful to them. The oral history of the Catholic Worker movement consists of a series of taped interviews with persons in the movement or knowledgeable of it made by Deane Mowrer of the Worker farm at Tivoli, New York. Copies of some of these tapes are in the Catholic Worker collection at Marquette University; all of them are in the keeping of Miss Mowrer at the Tivoli farm. Miss Mowrer's interviewing has been well done and these tapes represent a valuable source of information. But for one who is seeking primary information through personal interviews there is no better person with whom to begin than Stanley Vishnewski. He is himself a rich source of information, and he represents a clearing house of Worker information by virtue of his knowledge of the sources.

There is a great store of information on the Catholic Worker movement in periodicals and newspapers. I used some of this and examined all of it that I could find. Anyone wishing a guide to this information should consult "A Bibliography on Peter Maurin, Dorothy Day, and the Catholic Worker" compiled by Alex Avitabile, S.J., of Fordham University. This exhaustive and well arranged bibliographical guide is a cornerstone to the historiography of the Catholic Worker movement. Perhaps it will soon be in print. Otherwise, a duplicated copy can be gotten from Mr. Avitabile at Fordham. It should also be noted that *The Catholic Worker*, Vols. 1–27 (1933–1961), has been reprinted in four volumes, with an Introduction by Dwight Macdonald, by The Greenwood Press of Westport, Connecticut.

In the first drafts of this work I included the traditional documentation represented by the use of superscripts and footnotes. I have omitted these devices in the final draft. My purpose in writing this book has not been to create a panoramic fact-mass which contains esoteric and perhaps startling bits of information that require even further documentation. The sources of my story—even those which historians call "primary"—are not obscure, and I felt that to encumber the text with the paraphernalia of facticity would be a waste of space and pretentious. In most cases my sources for quotations and original idea material are indicated in a prefactory phrase, sentence, or chapter introduction. Quoted letters, except those designated as having come from other sources, are from the Catholic Worker papers, as are the occasional quotations from Dorothy Day's fragmentary journal. Ordinarily, quoted opinions and reflections that are unsupported in the text are from the oral history tapes made by Deane Mowrer.

There remains, however, a supporting body of information for this work that consists of books, articles, and sometimes unpublished matter. Some of this I regard as primary also, because it contains or suggests the ideas I have used to form the real structure of this history. Since the establishment of the Catholic Worker idea is accomplished mainly in the first half of the book, it is for chapters and sections of chapters in this part that I add these bibliographical notes. Beginning with the chapter on World War II and following, the story is mostly narration and relies for its development on the four principal sources mentioned above. The exceptions are the two chapters on Ammon Hennacy, where Hennacy's *The Book of Ammon* (Salt Lake City: Ammon Hennacy Publications, 1970) is the basic source for my narration and quotation.

INTRODUCTION: *The Radical Idea of the Catholic Worker.* This introduction was organized out of ideas from Dostoevsky's *The Brothers Karamazov* and the philosophical works of Nikolai Berdyaev. It seems to me that Dostoevsky deals with three main problems of human existence: evil, freedom, and community. These are the problems with which, finally, the Catholic Worker movement is concerned and which it perceives as Dostoevsky perceived them. Berdyaev emphasizes those special insights that make the connection between Dostoevsky and the Worker movement in his essay on Dostoevsky. A brief Berdyaev bibliography would include *The Destiny of Man* (New York: Harper Torchbooks, 1960), *Slavery and Freedom* (New York: Charles Scribner's Sons, 1944, paperback edition, 1970).

There is a substantial bibliography on the Christian personalist idea. Philosopher Jacques Maritain's writings are in this tradition and should be reread by this generation, especially *The Person and the Common Good* (University of Notre Dame paperback, 1971). Emmanuel Mounier's *The Personalist Manifesto* was published in the United States in 1938, and Catholic Workers studied this book. (See also *Personalism* by Emmanuel Mounier, University of Notre Dame paperback, 1971.) Mounier has been treated in a recent Harvard University dissertation by John Hellman, *Emmanuel Mounier and L'Esprit, A Personalist Dialogue with Marxism and Existentialism.*

There are essential interconnections between Christian thought as the personalists developed it and anarchism and socialism. Catholic Worker thought has sensed these interconnections and has developed accordingly, but they are subjects that need more study.

Chapter 1: *Peter Maurin.* The Maurin chapter is largely biographical. The principal published source is Arthur Sheehan's *Peter Maurin: Gay Believer* (Garden City, New York: Hanover House, 1959). This book can be supplemented by the chapters on Maurin in two of Dorothy Day's books on the Catholic Worker movement: *The Long Loneliness* (New York: Harper and Row, 1963; New York: Curtis paperback, 1972) and *Loaves and Fishes* (Garden City, New York; Harper & Brothers, 1952; New York: Curtis paperback, 1972). There is not, however, a book that systematically analyzes Maurin's thought, and one is needed. It is not a simple matter to get the weight of his ideas from his writing, since his curious terminology is apt to cause wonderment. Over the years *The Catholic Worker* has printed and reprinted his verses, which can also be found in several paperback editions. The first book collection of his writings was *Easy Essays,* published by Sheed and Ward in 1936. In 1949 the Catholic Worker published *Catholic Radicalism,* and in 1961 The Academy Guild Press brought out *The Green Revolution.* In 1971 another edition of Maurin's verses was published by the Green Revolution Press under the title *Radical Christian Thought: Easy Essays by Peter Maurin.*

Chapter 2 and Chapter 3: *Dorothy Day* and *The Young Journalist.* The two biographical chapters on Miss Day are derived from facts all supplied by Miss Day in her several autobiographical works. Two relate to her life in the Catholic Worker movement: *From Union Square to Rome* (Silver Spring, Maryland: Preservation of the Faith Press, 1938) and *The Long Loneliness* (1952). Altogether she has written seven books and over seventy published articles, a complete listing of which can be found in the Avitabile bibliography. Dorothy Day is not a philosopher. Her response to life is direct and reflective, and it is her sense of a Christian proportion and significance to things that make her reflections valuable. In this respect, much that is most valuable in her writing is to be found in her column in *The Catholic Worker,* which has now been running for nearly forty years. Since ordinarily a person cannot survey all of this material, I would recommend as a substitute a fine collection of Dorothy Day's reflections, selected and arranged by Stanley Vishnewski. The title is *Dorothy Day—Meditations,* published by the Newman Press. A volume of her recent writings is *On Pilgrimage: The Sixties* (Curtis paperback, 1972).

CHAPTER 4 THROUGH CHAPTER 6: *Union Square* through *Mott Street.* These chapters concern the first departures of the Catholic Worker movement from those areas of sacred affirmation whose precepts, centered on the competitive principle, were seldom questioned. These were the areas subsumed under the headings of state, race, and the economy. The best survey of this subject, including the pros and cons with respect to the Worker position, is David J. O'Brien's *American Catholics and Social Reform, the New Deal Years* (New York: Oxford University Press, 1968).

It is interesting that the "liberal" Catholic position, until the time of the Catholic Worker, had been that of identifying Catholicism with Americanism. This subject is emphasized in Raymond J. Cunningham's "Catholicism and American Nationalism," a Johns Hopkins University doctoral dissertation prospectus.

On the matter of race, the historic tradition of the Catholic Church was so clearly defined that there was not much argument against the Workers' position. Those who opposed it invoked the virtue of prudence, so much so that one concludes that at no other time was this virtue dragged so ruthlessly into the mire in order to justify prejudice.

The theoretical position of the Catholic Worker on the economy was that of voluntary socialism, a description of which can be found in Berdyaev's *Slavery and Freedom,* beginning page 218 of the 1944 Scribner's edition. Yet even on the matter of the economy one can find a statement of the Worker position in *The Brothers Karamazov.* It is in the lines where a police official is quoted as saying that he is not particularly afraid of the revolutionaries who profess atheism: "We keep watch on them and know all their goings on. But there are a few peculiar men among them who believe in God and are Christians, but at the same time are socialists. Those are the people we are most afraid of."

Within the Worker movement positions as to how economic justice was to be obtained were polarized: through Dorothy Day's agrarian "anarchism" or through the use of the traditional structures of capital and labor. The arguments with respect to these positions were set forth in the contemporary Catholic periodical literature, principally in *Commonweal*. David O'Brien has a balanced survey of this controversy in his book, and it is also touched on by Neil Betten, "Urban Catholicism and Industrial Reform, 1937–1940," *Thought* (Autumn, 1969).

The Child Labor amendment issue, so prominent in the thirties, is surveyed in "The Child Labor Issue," *Commonweal* (March 5, 1937).

CHAPTER 7: *The Spread of Maurin's Ideas.* This chapter concerns the expansion of the house of hospitality idea and that of the farm commune. Perhaps somewhere there are records left by the early houses of hospitality. If there are, and if they are in danger of being lost, they should be sent to the Catholic Worker collection at Marquette University to provide the source for the future histories of these houses. The records of the Cleveland house have been kept intact by Bill Gauchat, and these I was able to examine.

Peter Maurin's farm commune ideas (his "Agronomic University"), have similarities to those of the kibbutzim of Israel and the collective farms of the Chinese People's Republic. The farm commune idea has a close bearing on the whole spectrum of crises in which modern man lives, ranging from those of the spirit to those of the flesh. Many of these problems have been related to the commune idea, but there is still a need for an integrated and fundamental approach to the question such as Peter Maurin tried to make. In the

Catholic Worker papers there are two unpublished manuscripts by Dorothy Day on the subject, "Farming Communes" and "Idea of an Agronomic University." There is in the Worker papers one box of material dealing with farm commune enterprises around the world.

CHAPTER 9: *Israel.* The rise of totalitarian regimes in the world during the thirties is a phenomenon that Hannah Arendt in her *The Origins of Totalitarianism* (Cleveland: Meridian Books) sees as developing out of middle class life and values. I think her position is eminently sound, although the personalist thinkers, Berdyaev especially, had an acute sense of the corruption of life through middle class values that went beyond Miss Arendt's position.

Peter Maurin had a transcendent sense of the place of Judaism in history that, again, was shared by the personalist thinkers. It was with the French essayist Leon Bloy that Maurin and the other personalists might claim the closest spiritual kinship where the subject of anti-Semitism is concerned. In Bloy's autobiography, *The Pilgrim of the Absolute,* there is a chapter, "The Mystery of Israel," which states Bloy's position. I also found what amounted to a personalist approach to the history of anti-Semitism in Edward H. Flannery's *The Anguish of the Jews* (New York: Macmillan paperback). Father Flannery's understanding of this phenomenon is much more penetrating than the customary "sociological" explanations.

# INDEX

William D. Miller was born in Jacksonville, Florida, December 3, 1916. He attended public schools there and graduated from the University of Florida in 1939. He did graduate work at Duke University and the University of North Carolina, where he received his PhD in 1953. He is married to the former Rhea Bond of Sarasota, Florida. They have eight children. Mr. Miller is professor of history and Chairman of the American Studies program at Florida State University, Tallahassee.